AMERICAN POLITICAL, ECONOMIC, AND SECURITY ISSUES

# INFORMATION SECURITY AND TECHNOLOGY REPORTS FOR DECEMBER 2018

# AMERICAN POLITICAL, ECONOMIC, AND SECURITY ISSUES

Additional books and e-books in this series can be found on Nova's website under the Series tab.

American Political, Economic, and Security Issues

# Information Security and Technology Reports for December 2018

Lauren Van Raalte
Editor

snova
New York

**Library of Congress Cataloging-in-Publication Data**

ISBN: 978-1-53615-621-8

*Published by Nova Science Publishers, Inc. † New York*

# CONTENTS

# PREFACE

This book is a comprehensive compilation of all reports, testimony, correspondence and other publications issued by the GAO (Government Accountability Office) during the month of December, grouped according to the topics Information Security and Technology.

Chapter 1 - The federal government planned to invest more than $96 billion in IT in fiscal year 2018. However, IT investments have often failed or contributed little to mission-related outcomes. Further, increasingly sophisticated threats and frequent cyber incidents underscore the need for effective information security. As a result, GAO added two areas to its high-risk list: cybersecurity in 1997 and the management of IT acquisitions and operations in 2015. This statement summarizes federal agencies' progress in improving the management, and ensuring the security, of federal IT. It is primarily based on GAO's reports issued between February 1997 and August 2018 (and an ongoing review) on (1) CIO responsibilities, (2) agency CIOs' involvement in approving IT contracts, (3) data center consolidation efforts, (4) the management of software licenses, and (5) compliance with cybersecurity requirements.

Chapter 2 - CISA encouraged the timely sharing of cyber threat information between the public and private sectors. To facilitate the implementation of provisions related to this information sharing, the act required the seven designated federal agencies to jointly develop publicly available policies, procedures, and guidelines to assist federal and nonfederal entities in sharing information on cyber threat indicators and defensive measures. Specifically, the act required DHS and DOJ to lead the development of procedures and guidelines to assist federal entities when receiving information on cyber threat indicators or defensive measures from federal and nonfederal entities. The act also required DHS and DOJ to work with DOD and ODNI to develop policies to facilitate the sharing of cyber threat indicators and defensive measures among federal and nonfederal entities. Further, the act required these four agencies to coordinate the development of these artifacts with DOC, DOE and the Treasury. In support of this information sharing, the White House released a memorandum in 2016 stating that all departments and agencies should use DHS's AIS capability for the purpose of sharing cyber threat information. In addition, the act included specific provisions for the protection of privacy and civil liberties. In this regard, CISA required DHS and DOJ, in coordination with the other five designated federal agencies, to develop government-wide guidelines for the protection of privacy and civil liberties when implementing provisions of the act. Among other things, the seven designated agencies were to:

- develop privacy and civil liberties guidance governing the receipt, retention, use, and dissemination of cyber threat indicators, consistent with the eight fair information practice principles;
- develop and implement the aforementioned real-time sharing capability in compliance with this privacy and civil liberties guidance; and
- incorporate appropriate security and privacy protections into all other policies, procedures, and guidance for receiving and sharing cyber threat indicators and defensive measures specified in the act.

Chapter 3 - The Consolidated Appropriations Act, 2018 required the Secretary of Agriculture to conduct a detailed cost-benefit analysis that includes a complete analysis of the department's National Finance Center (NFC) data center and two other data centers of comparable size and complexity. According to the act, this analysis was also to include an assessment of each center's (1) cost-effectiveness; (2) security; (3) Federal Risk and Authorization Management Program (FedRAMP) certification status; and (4) demonstrated record of maintaining Continuity of Operations Plan (COOP) functions without disruption of critical operations. The act required the Department of Agriculture (USDA) to submit the cost-benefit analysis to the Committees on Appropriations of the Senate and House of Representatives within 90 days of the act's March 23, 2018 enactment. In response to the act, USDA requested that the General Services Administration's (GSA) Infrastructure Optimization Center of Excellence conduct the cost-benefit analysis on its behalf. Subsequently, GSA conducted an assessment of the NFC data center and three other data centers operated by USDA, the National Aeronautics and Space Administration (NASA), and the Department of Transportation (DOT). Following its completion, USDA submitted the assessment to the Committees on Appropriations on July 27, 2018 (36 days after the required June 21, 2018 deadline). In addition, the act included a provision for GAO to review the sufficiency of USDA's cost-benefit analysis, and to submit the results of its review to the Committees on Appropriations. Our objective was to determine the extent to which the assessment analyzed the cost-effectiveness, security, and continuity of operations of the selected data centers in accordance with federal guidance and leading practices. To accomplish this objective, we compared the assessment's analysis of each data center's cost-benefit and cost-effectiveness, security, and continuity of operations with relevant federal guidelines and leading practices established by the Office of Management and Budget (OMB), GAO, and others. Specifically, we evaluated relevant portions of the assessment against the elements of an economic analysis as defined in GAO's Assessment Methodology for Economic Analysis and consistent with OMB Circular A-94. Based on our evaluation, we determined whether the assessment considered and properly dealt with each of these defined elements. To evaluate the assessment's analysis of security, we first identified whether each data center's facility security level was reported, and then examined whether the information security posture of each data center was analyzed. In addition, to evaluate each center's FedRAMP certification status, we consulted the FedRAMP Marketplace to verify whether the assessment accurately reflected the authority to operate status for each of the selected data centers. Further, we evaluated whether the assessment's continuity of operations data reflected each data center's demonstrated ability to maintain continuity of operations plan functions in the event of a service disruption. We met with the GSA officials who conducted the assessment to discuss their methodology and to determine which, if any, federal or agency-specific policies or guidance were used to develop the assessment. We also interviewed officials responsible for the USDA, DOT, and NASA data centers included in the assessment. We obtained clarifying information about the applicability of their data centers as a basis for comparison to NFC, as well as their views on the extent to which GSA had consulted their offices during the completion of the assessment. We conducted this performance audit from July 2018 through December 2018 in accordance with generally accepted government auditing standards. Those standards require that we plan and perform the audit to obtain sufficient, appropriate evidence to provide a reasonable basis for our findings and conclusions based on our audit objectives. We believe that the evidence obtained provides a reasonable basis for our findings and conclusions based on our audit objectives.

Chapter 4 - CDC is responsible for detecting and responding to emerging health threats and controlling dangerous substances. In carrying out its mission, CDC relies on information technology systems to receive, process, and maintain sensitive data. Accordingly, effective information security controls are essential to ensure that the agency's systems and information are protected from misuse and modification. GAO was asked to examine information security at CDC. In June 2018, GAO issued a limited official use only report on the extent to which CDC had effectively implemented technical controls and an information security program to protect the confidentiality, integrity, and availability of its information on selected information systems. This current chapter is a public version of the June 2018 report. In addition, for this public report, GAO determined the extent to which CDC has taken corrective actions to address the previously identified security program and technical control deficiencies and related recommendations for improvement. For this chapter, GAO reviewed supporting documents regarding CDC's actions on previously identified recommendations and interviewed personnel at CDC.

Chapter 5 - The federal government spends tens of billions of dollars each year on IT products and services. Competition is a key component to achieving the best return on investment for taxpayers. Federal acquisition regulations allow for noncompetitive contracts in certain circumstances. Some noncompetitive contracts act as "bridge contracts"— which can be a useful tool to avoid a lapse in service but can also increase the risk of the government overpaying. There is currently no government-wide definition of bridge contracts. GAO was asked to review the federal government's use of noncompetitive contracts for IT. This chapter examines (1) the extent that agencies used noncompetitive contracts for IT, (2) the reasons for using noncompetitive contracts for selected IT procurements, (3) the extent to which IT procurements at selected agencies were bridge contracts, and (4) the extent to which IT procurements were in support of legacy systems. GAO analyzed FPDSNG data from fiscal years 2013 through 2017 (the most recent and complete data available). GAO developed a generalizable sample of 171 fiscal year 2016 noncompetitive IT contracts and orders awarded by DOD, DHS, and HHS—the agencies with the most spending on IT, to determine the reasons for using noncompetitive contracts and orders, and the extent to which these were bridge contracts or supported legacy systems.

In: Information Security …
Editor: Lauren Van Raalte

ISBN: 978-1-53615-621-8


*Chapter 1*

# INFORMATION TECHNOLOGY: IMPLEMENTATION OF RECOMMENDATIONS IS NEEDED TO STRENGTHEN ACQUISITIONS, OPERATIONS, AND CYBERSECURITY*

*Carol C. Harris*

## WHY GAO DID THIS STUDY

The federal government planned to invest more than $96 billion in IT in fiscal year 2018. However, IT investments have often failed or contributed little to mission-related outcomes. Further, increasingly sophisticated threats and frequent cyber incidents underscore the need for effective information security. As a result, GAO added two areas to its

* This is an edited, reformatted and augmented version of United States Government Accountability Office; Testimony before the Subcommittees on Government Operations and Information Technology, Committee on Oversight and Government Reform, House of Representatives, Accessible Version, Publication No. GAO-19-275T, dated December 12, 2018.

high-risk list: cybersecurity in 1997 and the management of IT acquisitions and operations in 2015.

This statement summarizes federal agencies' progress in improving the management, and ensuring the security, of federal IT. It is primarily based on GAO's reports issued between February 1997 and August 2018 (and an ongoing review) on (1) CIO responsibilities, (2) agency CIOs' involvement in approving IT contracts, (3) data center consolidation efforts, (4) the management of software licenses, and (5) compliance with cybersecurity requirements.

## What GAO Recommends

Since fiscal year 2010, GAO has made 1,242 recommendations to OMB and agencies to address shortcomings in IT acquisitions and operations. Since fiscal year 2010, GAO also has made over 3,000 recommendations to federal agencies to improve the security of federal systems. These recommendations include those to improve the implementation of CIO responsibilities, the oversight of the data center consolidation initiative, software license management efforts, and the strength of security programs and technical controls. Most agencies agreed with the recommendations, and GAO will continue to monitor their implementation.

## What GAO Found

The Office of Management and Budget (OMB) and federal agencies have taken steps to improve the management of information technology (IT) acquisitions and operations and ensure federal cybersecurity through a series of initiatives. As of November 2018, agencies had fully implemented about 59 percent of the 1,242 IT management-related recommendations that GAO has made since fiscal year 2010. Likewise, agencies had implemented about 73 percent of the approximately 3,000 security-related recommendations that GAO has made since 2010. Even with this progress, significant actions remain to be completed.

- Chief Information Officer (CIO) responsibilities. Laws such as the Federal Information Technology Acquisition Reform Act (FITARA) and related guidance assigned 35 key IT management responsibilities to CIOs to help address longstanding challenges. However, in August 2018, GAO reported that none of the 24 selected agencies had policies that fully addressed the role of their CIO, as called for by laws and guidance. GAO recommended that OMB and each of the 24 agencies take actions to improve the effectiveness of CIOs' implementation of their responsibilities. As of November 2018, none of the 27 recommendations had been implemented.
- IT contract approval. According to FITARA, covered agencies' CIOs are required to review and approve IT contracts. Nevertheless, in January 2018, GAO reported that most of the CIOs at 22 covered agencies were not adequately involved in reviewing billions of dollars of IT acquisitions. Consequently, GAO made 39 recommendations to improve CIO oversight over these acquisitions. As of November 2018, 27 of the recommendations had not been addressed.
- Consolidating data centers. OMB launched an initiative in 2010 to reduce data centers. According to agencies, data center consolidation and optimization efforts have resulted in approximately $4.5 billion in cost savings through 2018. Even so, additional work remains. GAO has made 160 recommendations to OMB and agencies to improve the reporting of related cost savings and to achieve optimization targets. However, as of November 2018, 47 of the recommendations had not been fully addressed.
- Managing software licenses. Effective management of software licenses can help avoid purchasing too many licenses that result in unused software. In May 2014, GAO reported that better

management of licenses was needed to achieve savings, and made 135 recommendations to improve such management. As of December 2018, 27 of the recommendations had not been implemented.

- Improving the security of federal IT systems. While the government has acted to protect federal information systems, agencies need to improve security programs, cyber capabilities, and the protection of personally identifiable information. The approximately 3,000 recommendations that GAO has made to agencies since 2010 were aimed at improving the security of federal systems and information. Specifically, these recommendations identified actions for agencies to take to strengthen their information security programs and technical controls over their computer networks and systems. As of November 2018, 688 of the security-related recommendations had not been implemented.

Chairmen Meadows and Hurd, Ranking Members Connolly and Kelly, and Members of the Subcommittees:

I am pleased to be here today to provide an update on federal agencies' efforts to address our high-risk areas on improving the management of information technology (IT) acquisitions and operations, as well as ensuring the security of federal information and IT. The federal government has spent billions of dollars on failed and poorly performing IT investments, which often suffered from ineffective management. Consequently, we added improving the management of IT acquisitions and operations to our high-risk areas for the federal government in February 2015.[1] In February 2017, we noted that, while progress had been made in addressing the high-

[1] GAO, *High-Risk Series: An Update*, GAO-15-290 (Washington, D.C.: Feb. 11, 2015). GAO maintains a high-risk program to focus attention on government operations that it identifies as high risk due to their greater vulnerabilities to fraud, waste, abuse, and mismanagement or the need for transformation to address economy, efficiency, or effectiveness challenges.

risk area of IT acquisitions and operations, significant work remained to be completed.[2]

With regard to cybersecurity, the increasingly sophisticated threats and frequent cyber incidents underscore the continuing and urgent need for effective information security. We first identified federal information security as a government-wide high-risk area in 1997.[3] Subsequently, in 2003,[4] we expanded this area to include computerized systems supporting the nation's critical infrastructure and, in 2015,[5] we further expanded this area to include protecting the privacy of personally identifiable information.[6] We continued to identify federal information security as a government-wide high-risk area in our February 2017 high-risk update report.[7]

My statement today provides an update on agencies' progress in improving the management of IT acquisitions and operations and the security of federal IT. The statement is based on our prior reports issued between February 1997 and August 2018 that discuss federal agencies' (1) implementation of Chief Information Officer (CIO) responsibilities, (2) fulfillment of CIO IT acquisition review requirements, (3) data center consolidation efforts, (4) management of software licenses, and (5) compliance with federal cybersecurity requirements. A more detailed discussion of the objectives, scope, and methodology for this work is included in each of the reports that are cited throughout this statement.

In addition, we have included preliminary results from our ongoing work reviewing the progress being made by federal agencies on data center

---

[2] GAO, *High-Risk Series: Progress on Many High-Risk Areas, While Substantial Efforts Needed on Others*, GAO-17-317 (Washington, D.C.: Feb. 15, 2017).

[3] GAO, *High-Risk Series: Information Management and Technology*, GAO-HR-97-9 (Washington, D.C.: February 1997).

[4] See GAO, *High-Risk Series: An Overview*, GAO-HR-97-1 (Washington, D.C.: February 1997) and *High-Risk Series: An Update*, GAO-03-119 (Washington, D.C.: January 2003).

[5] GAO-15-290.

[6] Personally identifiable information is any information that can be used to distinguish or trace an individual's identity, such as name, date and place of birth, Social Security number, or other types of personal information that can be linked to an individual, such as medical, educational, financial, and employment information.

[7] GAO-17-317.

optimization. The draft report related to this work is currently being reviewed by the agencies and we expect to issue it in early 2019.

We conducted the work upon which this statement is based in accordance with generally accepted government auditing standards. Those standards require that we plan and perform the audit to obtain sufficient, appropriate evidence to provide a reasonable basis for our findings and conclusions based on our audit objectives. We believe that the evidence obtained provides a reasonable basis for our findings and conclusions based on our audit objectives.

## BACKGROUND

According to the President's budget, the federal government planned to invest more than $96 billion for IT in fiscal year 2018—the largest amount ever budgeted. Despite such large IT expenditures, we have previously reported that investments in federal IT too often resulted in failed projects that incurred cost overruns and schedule slippages, while contributing little to the desired mission-related outcomes. For example:

- The tri-agency[8] National Polar-orbiting Operational Environmental Satellite System was disbanded in February 2010 at the direction of the White House's Office of Science and Technology Policy after the program spent 16 years and almost $5 billion.[9]

---

[8] The weather satellite program was jointly managed by the National Oceanic and Atmospheric Administration, the Department of Defense, and the National Aeronautics and Space Administration.

[9] See, for example, GAO, Polar-Orbiting Environmental Satellites: With Costs Increasing and Data Continuity at Risk, Improvements Needed in Tri-agency Decision Making, GAO-09-564 (Washington, D.C.: June 17, 2009) and Environmental Satellites: Polar-Orbiting Satellite Acquisition Faces Delays; Decisions Needed on Whether and How to Ensure Climate Data Continuity, GAO-08-518 (Washington, D.C.: May 16, 2008).

- The Department of Homeland Security's (DHS) Secure Border Initiative Network program was ended in January 2011, after the department obligated more than $1 billion for the program.[10]
- The Department of Veterans Affairs' Financial and Logistics Integrated Technology Enterprise program was intended to be delivered by 2014 at a total estimated cost of $609 million, but was terminated in October 2011.[11]
- The Department of Defense's Expeditionary Combat Support System was canceled in December 2012 after spending more than a billion dollars and failing to deploy within 5 years of initially obligating funds.[12]
- The United States Coast Guard (Coast Guard) decided to terminate its Integrated Health Information System project in 2015. As reported by the agency in August 2017, the Coast Guard spent approximately $60 million over 7 years on this project, which resulted in no equipment or software that could be used for future efforts.[13]

Our past work has found that these and other failed IT projects often suffered from a lack of disciplined and effective management, such as project planning, requirements definition, and program oversight and

---

[10] See, for example, GAO, Secure Border Initiative: DHS Needs to Strengthen Management and Oversight of Its Prime Contractor, GAO-11-6 (Washington, D.C.: Oct. 18, 2010); Secure Border Initiative: DHS Needs to Reconsider Its Proposed Investment in Key Technology Program, GAO-10-340 (Washington, D.C.: May 5, 2010); and Secure Border Initiative: DHS Needs to Address Testing and Performance Limitations That Place Key Technology Program at Risk, GAO-10-158 (Washington, D.C.: Jan. 29, 2010).

[11] GAO, Information Technology: Actions Needed to Fully Establish Program Management Capability for VA's Financial and Logistics Initiative, GAO-10-40 (Washington, D.C.: Oct. 26, 2009).

[12] GAO, DOD Financial Management: Implementation Weaknesses in Army and Air Force Business Systems Could Jeopardize DOD's Auditability Goals, GAO-12-134 (Washington, D.C.: Feb. 28, 2012) and DOD Business Transformation: Improved Management Oversight of Business System Modernization Efforts Needed, GAO-11-53 (Washington, D.C.: Oct. 7, 2010).

[13] GAO, Coast Guard Health Records: Timely Acquisition of New System Is Critical to Overcoming Challenges with Paper Process, GAO-18-59 (Washington, D.C.: Jan. 24, 2018).

governance. In many instances, agencies had not consistently applied best practices that are critical to successfully acquiring IT.

Such projects have also failed due to a lack of oversight and governance. Executive-level governance and oversight across the government has often been ineffective, specifically from CIOs. For example, we have reported that some CIOs' roles were limited because they did not have the authority to review and approve the entire agency IT portfolio.[14]

In addition to failures when acquiring IT, security deficiencies can threaten systems. As we previously reported, in order to counter security threats, the 23 civilian Chief Financial Officers (CFO) Act agencies spent a combined total of approximately $4 billion on IT security-related activities in fiscal year 2016.[15] Even so, our cybersecurity work at federal agencies continues to highlight information security deficiencies. The following examples describe the types of risks we have found at federal agencies.

- In September 2018, we reported that the Department of Education's Office of Federal Student Aid exercises minimal oversight of lenders' protection of student data and lacks assurance that appropriate risk-based safeguards are being effectively implemented, tested, and monitored.[16]

---

[14] GAO, Federal Chief Information Officers: Opportunities Exist to Improve Role in Information Technology Management, GAO-11-634 (Washington, D.C.: Sept. 15, 2011).

[15] The agencies included were the others covered by the CFO Act of 1990, 31 U.S.C. § 901(b): the Departments of Agriculture, Commerce, Education, Energy, Health and Human Services, Homeland Security, Housing and Urban Development, the Interior, Justice, Labor, State, Transportation, the Treasury, and Veterans Affairs; the Environmental Protection Agency; General Services Administration; National Aeronautics and Space Administration; National Science Foundation; Nuclear Regulatory Commission; Office of Personnel Management; Small Business Administration; Social Security Administration; and the U.S. Agency for International Development. See GAO, Federal Information Security: Weaknesses Continue to Indicate Need for Effective Implementation of Policies and Practices, GAO-17-549 (Washington, D.C.: Sept. 28, 2017). According to the Department of Defense, at the time of our review, the department had not submitted its FISMA report, nor was it required to issue a financial report for fiscal year 2016.

[16] GAO, Cybersecurity: Office of Federal Student Aid Should Take Additional Steps to Oversee Non-School Partners' Protection of Borrower Information, GAO-18-518 (Washington, D.C.: Sept. 17, 2018).

- In August 2017, we reported that, since the 2015 data breaches, the Office of Personnel Management (OPM) had taken actions to prevent, mitigate, and respond to data breaches involving sensitive personal and background investigation information.[17] However, we noted that the agency had not fully implemented recommendations made to OPM by DHS's United States Computer Emergency Readiness Team to help the agency improve its overall security posture and improve its ability to protect its systems and information from security breaches.
- In July 2017, we reported that information security at the Internal Revenue Service had weaknesses that limited its effectiveness in protecting the confidentiality, integrity, and availability of financial and sensitive taxpayer data. An underlying reason for these weaknesses was that the Internal Revenue Service had not effectively implemented elements of its information security program.[18]
- In May 2016, we reported that the National Aeronautics and Space Administration, the Nuclear Regulatory Commission, OPM, and the Department of Veteran Affairs did not always control access to selected high-impact systems, patch known software vulnerabilities, and plan for contingencies. An underlying reason for these weaknesses was that the agencies had not fully implemented key elements of their information security programs.[19]
- In August 2016, we reported that the information security of the Food and Drug Administration had significant weaknesses that

[17] GAO, Information Security: OPM Has Improved Controls, but Further Efforts Are Needed, GAO-17-614 (Washington, D.C.: Aug. 3, 2017).

[18] GAO, Information Security: Control Deficiencies Continue to Limit IRS's Effectiveness in Protecting Sensitive Financial and Taxpayer Data, GAO-17-395 (Washington, D.C.: July 26, 2017).

[19] GAO, Information Security: Agencies Need to Improve Controls over Selected High-Impact Systems, GAO-16-501 (Washington, D.C.: May 18, 2016).

jeopardized the confidentiality, integrity, and availability of its information systems and industry and public health data.[20]

## FITARA Increases CIO Authorities and Responsibilities for Managing IT

Congress and the President have enacted various key pieces of reform legislation to address IT management issues. These include the federal IT acquisition reform legislation commonly referred to as the Federal Information Technology Acquisition Reform Act (FITARA).[21] This legislation was intended to improve covered agencies' acquisitions of IT and enable Congress to monitor agencies' progress and hold them accountable for reducing duplication and achieving cost savings.[22] The law includes specific requirements related to seven areas:

- Agency CIO authority enhancements. CIOs at covered agencies have the authority to, among other things, (1) approve the IT budget requests of their respective agencies and (2) review and approve IT contracts.
- Federal data center consolidation initiative (FDCCI). Agencies covered by FITARA are required, among other things, to provide a strategy for consolidating and optimizing their data centers and issue quarterly updates on the progress made.

---

[20] GAO, Information Security: FDA Needs to Rectify Control Weaknesses That Place Industry and Public Health Data at Risk, GAO-16-513 (Washington, D.C.: Aug. 30, 2016).

[21] *Carl Levin and Howard P. 'Buck' McKeon National Defense Authorization Act for Fiscal Year 2015*, Pub. L. No. 113-291, div. A, title VIII, subtitle D, 128 Stat. 3292, 3438-3450 (Dec. 19, 2014).

[22] The provisions apply to the agencies covered by the CFO Act of 1990, 31 U.S.C. § 901(b). These agencies are the Departments of Agriculture, Commerce, Defense, Education, Energy, Health and Human Services, Homeland Security, Housing and Urban Development, Justice, Labor, State, the Interior, the Treasury, Transportation, and Veterans Affairs; the Environmental Protection Agency, General Services Administration, National Aeronautics and Space Administration, National Science Foundation, Nuclear Regulatory Commission, Office of Personnel Management, Small Business Administration, Social Security Administration, and U.S. Agency for International Development. However, parts of FITARA do not apply to the Department of Defense.

- Enhanced transparency and improved risk management. The Office of Management and Budget (OMB) and covered agencies are to make detailed information on federal IT investments publicly available, and agency CIOs are to categorize their investments by level of risk.
- Portfolio review. Covered agencies are to annually review IT investment portfolios in order to, among other things, increase efficiency and effectiveness and identify potential waste and duplication.
- Expansion of training and use of IT acquisition cadres. Covered agencies are to update their acquisition human capital plans to support timely and effective IT acquisitions. In doing so, the law calls for agencies to consider, among other things, establishing IT acquisition cadres (i.e., multi-functional groups of professionals to acquire and manage complex programs), or developing agreements with other agencies that have such cadres.
- Government-wide software purchasing program. The General Services Administration is to develop a strategic sourcing initiative to enhance government-wide acquisition and management of software. In doing so, the law requires that, to the maximum extent practicable, the General Services Administration should allow for the purchase of a software license agreement that is available for use by all executive branch agencies as a single user.[23]
- Maximizing the benefit of the Federal Strategic Sourcing Initiative.[24] Federal agencies are required to compare their purchases of services and supplies to what is offered under the Federal Strategic Sourcing Initiative.

---

[23] The Making Electronic Government Accountable by Yielding Tangible Efficiencies Act of 2016, or the "MEGABYTE Act" further enhances CIOs' management of software licenses by requiring agency CIOs to establish an agency software licensing policy and a comprehensive software license inventory to track and maintain licenses, among other requirements. Pub. L. No. 114-210, 130 Stat. 824 (2016).

[24] The Federal Strategic Sourcing Initiative is a program established by the General Services Administration and the Department of the Treasury to address government-wide opportunities to strategically source commonly purchased goods and services and eliminate duplication of efforts across agencies.

In June 2015, OMB released guidance describing how agencies are to implement FITARA.[25] This guidance is intended to, among other things:

- assist agencies in aligning their IT resources with statutory requirements;
- establish government-wide IT management controls to meet the law's requirements, while providing agencies with flexibility to adapt to unique agency processes and requirements;
- strengthen the relationship between agency CIOs and bureau CIOs; and strengthen CIO accountability for IT costs, schedules, performance, and security.

The guidance identifies a number of actions that agencies are to take to establish a basic set of roles and responsibilities (referred to as the common baseline) for CIOs and other senior agency officials and, thus, to implement the authorities described in the law. For example, agencies are to conduct a self-assessment and submit a plan describing the changes they intend to make to ensure that common baseline responsibilities are implemented.

In addition, in August 2016, OMB released guidance intended to, among other things, define a framework for achieving the data center consolidation and optimization requirements of FITARA.[26] The guidance directed agencies to develop a data center consolidation and optimization strategic plan that defined the agency's data center strategy for fiscal years 2016, 2017, and 2018. This strategy was to include, among other things, a statement from the agency CIO indicating whether the agency had complied with all data center reporting requirements in FITARA. Further, the guidance states that OMB is to maintain a public dashboard to display

---

[25] OMB, *Management and Oversight of Federal Information Technology*, Memorandum M15-14 (Washington, D.C.: June 10, 2015).

[26] OMB, *Data Center Optimization Initiative (DCOI),* Memorandum M-16-19 (Washington D.C.: Aug. 1, 2016).

consolidation-related costs savings and optimization performance information for the agencies.

## Congress Has Undertaken Efforts to Continue Selected FITARA Provisions and Modernize Federal IT

Congress has recognized the importance of agencies' continued implementation of FITARA provisions, and has taken legislative action to extend selected provisions beyond their original dates of expiration. Specifically, Congress and the President enacted laws to:

- remove the expiration dates for the enhanced transparency and improved risk management provisions, which were set to expire in 2019;
- remove the expiration date for portfolio review, which was set to expire in 2019; and
- extend the expiration date for FDCCI from 2018 to 2020.[27]

In addition, Congress and the President enacted a law to authorize the availability of funding mechanisms to help further agencies' efforts to modernize IT. The law, known as the Modernizing Government Technology (MGT) Act, authorizes agencies to establish working capital funds for use in transitioning from legacy IT systems, as well as for addressing evolving threats to information security.[28] The law also creates the Technology Modernization Fund, within the Department of the Treasury, from which agencies can "borrow" money to retire and replace legacy systems, as well as acquire or develop systems. Further, in February 2018, OMB issued guidance for agencies on implementing the MGT Act.[29] The guidance was intended to provide agencies additional information

---

[27] *FITARA Enhancement Act of 2017*, Pub. L. No. 115-88, 131 Stat. 1278 (2017).

[28] *National Defense Authorization Act for Fiscal Year 2018*, Pub. L. No. 115-91, Div. A, Title X, Subtitle G (2017).

[29] OMB, Implementation of the Modernizing Government Technology Act, M-18-12 (Washington, D.C.: Feb. 27, 2018).

regarding the Technology Modernization Fund, and the administration and funding of the related IT working capital funds. Specifically, the guidance encouraged agencies to begin submitting initial project proposals for modernization on February 27, 2018. In addition, in accordance with the MGT Act, the guidance provides details regarding a Technology Modernization Board, which is to consist of (1) the Federal CIO; (2) a senior IT official from the General Services Administration; (3) a member of DHS's National Protection and Program Directorate;[30] and (4) four federal employees with technical expertise in IT development, financial management, cybersecurity and privacy, and acquisition, appointed by the Director of OMB.

## FISMA Establishes Responsibilities for Agencies to Address Federal Cybersecurity

Congress and the President enacted the *Federal Information Security Modernization Act of 2014* (FISMA) to improve federal cybersecurity and clarify government-wide responsibilities.[31] The act addresses the increasing sophistication of cybersecurity attacks, promotes the use of automated security tools with the ability to continuously monitor and diagnose the security posture of federal agencies, and provides for improved oversight of federal agencies' information security programs. Toward this end, the act clarifies and assigns specific responsibilities to entities such as OMB, DHS, and the federal agencies. Table 1 describes a selection of the OMB, DHS, and agency responsibilities.

---

[30] The National Protection and Program Directorate (NPPD) was the Department of Homeland Security component responsible for addressing physical and cyber infrastructure protection. The recently enacted Cybersecurity and Infrastructure Security Agency Act of 2018 renames NPPD the Cybersecurity and Infrastructure Security Agency and establishes a Director and responsibilities for the agency.

[31] T*he Federal Information Security Modernization Act of 2014* (FISMA 2014) (Pub. L. No. 113-283, Dec. 18, 2014) largely superseded the *Federal Information Security Management Act of 2002* (FISMA 2002), enacted as Title III, E-Government Act of 2002, Pub. L. No. 107-347, 116 Stat. 2899, 2946 (Dec. 17, 2002). As used in this testimony, FISMA refers both to FISMA 2014 and to those provisions of FISMA 2002 that were either incorporated into FISMA 2014 or were unchanged and continue in full force and effect.

## Table 1. Selected Federal Information Security Modernization Act of 2014 (FISMA) Responsibilities

| Responsible agency or agencies | FISMA responsibilities |
|---|---|
| Office of Management and Budget (OMB) | • Develop and oversee the implementation of policies, principles, standards, and guidelines on information security in federal agencies, except with regard to national security systems.<br>• Require agencies to identify and provide information security protections commensurate with assessments of risk to their information and information systems.<br>• Report annually, in consultation with the Department of Homeland Security (DHS), on the effectiveness of information security policies and practices.<br>• Ensure that data breach notification policies and guidelines are periodically updated and require notification to congressional committees and affected individuals.<br>• Ensure development of guidance for evaluating the effectiveness of an information security program and practices, in consultation with DHS, the Chief Information Officers Council, the Council of the Inspectors General on Integrity and Efficiency, and other interested parties, as appropriate. |
| DHS | • Consult with OMB to administer the implementation of agency information security policies and practices for non-national security information systems. |
| Executive branch agencies covered by FISM | • Develop, document, and implement an agency-wide information security program that includes, among other things, periodic risk assessments, policies and procedures, plans for providing adequate information security, security awareness training, and periodic testing and evaluation.<br>• ·Ensure that senior officials carry out assigned responsibilities and that all personnel are held accountable for complying with the agency's information security program.<br>• ·Submit an annual report on the adequacy and effectiveness of information security policies, procedures, and practices, as well as compliance with the act to OMB, certain congressional committees, and the Comptroller General of the United States. The annual report is to include descriptions of major security incidents. |
| Executive branch agencies' Office of the Inspector General or independent auditor | • Assess the effectiveness of the agency's information security policies, procedures, and practices |

Source: GAO analysis. \| GAO-19-275T.

## The Administration Has Undertaken Efforts to Improve, Modernize, and Strengthen the Security of Federal IT

Beyond the implementation of FITARA, FISMA, and related actions, the administration has also initiated other efforts intended to improve federal IT. Specifically, in March 2017, the administration established the Office of American Innovation, which has a mission to, among other things, make recommendations to the President on policies and plans aimed at improving federal government operations and services. In doing so, the office is to consult with both OMB and the Office of Science and Technology Policy on policies and plans intended to improve government operations and services, improve the quality of life for Americans, and spur job creation.[32]

In May 2017, the Administration also established the American Technology Council, which has a goal of helping to transform and modernize federal agency IT and how the federal government uses and delivers digital services.[33] The President is the chairman of this council, and the Federal CIO and the United States Digital Service Administrator are among the members.[34]

In addition, on May 11, 2017, the President signed Executive Order 13800, *Strengthening the Cybersecurity of Federal Networks and Critical Infrastructure*.[35] This executive order outlined actions to enhance cybersecurity across federal agencies and critical infrastructure to improve the nation's cyber posture and capabilities against cybersecurity threats. Among other things, the order tasked the Director of the American

---

[32] The White House Office of Science and Technology Policy provides the President and others within the Executive Office of the President with advice on the scientific, engineering, and technological aspects of the economy, national security, homeland security, health, foreign relations, the environment, and the technological recovery and use of resources, among other topics.

[33] Exec. Order No. 13794, *Establishment of the American Technology Council*, 82 Fed. Reg. 20811 (May 3, 2017).

[34] The United States Digital Service is an office within OMB which aims to improve the most important public-facing federal digital services.

[35] Exec. Order No. 13800, 82 Fed Reg. 22391 (May 16, 2017).

Technology Council[36] to coordinate a report to the President from the Secretary of DHS, the Director of OMB, and the Administrator of the General Services Administration, in consultation with the Secretary of Commerce, regarding the modernization of federal IT.

As a result, the *Report to the President on Federal IT Modernization* was issued on December 13, 2017, and outlined the current and envisioned state of federal IT. The report focused on modernization efforts to improve the security posture of federal IT and recognized that agencies have attempted to modernize systems but have been stymied by a variety of factors, including resource prioritization, ability to procure services quickly, and technical issues. The report provided multiple recommendations intended to address these issues through the modernization and consolidation of networks and the use of shared services to enable future network architectures.

Further, in March 2018, the Administration issued the *President's Management Agenda,* which lays out a long-term vision for modernizing the federal government.[37] The agenda identifies three related drivers of transformation—IT modernization; data, accountability, and transparency; and the workforce of the future—that are intended to push change across the federal government.

The Administration also established 14 related Cross-Agency Priority goals, many of which have elements that involve IT.[38] In particular, the Cross-Agency Priority goal on IT modernization states that modern IT must function as the backbone of how government serves the public in the digital age. This goal establishes three priorities that are to guide the Administration's efforts to modernize federal IT: (1) enhancing mission effectiveness by improving the quality and efficiency of critical services, including the increased utilization of cloud-based solutions; (2) reducing cybersecurity risks to the federal mission by leveraging current commercial

---

[36] This position is held by an employee of the Executive Office of the President, as designated by the President.

[37] President's Management Council and Executive Office of the President, *President's Management Agenda* (Washington, D.C.: Mar. 20, 2018).

[38] Cross-Agency Priority goals were established in response to the Government Performance and Results Act Modernization Act of 2010, Sec. 5, Pub. L. No. 111-352 (Jan. 4, 2011); 124 Stat. 3866, 3873; 31 U.S.C. § 1120(a)(1)(B).

capabilities and implementing cutting edge cybersecurity capabilities; and (3) building a modern IT workforce by recruiting, reskilling, and retaining professionals able to help drive modernization with up-to-date technology.

More recently, on May 15, 2018, the President signed Executive Order 13833, *Enhancing the Effectiveness of Agency Chief Information Officers.* Among other things, this executive order is intended to better position agencies to modernize their IT systems, execute IT programs more efficiently, and reduce cybersecurity risks.[39] The order pertains to 22 of the 24 CFO Act agencies: the Department of Defense and the Nuclear Regulatory Commission are exempt. For the covered agencies, the executive order strengthens the role of agency CIOs by, among other things, requiring them to report directly to their agency head; serve as their agency head's primary IT strategic advisor; and have a significant role in all management, governance, and oversight processes related to IT. In addition, one of the cybersecurity requirements directs agencies to ensure that the CIO works closely with an integrated team of senior executives, including those with expertise in IT, security, and privacy, to implement appropriate risk management measures.

## Agencies Have Not Fully Addressed the IT Acquisitions and Operations High-Risk Area

In the February 2017 update to our high-risk series, we reported that agencies still needed to complete significant work related to the management of IT acquisitions and operations.[40] We stressed that OMB and federal agencies should continue to expeditiously implement FITARA and OMB's related guidance, which includes enhancing CIO authority, consolidating data centers, and acquiring and managing software licenses.

Our update to this high-risk area also stressed that OMB and agencies needed to continue to implement our prior recommendations in order to

[39] Exec. Order No. 13833, Enhancing the Effectiveness of Agency Chief Information Officers (May 15, 2018).

[40] GAO-17-317.

improve their ability to effectively and efficiently invest in IT. Specifically, since fiscal year 2010, we have made 1,242 recommendations to OMB and federal agencies to address shortcomings in IT acquisitions and operations.

As stated in the update, OMB and agencies should demonstrate government-wide progress in the management of IT investments by, among other things, implementing at least 80 percent of our recommendations related to managing IT acquisitions and operations. As of November 2018, OMB and agencies had fully implemented 732 (or about 59 percent) of the 1,242 recommendations. Figure 1 summarizes the progress that OMB and agencies have made in addressing our recommendations compared to the 80 percent target.

Overall, federal agencies would be better positioned to realize billions in cost savings and additional management improvements if they address these recommendations, including those aimed at implementing CIO responsibilities, reviewing IT acquisitions; improving data center consolidation; and managing software licenses.

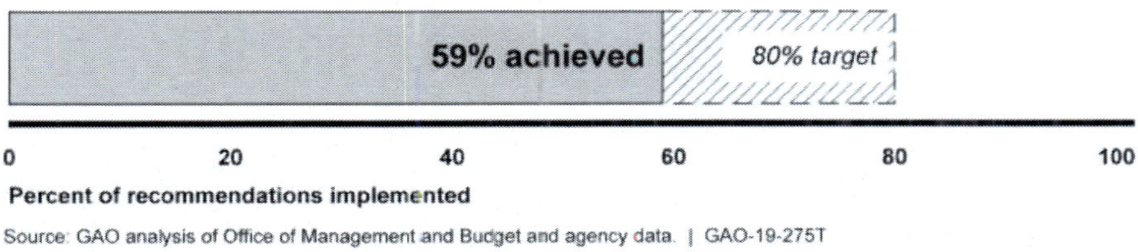


Figure 1. Summary of the Office of Management and Budget's and Federal Agencies' Progress in Addressing GAO's Information Technology Acquisitions and Operations Recommendations, as of November 2018.

## Agencies Need to Address Shortcomings and Challenges in Implementing CIO Responsibilities

In all, the various laws, such as FITARA,[41] and related guidance assign 35 IT management responsibilities to CIOs in six key areas. These areas

[41] In addition to FITARA, these laws include FISMA (44 U.S.C. § 3554), the Paperwork Reduction Act (44 U.S.C. § 3506), and the Clinger-Cohen Act (40 U.S.C. §§ 11312 and 11313).

are: leadership and accountability, budgeting, information security, investment management, workforce, and strategic planning.

In August 2018, we reported that none of the 24 agencies we reviewed had policies that fully addressed the role of their CIO, as called for by federal laws and guidance.[42] In this regard, a majority of the agencies had fully or substantially addressed the role of their CIOs for the area of leadership and accountability. In addition, a majority of the agencies had substantially or partially addressed the role of their CIOs for two areas: information security and IT budgeting.

However, most agencies partially or minimally addressed the role of their CIOs for two areas: investment management and strategic planning. Further, the majority of the agencies minimally addressed or did not address the role of their CIOs for the remaining area: IT workforce. Figure 2 depicts the extent to which the 24 agencies addressed the role of their CIOs for the six areas.

Despite the shortfalls in agencies' policies addressing the roles of their CIOs, most agency officials stated that their CIOs are implementing the responsibilities even if the agencies do not have policies requiring implementation.

Nevertheless, the CIOs of the 24 selected agencies acknowledged in responses to a survey that we administered that they were not always very effective in implementing the six IT management areas. Specifically, at least 10 of the CIOs indicated that they were less than very effective for each of the six areas of responsibility. We believe that until agencies fully address the role of CIOs in their policies, agencies will be limited in addressing longstanding IT management challenges.

Figure 3 depicts the extent to which the CIOs reported their effectiveness in implementing the six areas of responsibility.

Beyond the actions of the agencies, however, shortcomings in agencies' policies also are partially attributable to two weaknesses in OMB's guidance. First, the guidance does not comprehensively address all

---

[42] GAO, Federal Chief Information Officers: Critical Actions Needed to Address Shortcomings and Challenges in Implementing Responsibilities, GAO-18-93 (Washington, D.C.: Aug. 2, 2018).

CIO responsibilities, such as those related to assessing the extent to which personnel meet IT management knowledge and skill requirements, and ensuring that personnel are held accountable for complying with the information security program. Correspondingly, the majority of the agencies' policies did not fully address nearly all of the responsibilities that were not included in OMB's guidance.

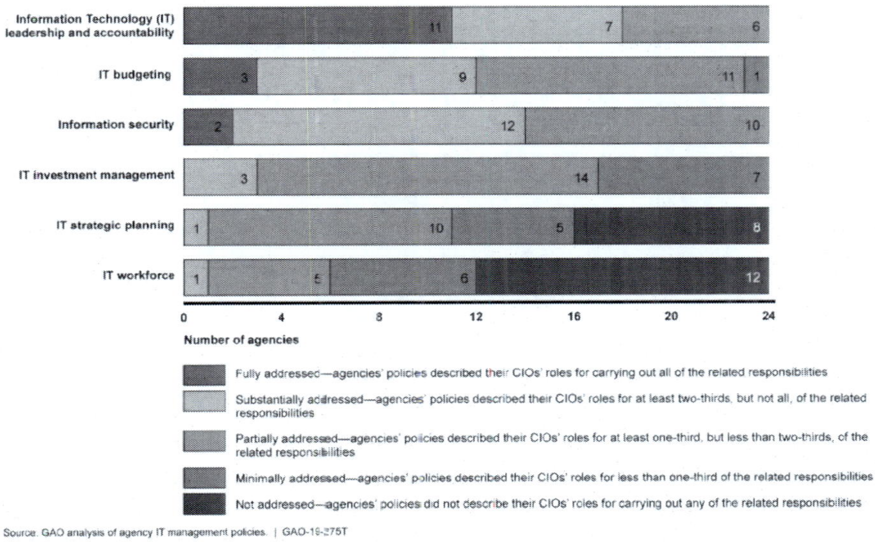


Figure 2. Extent to Which 24 Selected Agencies' Policies Addressed the Role of Their Chief Information Officers (CIO), Presented from Most Addressed to Least Addressed Area.

Second, OMB's guidance does not ensure that CIOs have a significant role in (1) IT planning, programming, and budgeting decisions; and (2) execution decisions and the management, governance, and oversight processes related to IT, as required by federal law and guidance. In the absence of comprehensive guidance, CIOs will not be positioned to effectively acquire, maintain, and secure their IT systems.

In response to the survey conducted for our August 2018 report, the 24 agency CIOs also identified a number of factors that enabled and challenged their ability to effectively manage IT. Specifically, most agency CIOs cited five factors as being enablers to effectively carry out their responsibilities: (1) NIST guidance, (2) the CIO's position in the agency hierarchy, (3) OMB guidance, (4) coordination with the Chief Acquisition Officer (CAO), and (5) legal authority. Further, three factors were cited by CIOs as major factors that have challenged their ability to effectively carry out responsibilities: (1) processes for hiring, recruiting, and retaining IT personnel; (2) financial resources; and (3) the availability of personnel/staff resources.

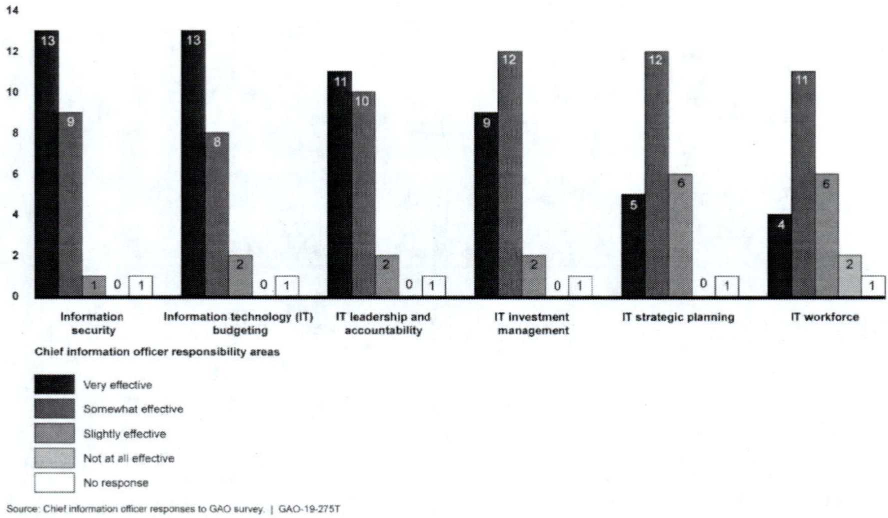


Figure 3. Extent to Which Agency Chief Information Officers (CIO) Reported Effective Implementation of Six Responsibility Areas, Presented from Most Effective to Least Effective Area, as of August 2018.

As shown in Figure 4, the five enabling factors were identified by at least half of the 24 CIOs and the three factors cited as major challenges were identified by at least half of the CIOs.

Although OMB has issued guidance aimed at addressing the three factors that were identified by at least half of the CIOs as major challenges, the guidance does not fully address those challenges. Further, regarding the financial resources challenge, OMB recently required agencies to provide data on CIO authority over IT spending; however, its guidance does not provide a complete definition of the authority. In the absence of such guidance, agencies have created varying definitions of CIO authority. Until OMB updates its guidance to include a complete definition of the authority that CIOs are to have over IT spending, it will be difficult for OMB to identify any deficiencies in this area and to help agencies make any needed improvements.

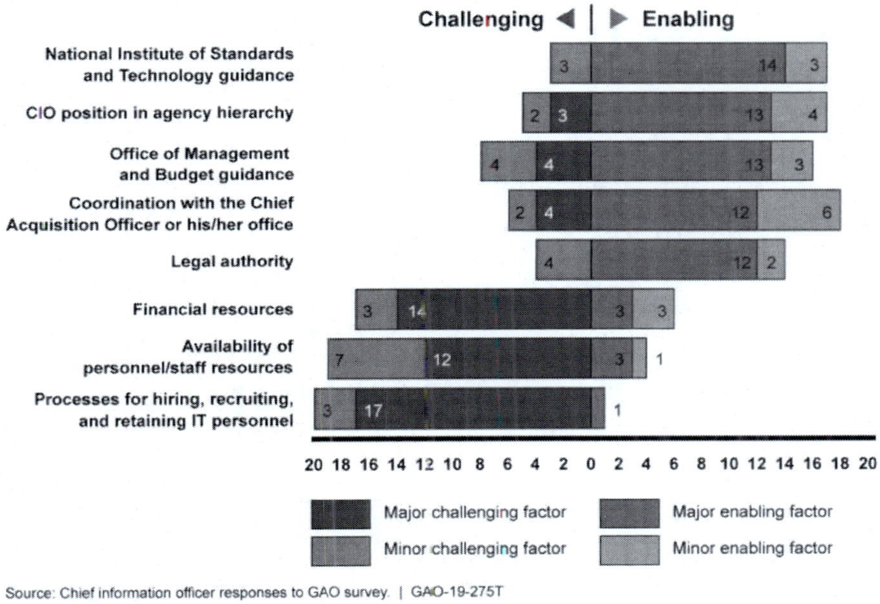


Figure 4. Factors Commonly Identified as Enabling and Challenging Chief Information Officers (CIO) to Effectively Manage Information Technology (IT), Presented from Most Enabling to Least Enabling Factor.

In order to address challenges in implementing CIO responsibilities, we made three recommendations to OMB and one recommendation to each of the selected 24 federal agencies to improve the effectiveness of CIOs' implementation of their responsibilities for each of the six IT management areas. Most agencies agreed with or had no comments on the recommendations. As of November 2018, all 27 of the recommendations had not been implemented. We will continue to monitor the implementation of these recommendations.

## Agencies Need to Ensure That IT Acquisitions Are Reviewed and Approved by CIOs

FITARA includes a provision to enhance covered agency CIOs' authority through, among other things, requiring agency heads to ensure that CIOs review and approve IT contracts. OMB's FITARA implementation guidance expanded upon this aspect of the legislation in a number of ways.[43] Specifically, according to the guidance:

- CIOs may review and approve IT acquisition strategies and plans, rather than individual IT contracts;[44]
- CIOs can designate other agency officials to act as their representatives, but the CIOs must retain accountability;[45]
- CAOs are responsible for ensuring that all IT contract actions are consistent with CIO-approved acquisition strategies and plans; and
- CAOs are to indicate to the CIOs when planned acquisition strategies and acquisition plans include IT.

In January 2018, we reported[46] that most of the CIOs at 22 selected agencies[47] were not adequately involved in reviewing billions of dollars of IT acquisitions. For instance, most of the 22 agencies did not identify all of

---

[43] OMB, Management and Oversight of Federal Information Technology, M-15-14 (Washington, D.C.: June 10, 2015).

[44] OMB's guidance states that CIOs should only review and approve individual IT contract actions if they are not part of an approved acquisition strategy or plan.

[45] OMB has interpreted FITARA's "governance process" provision to permit such delegation. That provision allows covered agencies to use the governance processes of the agency to approve a contract or other agreement for IT if the CIO of the agency is included as a full participant in the governance process.

[46] GAO, Information Technology: Agencies Need to Involve Chief Information Officers in Reviewing Billions of Dollars in Acquisitions, GAO-18-42 (Washington, D.C.: Jan. 10, 2018).

[47] The 22 agencies are the Departments of Agriculture, Commerce, Education, Energy, Health and Human Services, Housing and Urban Development, Justice, Labor, State, the Interior, the Treasury, Transportation, and Veterans Affairs; the Environmental Protection Agency; General Services Administration; National Aeronautics and Space Administration; National Science Foundation; Nuclear Regulatory Commission; Office of Personnel Management; Small Business Administration; Social Security Administration; and U.S. Agency for International Development.

their IT contracts. In this regard, the agencies identified 78,249 IT-related contracts, to which they obligated $14.7 billion in fiscal year 2016. However, we identified 31,493 additional contracts with $4.5 billion obligated, raising the total amount obligated to IT contracts by these agencies in fiscal year 2016 to at least $19.2 billion. Figure 5 reflects the obligations that the 22 selected agencies reported to us relative to the obligations we identified.

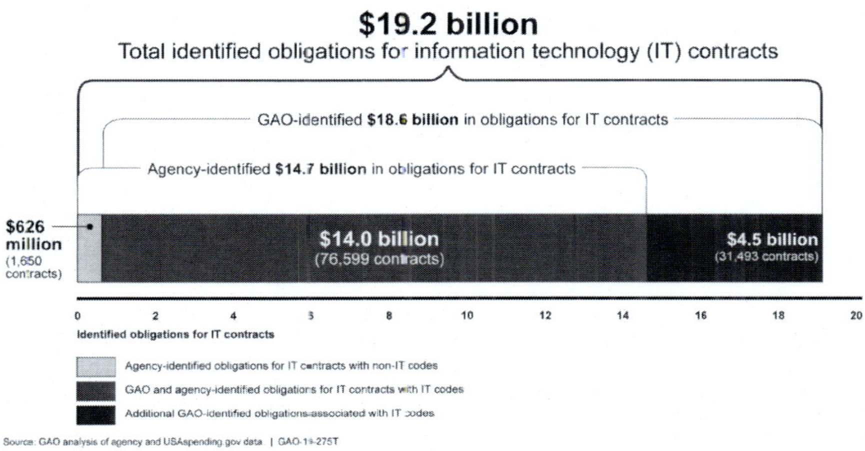


Figure 5. Agency- and GAO-Identified Approximate Dollars Obligated to Fiscal Year 2016 IT Contracts at 22 Selected Agencies.

The percentage of additional IT contract obligations we identified varied among the selected agencies. For example, the Department of State did not identify 1 percent of its IT contract obligations. Conversely, eight agencies did not identify over 40 percent of their IT contract obligations.

Many of the selected agencies that did not identify these IT contract obligations also did not follow OMB guidance. Specifically, 14 of the 22 agencies did not involve the acquisition office in their process to identify IT acquisitions for CIO review, as required by OMB. In addition, 7 agencies did not establish guidance to aid officials in recognizing IT. We concluded that until these agencies involve the acquisitions office in their IT acquisition identification processes and establish supporting guidance, they cannot ensure that they will identify all such acquisitions. Without proper identification of IT acquisitions, these agencies and CIOs cannot effectively provide oversight of these acquisitions.

In addition to not identifying all IT contracts, 14 of the 22 selected agencies did not fully satisfy OMB's requirement that the CIO review and approve IT acquisition plans or strategies. Further, only 11 of 96 randomly selected IT contracts at 10 agencies that we evaluated were CIO-reviewed and approved as required by OMB's guidance. The 85 contracts not reviewed had a total possible value of approximately $23.8 billion.

Until agencies ensure that CIOs are able to review and approve all IT acquisitions, CIOs will continue to have limited visibility and input into their agencies' planned IT expenditures and will not be able to effectively use the increased authority that FITARA's contract approval provision is intended to provide. Further, agencies will likely miss an opportunity to strengthen their CIOs' authority and the oversight of acquisitions. As a result, agencies may award IT contracts that are duplicative, wasteful, or poorly conceived.

As a result of these findings, we made 39 recommendations in our January 2018 report. Among these, we recommended that agencies ensure that their acquisition offices are involved in identifying IT acquisitions and issuing related guidance, and that IT acquisitions are reviewed in accordance with OMB guidance. OMB and the majority of the agencies generally agreed with or did not comment on the recommendations. As of November 2018, 27 of the recommendations had not been implemented.

## Agencies Have Made Progress in Consolidating Data Centers, but Need to Take Action to Achieve Planned Cost Savings

In our February 2017 high-risk update, we stressed that OMB and agencies needed to demonstrate additional progress on achieving data center consolidation savings in order to improve the management of IT acquisitions and operations. Further, data center consolidation efforts are key to implementing FITARA. Specifically, OMB established the FDCCI in February 2010 to improve the efficiency, performance, and environmental footprint of federal data center activities. The enactment of FITARA in 2014 codified and expanded the initiative.

In addition, in August 2016, OMB issued a memorandum which established the Data Center Optimization Initiative (DCOI) and included guidance on how to implement the data center consolidation and optimization provisions of FITARA.[48] Among other things, the guidance required agencies to consolidate inefficient infrastructure, optimize existing facilities, improve their security posture, and achieve cost savings.

According to agencies, data center consolidation and optimization efforts have resulted in approximately $4.5 billion in cost savings through 2018. However, additional work remains to fully carry out the initiative. Specifically, in a series of reports that we issued from July 2011 through May 2018, we noted that, while data center consolidation could potentially save the federal government billions of dollars, weaknesses existed in several areas, including agencies' data center consolidation plans, data center optimization, and OMB's tracking and reporting on related cost savings.[49] In these reports, we made a total of 160 recommendations to OMB and 24 agencies to improve the execution and oversight of the initiative. Most agencies and OMB agreed with our recommendations or had no comments. As of November 2018, 47 of these 160 recommendations remained unimplemented.

---

[48] OMB, Memorandum M-16-19.

[49] GAO, Data Center Optimization: Continued Agency Actions Needed to Meet Goals and Address Prior Recommendations, GAO-18-264 (Washington, D.C.: May 23, 2018); Data Center Optimization: Agencies Need to Address Challenges and Improve Progress to Achieve Cost Savings Goal, GAO-17-448 (Washington, D.C.: Aug. 15, 2017); Data Center Optimization: Agencies Need to Complete Plans to Address Inconsistencies in Reported Savings, GAO-17-388 (Washington, D.C: May 18, 2017); Data Center Consolidation: Agencies Making Progress, but Planned Savings Goals Need to Be Established [Reissued on March 4, 2016], GAO-16-323 (Washington, D.C.: Mar. 3, 2016); Data Center Consolidation: Reporting Can Be Improved to Reflect Substantial Planned Savings, GAO-14-713 (Washington, D.C.: Sept. 25, 2014); Data Center Consolidation: Strengthened Oversight Needed to Achieve Cost Savings Goal, GAO-13-378 (Washington, D.C.: Apr. 23, 2013); Data Center Consolidation: Agencies Making Progress on Efforts, but Inventories and Plans Need to Be Completed, GAO-12-742 (Washington, D.C.: July 19, 2012); and Data Center Consolidation: Agencies Need to Complete Inventories and Plans to Achieve Expected Savings, GAO-11-565 (Washington, D.C.: July 19, 2011).

In addition, in a draft report on data center optimization that we have provided to the agencies for comment and plan to issue in early 2019, our preliminary results indicate that agencies continued to report mixed progress toward achieving OMB's goals for closing data centers and realizing the associated savings by September 2018. Specifically, as of August 2018, over half of the agencies reported that they had met, or planned to meet, all of their OMB-assigned closure goals for tiered data centers by the deadline.[50] However, 6 agencies reported that they did not plan to meet their goals for tiered data centers. In addition, as of August 2018, 11 agencies reported that they had already met the goal for closing 60 percent of their non-tiered centers, 3 agencies reported that they planned to meet the goal by the end of fiscal year 2018, and 9 agencies reported that they did not plan to meet the goal by the end of fiscal year 2018.

In all, the 24 agencies reported a total of 6,250 data center closures as of August 2018, which represented about half of the total reported number of federal data centers. In addition, the agencies reported 1,009 planned closures by the end of fiscal year 2018, with an additional 191 closures planned through fiscal year 2023, for a total of 1,200 further closures.

Further, in August 2018, 22 agencies reported that they had achieved $1.94 billion in cost savings for fiscal years 2016 through 2018, while 2 agencies reported that they had not achieved any savings. In addition to that amount, 21 agencies identified a further $0.42 billion in planned savings through fiscal year 2018—for a total of $2.36 billion in planned cost savings from fiscal years 2016 through 2018. Nevertheless, this total is about $0.38 billion less than OMB's goal of $2.74 billion for overall DCOI savings.

[50] OMB's Memorandum M-16-19 directs agencies to categorize its data centers as a tiered data center, or a non-tiered data center. A tiered data center is defined as one using each of the following: (1) a separate physical space for IT infrastructure; (2) an uninterruptible power supply; (3) a dedicated cooling system or zone; and (4) a backup power generator for a prolonged power outage. All other data centers are to be considered non-tiered data centers.

## Agencies Need to Better Manage Software Licenses to Achieve Savings

In our 2015 high-risk report's discussion of IT acquisitions and operations, we identified the management of software licenses as an area of concern, in part because of the potential for cost savings. Federal agencies engage in thousands of software licensing agreements annually. The objective of software license management is to manage, control, and protect an organization's software assets. Effective management of these licenses can help avoid purchasing too many licenses, which can result in unused software, as well as too few licenses, which can result in noncompliance with license terms and cause the imposition of additional fees.

As part of its PortfolioStat initiative, OMB has developed a policy that addresses software licenses. This policy requires agencies to conduct an annual, agency-wide IT portfolio review to, among other things, reduce commodity IT spending. Such areas of spending could include software licenses.

In May 2014, we reported on federal agencies' management of software licenses and determined that better management was needed to achieve significant savings government-wide.[51] Of the 24 selected agencies we reviewed, only 2 had comprehensive policies that included the establishment of clear roles and central oversight authority for managing enterprise software license agreements, among other things. Of the remaining 22 agencies, 18 had policies that were not comprehensive, and 4 had not developed any policies.

Further, we found that only 2 of the 24 selected agencies had established comprehensive software license inventories, a leading practice that would help them to adequately manage their software licenses. The inadequate implementation of this and other leading practices in software license management was partially due to weaknesses in agencies' policies. As a result, we concluded that agencies' oversight of software license

[51] GAO, Federal Software Licenses: Better Management Needed to Achieve Significant Savings Government-Wide, GAO-14-413 (Washington, D.C.: May 22, 2014).

spending was limited or lacking, thus potentially leading to missed savings. However, the potential savings could be significant considering that, in fiscal year 2012, 1 major federal agency reported saving approximately $181 million by consolidating its enterprise license agreements, even when its oversight process was ad hoc.

**Table 2. Agencies' Implementation of GAO's Software License Management Recommendations, as of December 2018**

| Agency | Tracks and | Uses inventory to |
|---|---|---|
| Department of Agriculture | Fully | Fully |
| Department of Commerce | Partially | Fully |
| Department of Defense | Fully | Fully |
| Department of Education | Fully | Fully |
| Department of Energy | Fully | Fully |
| Department of Health and Human Services | Fully | Fully |
| Department of Homeland Security | Fully | Fully |
| Department of Housing and Urban Development | Partially | Partially |
| Department of Justice | Fully | Fully |
| Department of Labor | Fully | Fully |
| Department of State | Fully | Fully |
| Department of the Interior | Partially | Fully |
| Department of the Treasury | Partially | Partially |
| Department of Transportation | Fully | Fully |
| Department of Veterans Affairs | Fully | Fully |
| Environmental Protection Agency | Partially | Partially |
| General Services Administration | Fully | Fully |
| National Aeronautics and Space Administration | Fully | Fully |
| Nuclear Regulatory Commission | Fully | Fully |
| National Science Foundation | Fully | Fully |
| Office of Personnel Management | Partially | Partially |
| Small Business Administration | Fully | Fully |
| Social Security Administration | Fully | Fully |
| U.S. Agency for International Development | Fully | Fully |

Legend: Fully—the agency provided evidence that it fully addressed this recommendation C
Partially—the agency had plans to address this recommendation.
Source: GAO analysis. | GAO-19-275T.

Accordingly, we recommended that OMB issue a directive to help guide agencies in managing software licenses. We also made 135 recommendations to the 24 agencies to improve their policies and practices for managing licenses. Among other things, we recommended that the agencies regularly track and maintain a comprehensive inventory of software licenses and analyze the inventory to identify opportunities to reduce costs and better inform investment decision making.

Most agencies generally agreed with the recommendations or had no comments. As of December 2018, 27 of the 135 recommendations had not been implemented. Table 2 reflects the extent to which the 24 agencies implemented the recommendations in these two areas.

## AGENCIES NEED TO ADDRESS SHORTCOMINGS IN INFORMATION SECURITY AREA

Since information security was added to the high-risk list in 1997, we have consistently identified shortcomings in the federal government's approach to cybersecurity.[52] In particular, in a September 2018 report, we identified four major cybersecurity challenges: (1) establishing a comprehensive cybersecurity strategy and performing effective oversight, (2) securing federal systems and information, (3) protecting cyber critical infrastructure, and (4) protecting privacy and sensitive data.[53]

To address these challenges, we identified 10 critical actions that the federal government and other entities need to take. For example, in order to address the challenge of securing federal systems and information, we identified 3 actions that the agencies should take: (1) improve implementation of government-wide cybersecurity initiatives, (2) address weaknesses in federal information security programs, and (3) enhance the federal response to cyber incidents. Figure 6 depicts the 10 critical actions to address the four major cybersecurity challenges.

---

[52] As of the February 2017 update to the high-risk list, this high-risk area is designated as Ensuring the Security of Federal Information Systems and Cyber Critical Infrastructure and Protecting the Privacy of Personally Identifiable Information.

[53] GAO, High-Risk Series: Urgent Actions Are Needed to Address Cybersecurity Challenges Facing the Nation, GAO-18-622 (Washington, D.C.: Sept. 6, 2018).

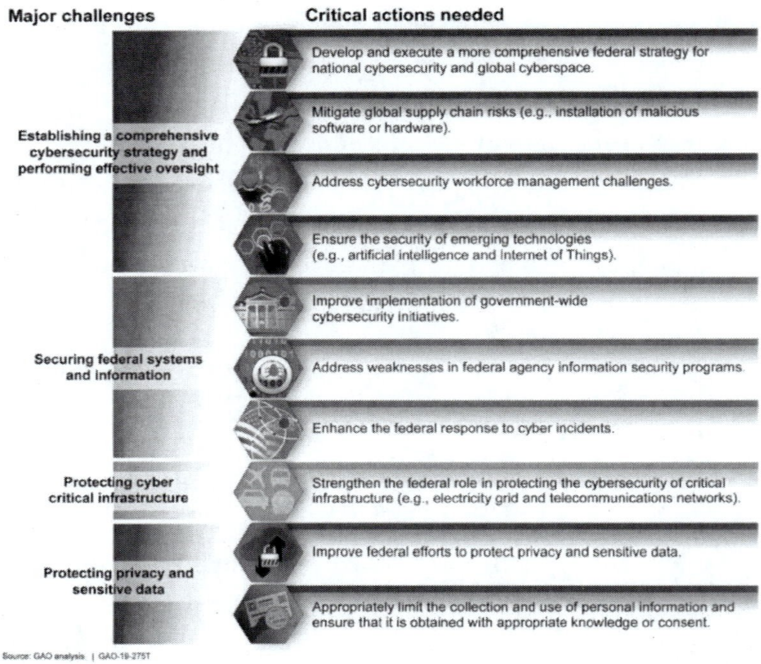


Figure 6. Ten Critical Actions Needed to Address Four Major Cybersecurity Challenges.

As we have previously noted, in order to strengthen the federal government's cybersecurity posture, agencies should fully implement the information security programs required by FISMA. In this regard, FISMA provides a framework for ensuring the effectiveness of information security controls for federal information resources. The law requires each agency to develop, document, and implement an agency-wide information security program. Such a program should include risk assessments; the development and implementation of policies and procedures to cost-effectively reduce risks; plans for providing adequate information security for networks, facilities, and systems; security awareness and specialized training; the testing and evaluation of the effectiveness of controls; the planning, implementation, evaluation, and documentation of remedial actions to address information security deficiencies; procedures for detecting, reporting, and responding to security incidents; and plans and procedures to ensure continuity of operations.

Since fiscal year 2010, we have made over 3,000 recommendations to agencies aimed at addressing the four cybersecurity challenges. These recommendations have identified actions for agencies to take to strengthen technical security controls over their computer networks and systems. They also have included recommendations for agencies to fully implement aspects of their information security programs, as mandated by FISMA. Nevertheless, many agencies continue to be challenged in safeguarding their information systems and information, in part, because many of these recommendations have not been implemented. Of the roughly 3,000 recommendations made since 2010, 73 percent had been implemented as of November 2018; leaving 688 recommendations unimplemented.

## Agencies' Inspectors General Are to Identify Information Security Program Weaknesses

In order to determine the effectiveness of the agencies' information security programs and practices, FISMA requires federal agencies' inspectors general to conduct annual independent evaluations. The agencies are to report the results of these evaluations to OMB, and OMB is to summarize the results in annual reports to Congress.

In these evaluations, the inspectors general are to frame the scope of their analyses, identify key findings, and detail recommendations to address the findings. The evaluations also are to capture maturity model ratings for their respective agencies. Toward this end, in fiscal year 2017, the inspector general community, in partnership with OMB and DHS, finalized a 3-year effort to create a maturity model for FISMA metrics. The maturity model aligns with the five function areas in the NIST Framework for Improving Critical Infrastructure Cybersecurity (Cybersecurity Framework): identify, protect, detect, respond, and recover.[54] This alignment is intended to help promote consistent and comparable metrics

[54] National Institute of Standards and Technology, *Framework for Improving Critical Infrastructure Cybersecurity* (Gaithersburg, Md.: Feb. 12, 2014).

and criteria and provide agencies with a meaningful independent assessment of their information security programs.

The maturity model is designed to summarize the status of agencies' information security programs on a five-level capability maturity scale. The five maturity levels are defined as follows:

- Level 1 Ad-hoc: Policies, procedures, and strategy are not formalized; activities are performed in an ad-hoc, reactive manner.
- Level 2 Defined: Policies, procedures, and strategy are formalized and documented but not consistently implemented.
- Level 3 Consistently Implemented: Policies, procedures, and strategy are consistently implemented, but quantitative and qualitative effectiveness measures are lacking.
- Level 4 Managed and Measurable: Quantitative and qualitative measures on the effectiveness of policies, procedures, and strategy are collected across the organizations and used to assess them and make necessary changes.
- Level 5 Optimized: Policies, procedures, and strategy are fully institutionalized, repeatable, self-generating, consistently implemented and regularly updated based on a changing threat and technology landscape and business/mission needs.

In March 2018, OMB issued its annual FISMA report to Congress, which showed the combined results of the inspectors general's fiscal year 2017 evaluations.[55] Based on data from 76 agency inspector general and independent auditor assessments, OMB determined that the government-wide median maturity model ratings across the five NIST Cybersecurity Framework areas did not exceed a level 3 (consistently implemented). Table 3 shows the inspectors general's median ratings for each of the NIST Cybersecurity Framework areas.

---

[55] Office of Management and Budget. Federal Information Security Modernization Act of 2014: Annual Report to Congress, Fiscal Year 2017 (Washington, D.C.: March 2018).

**Table 3. Median Government-Wide Inspectors General Maturity Model Ratings for Fiscal Year 2017**

| National Institute of Standards and Technology Cybersecurity Framework area | Median maturity model rating |
|---|---|
| Identify | Level 3: Consistently implemented |
| Protect | Level 3: Consistently implemented |
| Detect | Level 2: Defined |
| Respond | Level 3: Consistently implemented |
| Recover | Level 3: Consistently implemented |

Source: Office of Management and Budget. | GAO-19-275T.

## OMB Requires Agencies to Meet Targets for Cybersecurity Metrics

In its efforts toward strengthening the federal government's cybersecurity, OMB also requires agencies to submit related cybersecurity metrics as part of its Cross-Agency Priority goals. In particular, OMB developed the IT modernization goal so that federal agencies will be able to build and maintain more modern, secure, and resilient IT. A key part of this goal is to reduce cybersecurity risks to the federal mission through three strategies: manage asset security, protect networks and data, and limit personnel access. The key targets supporting each of these strategies correspond to areas within the FISMA metrics. Table 4 outlines the strategies, their associated targets, and the 23 civilian CFO Act agencies' progress in meeting those targets, as of June 2018.

In conclusion, FITARA and FISMA present opportunities for the federal government to address the high-risk areas on improving the management of IT acquisitions and operations and ensuring the security of federal IT, thereby saving billions of dollars. Most agencies have taken steps to execute key IT management and cybersecurity initiatives, including implementing CIO responsibilities, requiring CIO reviews of IT acquisitions, realizing data center consolidation cost savings, managing software assets, and complying with FISMA requirements.

**Table 4. Civilian Agencies' Progress in Meeting the Office of Management and Budget's (OMB) Targets to Reduce Cybersecurity Risks, as Reported by OMB, as of June 2018**

| Strategies to reduce cybersecurity risks | OMB's target(s) | Civilian agencies' progress in meeting target (average of 23 agencies) | Number of civilian agencies meeting the target (out of 23 agencies) |
|---|---|---|---|
| Limit Personnel Access | Privileged Network Access Management: 100 percent of privileged users are required to use a personal identity verification (PIV) card or Authenticator Assurance Level 3 (AAL3) multifactor authentication method to access the agency's network. | 96% | 17 |
| | High Value Asset (HVA) Access Management: 95 percent of High Value Assets require all users to authenticate using a PIV card or AAL3 multifactor authentication method. | 59% | 12 |
| | Automated Access Management: 95 percent of users are covered by an automated, dynamic access management solution that centrally tracks access and privilege levels. | 51% | 13 |
| Manage Asset Security | Hardware Asset Management: 95 percent of hardware assets covered by a capability to detect and alert upon the connection of an unauthorized hardware asset. | 61% | 15 |
| | Software Asset Management: 95 percent of software assets covered by a whitelisting capability. | 59% | 11 |
| | Authorization Management: 100 percent of high and moderate impact systems covered by a valid security authorization to operate. | 94% | 12 |
| | Mobile Device Management: 95 percent of mobile devices covered by a capability to remotely wipe contents if the device is lost or compromised. | 97% | 18 |

| Strategies to reduce cybersecurity risks | OMB's target(s) | Civilian agencies' progress in meeting target (average of 23 agencies) | Number of civilian agencies meeting the target (out of 23 agencies) |
|---|---|---|---|
| Protect Networks and Data | Intrusion Detection and Prevention: At least four of six intrusion prevention metrics have met an implementation target of at least 90 percent and 100 percent of email traffic is analyzed using domain-based message authentication, reporting, and conformance email authentication protocols. | 4.5 of 6[a] | 3[a] |
| | Exfiltration and Enhanced Defenses: At least three of four exfiltration and enhanced defenses metrics have met an implementation target of at least 90 percent. | 3.7 of 4 | 23 |
| | Data Protection: At least four of six data protection metrics have met an implementation target of at least 90 percent. | 3.4 of 6 | 12 |

Source: GAO summary of Office of Management and Budget data. | GAO-19-275T.

Note: [a]Many agencies did not meet this goal because not all of their email is analyzed using domain-based message authentication, reporting, and conformance email authentication protocols, as required by Department of Homeland Security's Binding Operational Directive 18-01.

The agencies have also continued to address the recommendations that we have made over the past several years. However, further efforts by OMB and federal agencies to implement our previous recommendations would better position them to improve the management and security of federal IT. To help ensure that these efforts succeed, we will continue to monitor agencies' efforts toward implementing the recommendations.

Chairmen Meadows and Hurd, Ranking Members Connolly and Kelly, and Members of the Subcommittees, this completes my prepared statement. I would be pleased to respond to any questions that you may have.

In: Information Security …
Editor: Lauren Van Raalte

ISBN: 978-1-53615-621-8


*Chapter 2*

# CYBERSECURITY: FEDERAL AGENCIES MET LEGISLATIVE REQUIREMENTS FOR PROTECTING PRIVACY WHEN SHARING THREAT INFORMATION*

***United States Government Accountability Office***

The Honorable Richard Burr
Chairman

The Honorable Mark R. Warner
Vice Chairman
Select Committee on Intelligence United States Senate

The Honorable Devin Nunes
Chairman

* This is an edited, reformatted and augmented Accessible version of the United States Government Accountability Office Report, Publication No. GAO-19-114R, dated December 6, 2018.

The Honorable Adam Schiff
Ranking Member
Permanent Select Committee on Intelligence
House of Representatives

Federal agencies and our nation's critical infrastructures, such as communications and financial services, are dependent on information technology systems and electronic data to carry out operations and to process, maintain, and report essential information.[1] The security of these systems and data is vital to public confidence and national security, prosperity, and well-being. Yet, cyber-based intrusions and attacks on federal and nonfederal systems have become not only more numerous and diverse, but also more damaging and disruptive. For example, a data breach reported in July 2015 at the Office of Personnel Management affected at least 21.5 million individuals and compromised federal employees' personal information, including Social Security numbers, residency and education history, employment history, financial history, and the fingerprints of approximately 5.6 million individuals.

Due to cyber-based threats to federal systems and critical infrastructure, the persistent nature of information security vulnerabilities, and associated risks, we have continued to designate information security as a government-wide high-risk area in our most recent biennial report to Congress—a designation we have made in each high-risk report since 1997.[2] We expanded this area beyond federal information systems to

---

[1] The term "critical infrastructure," as defined in the Critical Infrastructures Protection Act of 2001, part of the Uniting and Strengthening America by Providing Appropriate Tools Required to Intercept and Obstruct Terrorism Act of 2001 (USA PATRIOT Act), refers to systems and assets so vital to the United States that their incapacity or destruction would have a debilitating impact on security, national economic security, national public health or safety, or any combination of these matters. 42 U.S.C.§5195c(e). Federal policy identifies 16 critical infrastructure sectors: chemical; commercial facilities; communications; critical manufacturing; dams; defense industrial base; emergency services; energy; financial services; food and agriculture; government facilities; health care and public health; information technology; nuclear reactors, materials, and waste; transportation systems; and water and wastewater systems.

[2] GAO, High-Risk Series: Progress on Many High-Risk Areas, While Substantial Efforts Needed on Others, GAO-17- 317, (Washington, D.C.: February 15, 2017).

include the protection of cyber critical infrastructure in 2003 and protecting the privacy of personally identifiable information in 2015.

In December 2015, the President signed the Cybersecurity Information Sharing Act of 2015 (hereafter referred to as CISA or the act) into law to encourage the sharing of cyber threat information between the public and private sectors in a timely manner.[3] The act designated seven federal agencies to coordinate and develop government-wide, publicly available policies, procedures, and guidance to assist federal and nonfederal entities[4] in their efforts to receive and share[5] cyber threat indicators and defensive measures.[6] These seven agencies were the Departments of Homeland Security (DHS), Justice (DOJ), Defense (DOD), Commerce (DOC), Energy (DOE), and the Treasury, and the Office of the Director of National Intelligence (ODNI).

In addition, the act included provisions related to ensuring the protection of privacy and civil liberties during the information sharing activities. It also incorporated language related to limitations on collection and use of personal information. According to the act, the designated agencies were to develop guidelines for the protection of privacy and civil liberties when implementing the CISA provisions.

The act further required that these guidelines on privacy and civil liberties be consistent with the eight fair information practice principles defined in appendix A of the National Strategy for Trusted Identities in

---

[3] Consolidated Appropriations Act, 2016, Pub. L. No. 114-113, div. N (Cybersecurity Act of 2015), Title I (Cybersecurity Information Sharing Act of 2015), 129 Stat. 2242, 2936-56 (2015) (*codified at* 6 U.S.C. §§ 1501-10).

[4] A federal entity is a department or agency of the United States or any component of such department or agency. Nonfederal entities include state and local governments, private sector entities, and academic institutions.

[5] The act established requirements to develop artifacts for the receipt of cyber threat indicators and defensive measures by federal entities and for the sharing of cyber threat indicators and defensive measures by both federal and nonfederal entities. Unless explicitly specified as either receiving or sharing as part of a requirement within the act, this correspondence will collectively refer to these activities as "information sharing".

[6] As defined in CISA, cyber threat indicators include threat-related information such as methods of defeating or causing users to unwittingly enable the defeat of security controls and methods of exploiting cybersecurity vulnerabilities. Defensive measures include any actions, devices, procedures, techniques, or other means that detect, prevent, or mitigate a known or suspected cybersecurity threat or vulnerability.

Cyberspace and other applicable provisions of law.[7] The fair information practice principles are the widely accepted framework of defining principles to be used in the evaluation and consideration of systems, processes, or programs that affect individual privacy.

Beyond the aforementioned requirements, the act included a provision for GAO to review actions taken by the federal government related to the removal of personal information from cyber threat indicators or defensive measures. Accordingly, our specific objective for this work was to determine the extent to which federal agencies have developed policies, procedures, and guidelines for the removal of personal information from cyber threat indicators and defensive measures, pursuant to CISA's provisions.[8]

To fulfill this objective, we gathered and analyzed policies, procedures, and guidelines that the seven designated federal agencies developed in response to requirements established within the act. We compared these documents to requirements established by the eight provisions in the act (identified in table 1 of this chapter) that relate to the removal of personal information from cyber threat indicators and defensive measures. We also compared the contents of these documents to the eight fair information practice principles (identified in table 2 of this chapter).

Further, we gathered and analyzed information from the seven designated federal agencies on their use of DHS's Automated Indicator Sharing (AIS) capability—the primary government-wide capability for real-time, automated receipt and sharing of cyber threat indicators and defensive measures that was called for in the act.[9] Specifically, we looked

---

[7] The White House, *National Strategy for Trusted Identities in Cyberspace,* Appendix A (Washington, D.C.: April 2011).

[8] CISA refers to the removal of "personal information" from cyber threat indicators and defensive measures. For the purposes of this correspondence, we consider personal information to include all information that an individual would consider sensitive and would not want to be released publicly. This information is generally referred to as personally identifiable information (PII) and is similar to, but may not be identical to, personal information.

[9] The AIS initiative is an automated capability that receives, processes, and disseminates cyber threat indicators and defensive measures in real-time by enabling DHS to receive indicators from federal and nonfederal entities, remove personally identifiable information and other sensitive information not directly related to the cybersecurity threat, and disseminate the

at how each designated agency's relevant policies and guidance incorporated the use of this capability, including for the handling of personal information. In addition, we supplemented our analyses with interviews of responsible security and privacy officials from each of the seven agencies.

We conducted this performance audit from February 2018 to October 2018 in accordance with generally accepted government auditing standards. Those standards require that we plan and perform the audit to obtain sufficient, appropriate evidence to provide a reasonable basis for our findings and conclusions based on our audit objectives. We believe that the evidence obtained provides a reasonable basis for our findings and conclusions based on our audit objectives.

## BACKGROUND

CISA encouraged the timely sharing of cyber threat information between the public and private sectors. To facilitate the implementation of provisions related to this information sharing, the act required the seven designated federal agencies to jointly develop publicly available policies, procedures, and guidelines to assist federal and nonfederal entities in sharing information on cyber threat indicators and defensive measures.[10]

Specifically, the act required DHS and DOJ to lead the development of procedures and guidelines to assist federal entities when receiving information on cyber threat indicators or defensive measures from federal and nonfederal entities. The act also required DHS and DOJ to work with DOD and ODNI to develop policies to facilitate the sharing of cyber threat indicators and defensive measures among federal and nonfederal entities. Further, the act required these four agencies to coordinate the development of these artifacts with DOC, DOE and the Treasury. In support of this

---

cyber threat indicators and defensive measures, as appropriate, to other federal and nonfederal entities.

[10] CISA designated these entities as the appropriate agencies to develop and coordinate regarding the required policies, procedures, and guidance.

information sharing, the White House released a memorandum in 2016 stating that all departments and agencies should use DHS's AIS capability for the purpose of sharing cyber threat information.

In addition, the act included specific provisions for the protection of privacy and civil liberties. In this regard, CISA required DHS and DOJ, in coordination with the other five designated federal agencies, to develop government-wide guidelines for the protection of privacy and civil liberties when implementing provisions of the act.

Among other things, the seven designated agencies were to:

- develop privacy and civil liberties guidance governing the receipt, retention, use, and dissemination of cyber threat indicators, consistent with the eight fair information practice principles;
- develop and implement the aforementioned real-time sharing capability in compliance with this privacy and civil liberties guidance; and
- incorporate appropriate security and privacy protections into all other policies, procedures, and guidance for receiving and sharing cyber threat indicators and defensive measures specified in the act.

## DESIGNATED FEDERAL AGENCIES MET REQUIREMENTS TO DEVELOP POLICIES, PROCEDURES, AND GUIDELINES FOR REMOVAL OF PERSONAL INFORMATION

The seven designated federal agencies developed policies, procedures, and guidelines that met the eight CISA provisions relevant to the removal of personal information from cyber threat indicators and defensive measures. Table 1 summarizes these CISA provisions and identifies the government-wide policies, procedures, and guidelines that the designated agencies created to fulfill each provision for the sharing of cyber threat indicators and defensive measures, and the removal of personal information. The table is followed by additional discussion of the provisions and related policies, procedures, and guidance.

**Table 1. Government-wide Policies, Procedures, and Guidelines Created to Fulfill Eight Provisions of the Cybersecurity Information Sharing Act of 2015 Related to the Removal of Personal Information from Cyber Threat Indicators and Defensive Measures**

| CISA section[a] | Requirement | Related policy, procedure, or guidance created by designated agencies |
|---|---|---|
| 103(a) | The Office of the Director of National Intelligence (ODNI), the Department of Defense (DOD), the Department of Justice (DOJ), and the Department of Homeland Security (DHS) are to develop and issue procedures for the timely sharing of cyber threat information to mitigate adverse effects | *Sharing of Cyber Threat Indicators and Defensive Measures by the Federal Government under the Cybersecurity Information Sharing Act of 2015,* February 16, 2016 |
| 103(b) | ODNI, DOD, DOJ, and DHS are to ensure that the secure real-time sharing of cyber threat information excludes personal information not directly related to a cybersecurity threat | *Sharing of Cyber Threat Indicators and Defensive Measures by the Federal Government under the Cybersecurity Information Sharing Act of 2015,* February 16, 2016 |
| 103(c) | Procedures developed shall be issued no later than 60 days after the date of enactment of CISA | *Sharing of Cyber Threat Indicators and Defensive Measures by the Federal Government under the Cybersecurity Information Sharing Act of 2015,* February 16, 2016 |
| 105(a)(1) | DOJ and DHS are to develop interim policies to guide in the receipt of cyber indicators and defensive measures by the federal government | *Interim Procedures Related to the Receipt of Cyber Threat Indicators and Defensive Measures by the Federal Government,* February 16, 2016 |
| 105(a)(2) | DOJ and DHS are to develop final policies to guide in the receipt of cyber indicators and defensive measures by the federal government | *Final Procedures Related to the Receipt of Cyber Threat Indicators and Defensive Measures by the Federal Government, June 16, 2016* |
| 105(a)(4) | DOJ and DHS are to develop guidance to assist nonfederal entities and promote sharing of cyber threat indicators with federal entities | *Guidance to Assist Nonfederal Entities to Share Cyber Threat Indicators and Defensive Measures with Federal Entities under the Cybersecurity Information Sharing Act of 2015, February 16, 2016* |

**Table 1. (Continued)**

| CISA section[a] | Requirement | Related policy, procedure, or guidance created by designated agencies |
|---|---|---|
| 105(b)(1) | DOJ and DHS are to develop interim guidelines relating to privacy and civil liberties that governs the receipt, retention, use, and dissemination of cyber threat information and are consistent with fair information practice principles | *Privacy and Civil Liberties Interim Guidelines: Cybersecurity Information Sharing Act of 2015, February 16, 2016* |
| 105(b)(2) | DOJ and DHS are to develop final guidelines relating to privacy and civil liberties that governs the receipt, retention, use, and dissemination of cyber threat information and are consistent with fair information practice principles | *Privacy and Civil Liberties Final Guidelines: Cybersecurity Information Sharing Act of 2015, June 16, 2016b* |

Source: GAO analysis of policies and procedures created by DOD, DOJ, DHS, and ODNI, and in response to CISA.

[a] CISA = Cybersecurity Information Sharing Act of 2015, and can be found at https://www.congress.gov/114/plaws/publ113/PLAW-114publ113.pdf.

[b] In accordance with CISA, DHS and DOJ produced an updated version of this document in June 2018. Changes between the two versions were non-substantial for the purposes of our analysis.

To satisfy subsections 103(a), (b), and (c) of CISA, which called for the development and issuance of procedures for the timely sharing of cyber threat information and defensive measures, DHS, DOJ, ODNI, and DOD, in coordination with the other three agencies designated in the act, developed the procedures in *Sharing of Cyber Threat Indicators and Defensive Measures by the Federal Government under the Cybersecurity Information Sharing Act of 2015*. As required by subsection 103(a), these procedures outline how federal entities are to share classified and unclassified cyber threat indicators and defensive measures in a timely manner and in a way that mitigates adverse effects from cybersecurity threats. For example, the procedures include details on existing government programs that facilitate the sharing of information on cybersecurity threats and the periodic publication of cybersecurity best practices—such as technical security guidelines for federal agency information systems, and recommended practices and references for technical and nontechnical users.

In addition, as required by subsection 103(b), the procedures include information on the existing roles and responsibilities of federal and nonfederal entities when sharing information. The procedures also incorporate requirements related to the security of cyber threat indicators and defensive measures prior to sending them to other entities, in order to assure that federal or nonfederal entities do not share personal information unnecessarily.[11] For example, the guidance includes requirements for notification when a cyber threat indicator or defensive measure is shared in error and for protection against unauthorized access to a cyber threat indicator or defensive measure. Further, as required by subsection 103(c), the designated agencies issued the procedures in less than 60 days after the enactment of the act. DOJ and DHS met the requirements in sections 105(a)(1) and 105(a)(2) of CISA, which call for the development of policies for the receipt and sharing of cyber threat indicators and defensive measures, including consideration of privacy and civil liberties as a part of the receipt process. Specifically, in coordination with the other five designated federal agencies, these departments developed the interim and final versions of the guidance document, *Procedures Related to the Receipt of Cyber Threat Indicators and Defensive Measures by the Federal Government.* This document describes the processes for receiving, handling, and disseminating cyber threat indicators and defensive measures shared through DHS's AIS, as well as through the submission of a website form or email.[12] For all federal entities that receive cyber threat indicators and defensive measures, this guidance states and provides context for the statutory requirements for privacy and civil liberties, and for the maintenance of data on the number of cyber threat indicators and defensive measures where personal information concerns were addressed.

DOJ and DHS also addressed the provision in section 105(a)(4) through creation of the *Guidance to Assist Nonfederal Entities to Share Cyber Threat Indicators and Defensive Measures with Federal Entities under the CISA of 2015.* Specifically, the stated intent of this guidance is to

---

[11] In some cases, personal information directly related to a cybersecurity threat may be shared.

[12] The final *Procedures Related to the Receipt of Cyber Threat Indicators and Defensive Measures by the Federal Government* was released in June 2016, replacing the February 2016 interim version.

assist nonfederal entities in identifying cyber threat information. Further, the guidance explains how to share such information with federal entities through both DHS's AIS and other means authorized by CISA.

**Table 2. Definitions of Fair Information Practice Principles**

| Principle | Definition |
|---|---|
| Transparency | Organizations should be transparent and notify individuals regarding the collection, use, dissemination, and maintenance of personally identifiable information (PII). |
| Individual participation | Organizations should involve the individual in the process of using PII and, to the extent practicable, seek individual consent for the collection, use, dissemination, and maintenance of PII. Organizations should also provide mechanisms for appropriate access, correction, and redress regarding the use of PII. |
| Purpose specification | Organizations should specifically articulate the authority that permits the collection of PII and specifically articulate the purpose or purposes for which the PII is intended to be used. |
| Data minimization | Organizations should only collect PII that is directly relevant and necessary to accomplish the specified purpose(s) and only retain PII for as long as is necessary to fulfill the specified purpose(s). |
| Use limitation | Organizations should use PII solely for the purpose(s) specified in the notice. Sharing PII should be for a purpose compatible with the purpose for which the PII was collected. |
| Data quality and integrity | Organizations should, to the extent practicable, ensure that PII is accurate, relevant, timely, and complete. |
| Accountability and auditing | Organizations should be accountable for complying with these principles, providing training to all employees and contractors who use PII, and auditing the actual use of PII to demonstrate compliance with these principles and all applicable privacy protection requirements against risks such as loss, unauthorized access or use, destruction, modification, or unintended or inappropriate disclosure. |

Source: The White House, *National Strategy for Trusted Identities in Cyberspace* (Washington, D.C.: April 2011).

In response to requirements in sections 105(b)(1) and 105(b)(2) of CISA, on the development of guidelines for the consideration of privacy and civil liberties when sharing cyber threat indicators, DHS and DOJ, in coordination with the other five designated federal agencies, issued the

*Privacy and Civil Liberties Interim Guidelines* and the *Privacy and Civil Liberties Final Guidelines*.[13]

These guidance documents govern the receipt, retention, use, and dissemination of cyber threat information. For example, according to the *Final Guidelines*, federal entities should follow requirements to safeguard cyber threat indicators prior to sharing the indicators, including in cases when the shared cyber threat indicators contain specific individuals' personal information or information that identifies specific individuals that is not directly related to a cybersecurity threat.

Beyond the aforementioned provisions, CISA section 105(b) requires that the guidance documents created to fulfill its provisions also address the fair information practice principles as applicable. Table 2 defines the eight fair information practice principles.

The *Privacy and Civil Liberties Final Guidelines* fully meets requirements in section 105(b) by addressing all eight fair information practice principles. Specifically, the guidelines do so by establishing or considering the fair information practice principles as the primary guiding principles for all federal entity activities related to the receipt, retention, use, and dissemination of cyber threat indicators, as authorized by CISA. For example:

- *Transparency principle*. The final guidelines state that federal entities are to be transparent about their receipt, retention, use, and dissemination of cyber threat indicators under CISA.
- *Individual participation principle*. The final guidelines state that, given the nature of a cyber threat indicator, an individual whose personal information is directly related to a cybersecurity threat does not have the ability to consent to, or to be involved in, the process used to collect, access, or correct that information.

[13] In accordance with CISA, DHS produced an updated version of this document in June 2018. Changes between the two versions were non-substantial for the purposes of our analysis.

Each of the other guidance documents refers to the requirements in the Privacy and Civil Liberties Final Guidelines as a necessary part of their own requirements.

Finally, DHS's guidance includes other related information on the consideration of the fair information practice principles specifically in support of its implementation of AIS. Specifically, the Final Procedures Related to the Receipt of Cyber Threat Indicators and Defensive Measures provides several examples to guide the implementation of fair information practice principles when federal and nonfederal entities use AIS. For example:

- *Purpose specification principle.* The procedures provide guidance to federal entities on using an AIS profile to standardize cyber threat indicator information received while adhering to all relevant privacy and civil liberties requirements.
- *Data minimization principle.* The procedures require nonfederal entity submissions to conform to the defined AIS profile. This ensures that submissions include input fields most directly related to cyber threat indicators. Furthermore, the procedures guide entities to add or delete fields when considering changes to the AIS profile, in compliance with CISA's provisions that are designed to limit the receipt, retention, use, and dissemination of cyber threat indicators containing personal information.
- *Use limitation principle.* The procedures state that failure by federal employees to abide by usage requirements will result in individual sanctions such as loss of access to information and loss of a security clearance.

## Agency Comments

We provided a draft of this chapter to DHS, DOJ, DOD, DOC, DOE, Treasury, and ODNI for review and comment. DHS, DOJ, and DOD provided technical comments, which we incorporated into the chapter as appropriate. The other four agencies stated via email that they had no comments on the chapter.

Sincerely yours,

Nick Marinos
Director, Cybersecurity & Data Protection Issues

In: Information Security ...
Editor: Lauren Van Raalte
ISBN: 978-1-53615-621-8


*Chapter 3*

# DEPARTMENT OF AGRICULTURE: ANALYSIS OF SELECTED DATA CENTERS DID NOT FOLLOW FEDERAL GUIDANCE AND LEADING PRACTICES*

***United States Government Accountability Office***

The Consolidated Appropriations Act, 2018 required the Secretary of Agriculture to conduct a detailed cost-benefit analysis[1] that includes a complete analysis of the department's National Finance Center (NFC) data center and two other data centers of comparable size and complexity.[2] According to the act,[3] this analysis was also to include an assessment of

* This is an edited, reformatted and augmented Accessible Version of the United States Government Accountability Office Report to Congressional Committees Publication No. GAO-19-146R, dated December 19, 2018.

[1] The Office of Management and Budget (OMB) defines a cost-benefit analysis as a systematic quantitative method for assessing the desirability of government projects or policies when it is important to take a long view of future effects and a broad view of possible side effects.

[2] Consolidated Appropriations Act, 2018, Pub. L. No. 115-141, div. A, title VII, § 702, 132 Stat. 348, 382 (March 23, 2018).

[3] In this report, "the act" refers to the Consolidated Appropriations Act, 2018.

each center's (1) cost-effectiveness;[4] (2) security; (3) Federal Risk and Authorization Management Program (FedRAMP) certification status;[5] and (4) demonstrated record of maintaining Continuity of Operations Plan (COOP) functions without disruption of critical operations. The act required the Department of Agriculture (USDA) to submit the cost-benefit analysis to the Committees on Appropriations of the Senate and House of Representatives within 90 days of the act's March 23, 2018 enactment.

In response to the act, USDA requested that the General Services Administration's (GSA) Infrastructure Optimization Center of Excellence conduct the cost-benefit analysis on its behalf.[6]

Subsequently, GSA conducted an assessment of the NFC data center and three other data centers operated by USDA, the National Aeronautics and Space Administration (NASA), and the Department of Transportation (DOT).[7] Following its completion, USDA submitted the assessment to the Committees on Appropriations on July 27, 2018 (36 days after the required June 21, 2018 deadline).

In addition, the act included a provision for GAO to review the sufficiency of USDA's cost-benefit analysis, and to submit the results of its

---

[4] OMB defines cost-effectiveness as a systematic quantitative method for comparing the costs of alternative means of achieving the same stream of benefits or a given objective. An alternative is considered cost-effective if, on the basis of life-cycle cost analysis of competing alternatives, it is determined to have the lowest costs expressed in present value terms for a given amount of benefits.

[5] FedRAMP is a government-wide program managed by GSA that is intended to provide a standardized approach to security assessment, authorization, and continuous monitoring for cloud services. Cloud services refer to any capabilities offered by ubiquitous, convenient, on-demand network access to a shared pool of configurable computing resources (e.g., networks, servers, storage, applications, and services) that can be rapidly provisioned and released with minimal management effort or service provider interaction. For the purpose of this report, "certification status" refers to the status of the FedRAMP-issued authorization to operate.

[6] GSA's Infrastructure Optimization Center of Excellence supports USDA's data center consolidation initiative. The Center of Excellence is responsible for assisting federal agencies with, among other things, developing a unified and optimized IT infrastructure and leveraging federally owned data centers, cloud computing services, and commercial data centers.

[7] GSA, *PL-115-141 Title VII § 702: Assessment of the National Finance Center Data Center* (June 1, 2018). The assessment compared NFC to three other data centers it considered to be operationally comparable, rather than to two data centers, as specified in the act.

review to the Committees on Appropriations.[8] Our objective was to determine the extent to which the assessment analyzed the cost-effectiveness, security, and continuity of operations of the selected data centers in accordance with federal guidance and leading practices. To accomplish this objective, we compared the assessment's analysis of each data center's cost-benefit and cost-effectiveness, security, and continuity of operations with relevant federal guidelines and leading practices established by the Office of Management and Budget (OMB), GAO, and others. Specifically, we evaluated relevant portions of the assessment against the elements of an economic analysis as defined in GAO's Assessment Methodology for Economic Analysis[9] and consistent with OMB Circular A-94.[10] Based on our evaluation, we determined whether the assessment considered and properly dealt with each of these defined elements.

To evaluate the assessment's analysis of security, we first identified whether each data center's facility security level was reported, and then examined whether the information security posture of each data center was analyzed. In addition, to evaluate each center's FedRAMP certification status, we consulted the FedRAMP Marketplace[11] to verify whether the assessment accurately reflected the authority to operate status for each of the selected data centers. Further, we evaluated whether the assessment's continuity of operations data reflected each data center's demonstrated

---

[8] On October 25, 2018, GAO submitted to the Committees on Appropriations a sufficiency review of USDA's cost-benefit analysis as required by the act. This numbered correspondence finalizes the review.

[9] GAO, *Assessment Methodology for Economic Analysis*, GAO-18-151SP (Washington, D.C.: Apr. 10, 2018). The methodology provides a framework for assessing the sufficiency of economic analyses, including cost-benefit and cost-effectiveness analyses. GAO developed this methodology by synthesizing economic concepts identified in federal and international agency guidance, and by consulting with experts on economic analysis.

[10] Office of Management and Budget, *Guidelines and Discount Rates for Benefit-Cost Analysis of Federal Programs*, OMB Circular No. A-94 (October 1992; discount rates revised February 2018). This circular provides guidelines that OMB directs agencies to follow when conducting benefit-cost (referred to in this report as cost-benefit) and cost-effectiveness analyses that are submitted to OMB in support of legislative proposals. It also provides specific guidance on the discount rates to be used in evaluating federal programs whose benefits and costs are distributed over time.

[11] The FedRAMP Marketplace is GSA's official list of FedRAMP-authorized cloud service providers.

ability to maintain continuity of operations plan functions in the event of a service disruption.

We met with the GSA officials who conducted the assessment to discuss their methodology and to determine which, if any, federal or agency-specific policies or guidance were used to develop the assessment. We also interviewed officials responsible for the USDA, DOT, and NASA data centers included in the assessment. We obtained clarifying information about the applicability of their data centers as a basis for comparison to NFC, as well as their views on the extent to which GSA had consulted their offices during the completion of the assessment.

We conducted this performance audit from July 2018 through December 2018 in accordance with generally accepted government auditing standards. Those standards require that we plan and perform the audit to obtain sufficient, appropriate evidence to provide a reasonable basis for our findings and conclusions based on our audit objectives. We believe that the evidence obtained provides a reasonable basis for our findings and conclusions based on our audit objectives.

## BACKGROUND

In 2010, OMB launched the Federal Data Center Consolidation Initiative to promote green information technology (IT) by, among other things, reducing the overall energy and real estate footprint of government data centers. Subsequently, in September 2011, USDA published its data center consolidation plan. In addition, as part of its IT modernization plan submitted to Congress in December 2017, the department set a goal of reducing its data center footprint from a baseline of 39 data centers providing end-user services—which includes NFC—to 1 data center and 1 backup site by the end of fiscal year 2019.

USDA's NFC data center is located in Lakewood, Colorado, and has a fiscal year 2019 projected operating budget of $21.1 million. NFC-hosted applications handle the payrolls for more than 650,000 federal employees, including those in USDA; the Departments of Homeland Security,

Commerce, the Treasury, and Justice; and more than 100 smaller agencies, including GAO. NFC also processes insurance claims for nonfederal organizations, as well as for federal and tribal entities across the federal government.

In addition to NFC, GSA selected three other data centers for the assessment:

- The Enterprise Services Center (ESC) data center. This data center is operated by the Federal Aviation Administration (within DOT) and is located in Oklahoma City, Oklahoma. GSA reported that it selected this data center because of the size and complexity of the applications that the center supports. This facility performs financial management shared-services business functions that are comparable to those formerly performed at NFC.
- The National Center for Critical Information Processing and Storage (NCCIPS) data center. Operated by NASA, this data center is located in Stennis, Mississippi. GSA reported selecting this data center because it serves as an enterprise data center for government-wide federal data center consolidation initiatives that are similar to those conducted by USDA.
- The National Information Technology Center (NITC) data center. Operated by USDA, this data center is located in Kansas City, with a backup site in St. Louis, Missouri. GSA reported that it selected this center for the assessment because it is the only remaining enterprise data center and disaster recovery center identified by the USDA chief information officer (CIO) in the department's December 2017 IT modernization plan submitted to Congress. NITC is also the proposed destination data center planned for NFC's infrastructure migration.

Table 1 provides details about the 4 data centers, as reported in the assessment.

**Table 1. Details on Selected Data Centers Operated by the Department of Transportation and Federal Aviation Administration, National Aeronautics and Space Administration, and Department of Agriculture**

| Data center | FedRAMP authorized | Size (square feet) | FY19 budget($, millions) |
|---|---|---|---|
| Enterprise Services Center, Department of Transportation, Federal Aviation Administration | not authorized | 7,660 | $13.4 |
| National Center for Critical Information Processing and Storage, National Aeronautics and Space Administration | not authorized | 86,000 | $16.9 |
| National Finance Center, Department of Agriculture | not authorized | 12,747 | $21.1 |
| National Information Technology Center, Department of Agriculture | authorized | 171,331 | $35 |

Source: USDA's Assessment of the National Finance Center Data Center data | GAO-19-146R .

Legend: ● Authorized by the Federal Risk and Authorization Management Program. ○ Not authorized by the Federal Risk and Authorization Management Program.

## The Assessment Lacked Key Elements for Analysis of Cost-Benefit and Cost-Effectiveness, Security, and Continuity of Operations

### *The Assessment Did Not Meet Three of Five Elements of a Cost-Benefit and Cost-Effectiveness Analysis*

GAO's *Assessment Methodology for Economic Analysis*[12] identifies five key methodological elements for the baseline structure of both a cost-benefit and cost-effectiveness analysis: objective and scope, methodology, analysis of effects, transparency, and documentation. However, USDA's assessment did not meet—that is, adequately consider and properly deal

---

[12] An economic analysis, such as a cost-benefit or cost-effectiveness analysis, is intended to inform decision makers and stakeholders about the cost-and-benefit effects of an action. The analysis may be prospective, examining an action that could be taken, or retrospective, examining the outcome of an action that has already been taken.

with—three of the five key elements, and only partially met the remaining two elements.

**Objective and Scope—Partially Met**

According to GAO's methodology, the assessment's objective should be stated and its scope should be designed to address this objective. Further, OMB Circular A-94 recommends that a cost-effectiveness or cost-benefit analysis clearly state the rationale for the examination being performed. OMB also states that it is important in a cost-benefit analysis to take a long view of future effects and a broad view of possible side effects.

USDA's assessment stated that its objective was to conduct a cost-benefit analysis of the NFC data center against operationally comparable data centers in accordance with the act. However, the scope of the assessment included an evaluation of the impact of migrating NFC to NITC, without clearly explaining how the migration addresses the objective. Further, the assessment reported its time horizon as "phased," without defining its duration.

**Methodology—Not Met**

GAO's methodology recommends that the assessment should consider all relevant alternatives, define an appropriate baseline, and identify the important economic effects for each alternative considered, along with their time horizons, and whether direct or ancillary effects exist. Similarly, OMB Circular A-94 recommends that agencies consider alternative means of achieving program objectives.

While the data center assessment reported its selection criteria for evaluating the selected data centers against the NFC baseline, the assessment did not report on the decision rules that led to the data centers' selection. For instance, the assessment reported that each data center's gross floor area was among the selection criteria for evaluation, but did not go on to explain what measures led GSA to the determination that NCCIPS, with 86,000 square feet of data center space, was comparable to the NFC baseline, with 12,747 square feet of space. Further, in the course of conducting its analysis, GSA only evaluated the NFC effect of migrating to NITC, and did not evaluate other selected data centers.

**Analysis of Effects—Not Met**

GAO's methodology recommends that the assessment should quantify the important cost and-benefit effects and monetize them using the concept of opportunity cost.[13] It should also apply the criterion of net present value, or related outcome measures, to compare these effects across alternatives. In addition, the assessment should control for inflation and use economically justified discount rates. Where important cost-and-benefit effects cannot be quantified, the assessment should show how they affect the comparison of alternatives. In addition, OMB Circular A-94 recommends that the net present value of the life-cycle cost of the alternatives be considered in a cost-effectiveness analysis. Further, OMB Circular A-94 states that social net benefits, and not the benefits and costs to the federal government, should be the basis for evaluating government programs or policies that have effects on private citizens or other levels of government.

USDA's assessment included a comparison of the current operating costs of the infrastructure and levels of service provided for each of the selected data centers. The assessment also identified potential cost savings and qualitative improvements to NFC. However, the assessment did not determine the net present value of the life-cycle costs of operating the data centers and provided only per-unit costs, such as floor space, server instances, or terabytes of data storage. Instead, the scope of the assessment focused on the impact of the NFC migration from the perspective of costs to the federal government rather than costs and benefits that would accrue to society (including citizens and residents of the United States) as a result of NFC moving to NITC.

---

[13] According to OMB, opportunity cost is the maximum worth of a good or input among possible alternatives.

**Transparency—Not Met**

GAO's methodology recommends that analytical choices, assumptions, and data used be described and justified. The methodology further recommends evaluating how plausible adjustments to each choice and assumption may impact the estimates of the cost-and benefit effects and results of the comparison of alternatives. Similarly, OMB Circular A-94 recommends that the sources and nature of uncertainty be characterized, ideally presenting probability distributions of potential benefits, costs, and net benefits.

However, the assessment lacked transparency with regard to how it arrived at the results it presented. For example, the assessment reported that USDA would incur a one-time cost to migrate NFC to NITC, estimated at $131,000, but did not provide support for this amount. The assessment also projected expected cost savings for migrating to NITC, but did not characterize the level of certainty for this projection, or the probability of this outcome. The assessment also lacked a sensitivity analysis on this projection.[14]

**Documentation—Partially Met**

GAO's methodology recommends that the assessment be clearly written; it should clearly describe data and results; its conclusions should be consistent with its results; and sources should be cited. The methodology also states that the assessment should document its compliance with a robust quality assurance process, such as those described in guidelines issued pursuant to the law referred to as the Information Quality Act.[15] Further, OMB Circular A-94 recommends that

---

[14] A sensitivity analysis identifies assumptions associated with key cost drivers, and then calculates the estimate's sensitivity to changes in the underlying assumptions.

[15] Section 515 of the Treasury and General Government Appropriations Act, 2001 is commonly referred to as the Information Quality Act or the Data Quality Act, Pub. L. No. 106-554, appendix C, title V, §515, 114 Stat. 2763, 2763A-153 (Dec. 21, 2000). It required OMB to issue guidance requiring agencies to develop guidelines ensuring and maximizing the quality (including the objectivity, utility, and integrity) of information before it is disseminated. Accordingly, in October 2001 OMB issued *Guidelines for Ensuring and Maximizing the Quality, Objectivity, Utility, and Integrity of Information Disseminated by Federal Agencies,* which were finalized in February 2002.

key data and results, such as year-by-year estimates of benefits and costs, be reported to promote independent analysis and review.

Although the assessment was clearly written and reported that cost data were supplied by each data center, the assessment did not always cite its sources. For example, the assessment reported that the migration cost of NFC to NITC was estimated at $131,000, but did not provide support for this amount. Further, the assessment did not provide year-by-year estimates of benefits and costs beyond fiscal year 2019. Further, GSA did not indicate that the assessment was developed in accordance with a quality assurance process, such as guidelines issued pursuant to the law referred to as the Information Quality Act. In addition, the executive summary of the assessment reported an upfront savings of up to $235 million from migrating NFC to NITC, but later in the assessment reported the upfront savings as only $23.5 million, which indicates that GSA did not apply a quality assurance process.

In discussing their approach to developing the assessment, GSA officials stated that they did not follow any policies or guidance for the development of this assessment. As such, the assessment lacks key elements and is not sufficient to serve as a cost-benefit or cost-effectiveness analysis, and, as a result, it does not effectively inform relevant decision makers and stakeholders on the Committees on Appropriations.

### *The Assessment Accurately Reported Each Data Center's FedRAMP Authorization Status, but Did Not Comprehensively Review the Centers' Security or Continuity of Operations*

USDA's assessment included each agency's FedRAMP authorization status, but did not provide a comprehensive review of security and continuity of operations plans for the selected data centers. The review of security was limited to physical security, while the continuity of operations review did not demonstrate each agency's ability to maintain continuity of operations functions, as required by the act.

The assessment accurately reported the FedRAMP authorization to operate (ATO) status for each data center. Consistent with the FedRAMP

Marketplace, the assessment noted that only one of the four selected data centers—NITC—currently holds a FedRAMP ATO. It further noted that one data center—NFC—lost its ATO in March 2017 for not maintaining appropriate security requirements for continuous monitoring and annual security control assessments. Representatives from the remaining two data centers reported that their data centers do not require a FedRAMP ATO because they do not provide cloud services.

The act required USDA to provide a security analysis of each selected data center. The National Institute of Standards and Technology (NIST) Special Publication 800-53A[16] provides a set of procedures for conducting such assessments of security— including both information and physical security controls—employed within federal information systems and organizations. USDA's assessment, however, did not provide an analysis of the information security controls for any of the selected data centers.

GSA officials stated that they did not evaluate the information security capabilities of the data centers because information on the information security posture for each data center was already available as part of the agencies' required reporting on Federal Information Security Modernization Act of 2014 (FISMA)[17] metrics. Without providing an analysis of the information security controls for each data center, USDA's assessment cannot comprehensively report on the effectiveness of each data center's information security capabilities.

USDA's assessment of physical security was also limited. USDA provided a summary of an assessment of physical security for only two—NFC and NITC—of the four data centers. The assessment, conducted in

[16] NIST, Assessing Security and Privacy Controls in Federal Information Systems and Organizations: Building Effective Assessment Plans, Special Publication 800-53A, Revision 4 (Gaithersburg, MD: December 2014).

[17] The Federal Information Security Modernization Act of 2014 (FISMA 2014), Pub. L. No. 113-283, 128 Stat. 3073 (Dec. 18, 2014) largely superseded the Federal Information Security Management Act of 2002 (FISMA 2002), enacted as Title III, E-Government Act of 2002, Pub. L. No. 107-347, 116 Stat. 2899, 2946 (Dec. 17, 2002). As used in this report, FISMA refers both to FISMA 2014 and to those provisions of FISMA 2002 that were either incorporated into FISMA 2014 or were unchanged and continue in full force and effect.

accordance with Interagency Security Committee guidelines,[18] identified the facility security levels for NFC (Level III) and NITC (Level IV). Facility security levels, ranging from Level I (lowest risk) to Level V (highest risk),[19] reflect the perceived risk to the data centers and establish baseline levels of protection and countermeasures for physical security. The assessment also identified examples of physical security countermeasures in place at NITC.

However, it did not assess physical security for the ESC and NCCIPS data centers. GSA officials stated that they excluded the data centers for ESC and NCCIPS from this portion of the assessment due to time limitations established by the mandate. Without completely reporting on each data center's facility security level, decision makers and stakeholders on the Committees on Appropriations will not be informed of the comparability of each data center's risk level.

Further, USDA's assessment only partially addressed each of the four selected data centers' demonstrated history of maintaining continuity of operation plan functions and not missing critical operations. FISMA requires agencies to have plans and procedures to ensure continuity of operations (COOP) for information systems that support the operations and assets of the agency.

The assessment reported that ESC had provided its incident response plan[20] as a validation of the data center's ability to recover from adverse events, but did not include the results of any tests of the plan. Additionally, the assessment reported that NCCIPS tests its failover systems semi-annually, although it did not include the result of such tests.[21] Further, the

---

[18] Interagency Security Committee guidance describes *facility* as a space built or established to serve a particular purpose. The facility is inclusive of a building or suite and associated support infrastructure (e.g., parking or utilities) and land.

[19] Facility security levels are determined by five factors. These include a facility's (1) mission criticality; (2) symbolic attractiveness as a threat target; (3) population; (4) square footage; and (5) threats to the tenant agencies.

[20] NIST, *Contingency Planning Guide for Federal Information Systems*, Special Publication 800-34, Revision 1 (Gaithersburg, MD: May 2010). Per NIST, federal directives distinguish COOP plans as a specific type of plan that should not be confused with information system contingency plans, disaster recovery plans, or business continuity plans.

[21] NIST, *Contingency Planning Guide for Federal Information Systems*, Special Publication 800-34, Revision 1 (Gaithersburg, MD: May 2010). Per NIST, federal directives distinguish

assessment included limited details on the expected annual maximum downtime for three of the four data centers—ESC, NFC, and NITC, but did not discuss the demonstrated history of the data centers for sustaining it.

GSA officials stated that they did not include the results of after-action reports in the assessment because the results were not seen as factors differentiating the data centers' demonstrated ability to maintain continuity of operations. However, without providing evidence such as the results of after-action reports, the assessment does not address each agency's demonstrated ability to not miss critical operations in the event of a service disruption.

## CONCLUSION

USDA's Assessment of the National Finance Center Data Center did not comprehensively address the objective for conducting the cost-benefit analysis and providing the assessment pursuant to the Consolidated Appropriations Act, 2018.[22] While providing cost comparisons, the assessment lacked key elements expected for a cost-benefit analysis. Further, the assessment provided only limited information on the security and continuity of operations for each data center. As a result, the assessment does not effectively inform stakeholders and congressional decision makers.

### Recommendations for Executive Action

GAO recommends that the Secretary of Agriculture take four actions:

The Secretary of Agriculture should amend its analysis of selected data centers to address key elements of a cost-benefit and cost-effectiveness

---

COOP plans as a specific type of plan that should not be confused with information system contingency plans, disaster recovery plans, or business continuity plans.

[22] Pub. L. No. 115-141, div. A, title VII, §702 (March 23, 2018).

analysis as defined by OMB Circular A-94 and relevant agency guidance. (Recommendation 1)

When amending its analysis of the selected data centers, the Secretary of Agriculture should report on the assessment of each facility's protective measures, as outlined by the Interagency Security Committee guidance. (Recommendation 2)

## Agency Comments and Our Evaluation

We provided a draft of this chapter to USDA, GSA, DOT, and NASA for comment. In response, USDA provided written comments, which are reprinted in enclosure I and further discussed below. A Management and Program Analyst within GSA's Office of the Executive Secretariat and Audit Management provided comments via email, dated November 21, 2018, which stated that the agency concurred with the report. DOT and NASA provided technical comments, which we incorporated into the report, as appropriate.

In its comments, USDA generally disagreed with the findings and recommendations in the report. The department stated that conducting another assessment in accordance with OMB guidance would be redundant and represent a waste of government and taxpayer resources. The agency further stated that performing a new cost-benefit analysis in accordance with OMB's guidance for conducting an economic analysis would yield the same results as its original assessment.

As previously stated in this letter, the relevant provisions of the Consolidated Appropriations Act of 2018 required USDA to conduct and submit a detailed cost-benefit analysis to the Committees on Appropriations that includes a complete analysis of the National Finance Center data center and two operationally comparable data centers. The act required this analysis to detail and provide an assessment of each center's (1) cost-effectiveness; (2) security; (3) FedRAMP certification status; and (4) demonstrated record of maintaining continuity of operations and planning functions without disruption of critical operations. However,

USDA's assessment lacked key elements, and was not sufficient to provide all of the necessary information called for by the act. Further, it is not GAO's intent to recommend that USDA perform any additional analysis that may have already been conducted. Rather, we believe it is important for USDA to provide to the Committees on Appropriations, all of the information that the act contemplated that the department omitted from its assessment. Accordingly, we have modified the language of our recommendations to more clearly reflect this intent. However, we continue to believe our recommendations are warranted.

USDA also provided the following additional comments:

In regard to recommendation 1, the department responded that its assessment had included a cost-effectiveness study. The department stated that it was directed to perform its assessment within 90 days, whereas a full cost-benefit analysis would typically require upwards of a year if conducted in accordance with OMB guidance and pursuant to the Information Quality Act. The department also stated that it conducted its assessment in accordance with criteria established in OMB memorandum M-16-19, *Data Center Optimization Initiative.*

GAO acknowledges the challenges associated with developing a cost-benefit analysis within 90 days. However, as stated in our report the assessment did not meet 3 of the 5 elements of a cost-benefit or cost-effectiveness analysis, and therefore was inadequate for the required "detailed cost-benefit analysis" that provides "a complete analysis" of the data centers. OMB memorandum M-16-19 cited by USDA, defines a framework for achieving the data center consolidation and optimization requirements of the statutory provisions referred to as the Federal Information Technology Acquisition Reform Act, but does not address the elements necessary for conducting sound cost-benefit or cost-effectiveness analyses. OMB Circular A-94, however, provides the relevant guidance for doing so. Accordingly, we believe our modified recommendation for USDA to amend its analysis of selected data centers to address key elements of a cost-benefit and cost-effectiveness analysis as defined by OMB Circular A-94 and relevant agency guidance is warranted.

With respect to recommendation 2, USDA concluded that conducting any testing of physical security controls for the purposes of its assessment would have been duplicative. The department added that the Department of Homeland Security (DHS) conducts facility security assessments in accordance with Interagency Security Committee (ISC) guidance, while USDA continually assesses the inventory of baseline security controls—including physical security controls—according to FISMA requirements. Further, the department reported that the mandated time frame was insufficient to complete a full assessment of physical security controls.

Nevertheless, USDA did not include the results of such a DHS review in its assessment to Congress. Further, the assessment's summary of physical security was limited to only 2 of the 4 selected data centers. The assessment did not include a discussion of the physical security for the NCCIPS and ESC data centers. Therefore, we believe the modified recommendation for USDA to report on the assessment of each facility's protective measures, as outlined by the Interagency Security Committee guidance, is warranted.

Regarding recommendation 3, USDA reported that it utilized private-sector best practices to develop a comparative analysis of relevant security controls to complete the assessment. Additionally, the department stated that it continuously assesses the inventory of baseline security controls according to NIST guidance and FISMA requirements.

However, USDA did not include the results of such an analysis in its assessment to Congress. Additionally, GSA officials, who conducted the assessment on USDA's behalf, stated that they did not evaluate the information security capabilities of the data centers because information on the information security posture for each data center was already available as part of the agencies' required reporting on Federal Information Security Modernization Act of 2014 (FISMA) metrics. Because the assessment did not include a comprehensive security analysis of each data center, we maintain that our modified recommendation to report on an analysis of the information security controls for each data center is warranted.

With respect to recommendation 4, USDA reported that it had addressed the continuity of operations by comparing the maximum downtime ceiling requirements that each center must demonstrate to maintain their overall tier rating. However, as stated in our report, the department provided self-classified tier ratings for only 3 of the 4 data centers selected for its assessment, and failed to provide validation that the 3 data centers actually met the downtime requirements needed to maintain their respective ratings. Additionally, the department did not provide validation of the selected data centers' demonstrated record for maintaining the centers' continuity of operations plan functions and not miss critical operations. Therefore, we stand by our recommendation to report on each data center's demonstrated history of restoring continuity of operation functions in the event of a service disruption.

Gregory C. Wilshusen
Director, Information Security Issues

Oliver M. Richard Chief Economist

USDA

**United States Department of Agriculture**

Office of the Assistant Secretary for Administration

1400 Independence Avenue SW

Washington, DC 20250-0103

**TO:** Gregory C. Wilshusen
Director, Information Security Issues
U.S. Government Accountability Office

**THROUGH:** Gary S. Washington
Chief Information Officer
Office of the Chief Information Officer

GARY WASHINGTON — Digitally signed by GARY WASHINGTON Date: 2018.12.11 12:48:14 -05'00'

**FROM:** Donald K. Bice
Deputy Assistant Secretary
for Administration

DONALD BICE — Digitally signed by DONALD BICE Date: 2018.12.11 13:19:53 -05'00'

**SUBJECT:** U.S. Government Accountability Office's (GAO) draft report, entitled: Department of Agriculture: Analysis of Selected Data Centers Did Not Follow Federal Guidance and Leading Practices, Job Code 102946

The U.S. Department of Agriculture (USDA) appreciates the opportunity to respond to the U.S. Government Accountability Office (GAO) draft report "Department of Agriculture: Analysis of Selected Data Centers Did Not Follow Federal Guidance and Leading Practices, Job Code 102946" dated October 25, 2018. The USDA acknowledges the findings and recommendations in the GAO draft report. However, we would like to provide the following comments.

Recommendation 1 – The Secretary of Agriculture should conduct a comprehensive analysis of selected data centers that includes the elements of a cost-benefit analysis and cost-effectiveness analysis as defined by OMB Circular A-94 and relevant agency guidance.

USDA Response – USDA was directed to do an assessment in 90 days. A full *Benefit-Cost Analysis* according to all the associated criteria from OMB Circular A-94 and the Information Quality Act would typically take up to a year to complete. In order to meet the timelines directed by Congress, high-risk elements were assessed according to directions within the Appropriations Bill PL-115-141 Title VII §702 and in a manner consistent with USDA Data Center Optimization Initiative (DCOI) and Data Center Consolidation policy. The USDA assessment did include a cost effectiveness study, a security analysis, a Federal Risk and Authorization Management Program (FedRAMP) certification status, and a Continuity of Operations Plan (COOP) capability evaluation of each data center. The USDA also conducted the assessment according to criteria within OMB Memorandum M-16-19, Consolidation and Closure of Existing Data Centers; as well as private industry Best Practices uniquely available through the Office of American Innovation - IT Modernization, Infrastructure Optimization Center of Excellence.

Recommendation 2 – When conducting its comprehensive analysis of the selected data centers, the Secretary of Agriculture should include a comprehensive review of each data centers' physical security, with an assessment of each facilities protective measures as outlined by the Interagency Security Committee guidance.

USDA Response – Given the timeframe, USDA could not complete a full assessment of physical security controls. The Department of Homeland Security (DHS) conducts facility security assessments that evaluate facility protective measures according to Interagency Security Committee guidance, and the USDA continuously assesses the inventory of baseline security controls - including physical security controls - according to the Federal Information Security Management Act (FISMA) requirements. The USDA concluded that conducting additional testing within the framework of the assessment, would have been duplicative.

Recommendation 3 – When conducting its comprehensive analysis of the selected data centers, the Secretary of Agriculture should include a comprehensive review of each data centers' security control assessments, in order to evaluate the data centers information security capabilities.

USDA Response – USDA utilized private industry Best Practices to develop a comparative analysis of relevant IT security controls to complete the assessment. The USDA also continuously assesses the inventory of baseline security controls according to National Institute of Standards and Technology (NIST) Risk Management Framework standard and FISMA requirements, and in compliance with DHS and USDA Cyber Security Policy.

Recommendation 4 – When conducting its comprehensive analysis of the selected data centers, the Secretary of Agriculture should ensure that each data center's demonstrated history of restoring continuity of operation functions in the event of a service disruption is reported.

USDA Response – The USDA assessment addressed continuity of operations functionality of selected data centers by comparing the stringent down time ceiling requirements each center must demonstrate to maintain their overall Tier Rating.

Overall, USDA believes that a thorough and appropriate analysis using industry Best Practices was completed, and the outcome would be the same if a full OMB Circular A-94 assessment had been performed. Performing an A-94 assessment at this point would be a waste of government and taxpayer resources and would be redundant of the assessment already completed. Therefore, USDA disagrees with reconducting the assessment and will utilize scarce taxpayer resources to align itself with the Federal Data Center Optimization Initiative, our National Information Technology Center (NITC) Modernization Plan and our overarching Agency strategic objectives by migrating National Finance Center systems into the target consolidated NITC data center environment.

Thank you again for the opportunity to review and respond to the report.

## List of Committees

The Honorable John Hoeven
Chairman

The Honorable Jeff Merkley
Ranking Member
Subcommittee on Agriculture, Rural Development,
Food and Drug Administration, and Related Agencies
Committee on Appropriations
United States Senate

The Honorable Robert Aderholt
Chairman

The Honorable Sanford Bishop
Ranking Member
Subcommittee on Agriculture, Rural Development,
Food and Drug Administration, and Related Agencies
Committee on Appropriations
House of Representatives

In: Information Security …
Editor: Lauren Van Raalte

ISBN: 978-1-53615-621-8


*Chapter 4*

# INFORMATION SECURITY: SIGNIFICANT PROGRESS MADE, BUT CDC NEEDS TO TAKE FURTHER ACTION TO RESOLVE CONTROL DEFICIENCIES AND IMPROVE ITS PROGRAM*

***United States Government Accountability Office***

## ABBREVIATIONS

| | |
|---|---|
| CDM | Continuous Diagnostics and Mitigation |
| CIO | Chief Information Officer |
| CISO | Chief Information Security Officer |
| CDC | Centers for Disease Control and Prevention |

* This is an edited, reformatted and augmented version of United States Government Accountability Office; Report to Congressional Requesters; Accessible Version, Publication No. GAO-19-70, dated December 2018.

| | |
|---|---|
| DMZ | Demilitarized Zone |
| ISCM | Information Security Continuous Monitoring |
| FIPS | Federal Information Processing Standards |
| FISMA | Federal Information Security Modernization Act of 2014 |
| HHS | Department of Health and Human Services |
| ISC | Interagency Security Committee |
| ISSO | Information Systems Security Officer |
| NIST | National Institute of Standards and Technology |
| OCIO | Office of the Chief Information Officer |
| PIV | Personal Identity Verification |
| POA&M | Plan Of Actions and Milestones |
| SP | Special Publication |

## Why GAO Did This Study

CDC is responsible for detecting and responding to emerging health threats and controlling dangerous substances. In carrying out its mission, CDC relies on information technology systems to receive, process, and maintain sensitive data. Accordingly, effective information security controls are essential to ensure that the agency's systems and information are protected from misuse and modification.

GAO was asked to examine information security at CDC. In June 2018, GAO issued a limited official use only report on the extent to which CDC had effectively implemented technical controls and an information security program to protect the confidentiality, integrity, and availability of its information on selected information systems.

This current report is a public version of the June 2018 report. In addition, for this public report, GAO determined the extent to which CDC has taken corrective actions to address the previously identified security program and technical control deficiencies and related recommendations for improvement. For this chapter, GAO reviewed supporting documents regarding CDC's actions on previously identified recommendations and interviewed personnel at CDC.

## WHAT GAO FOUND

As GAO reported in June 2018, the Centers for Disease Control and Prevention (CDC) implemented technical controls and an information security program that were intended to safeguard the confidentiality, integrity, and availability of its information systems and information. However, GAO identified control and program deficiencies in the core security functions related to identifying risk, protecting systems from threats and vulnerabilities, detecting and responding to cyber security events, and recovering system operations (see table below). GAO made 195 recommendations to address these deficiencies.

As of August 2018, CDC had made significant progress in resolving many of the security deficiencies by implementing 102 of 184 (about 55 percent) technical control recommendations, and partially implementing 1 of 11 information security program recommendations made in the June 2018 report. The figure shows the status of CDC's efforts to implement the 195 recommendations.

**Number of GAO-Identified Technical Control and Information Security Program Deficiencies at the Centers for Disease Control and Prevention and Associated Recommendations by Core Security Function**

| Core security function | Number of technical control deficiencies | Number of technical control recommendations | Number of information security program deficiencies | Number of information security program recommendations |
|---|---|---|---|---|
| Identify | 0 | 0 | 5 | 5 |
| Protect | 85 | 161 | 1 | 1 |
| Detect | 8 | 18 | 3 | 3 |
| Respond | 1 | 5 | 1 | 1 |
| Recover | 0 | 0 | 1 | 1 |
| Total | 94 | 184 | 11 | 11 |

Source: GAO. | GAO-19-70.

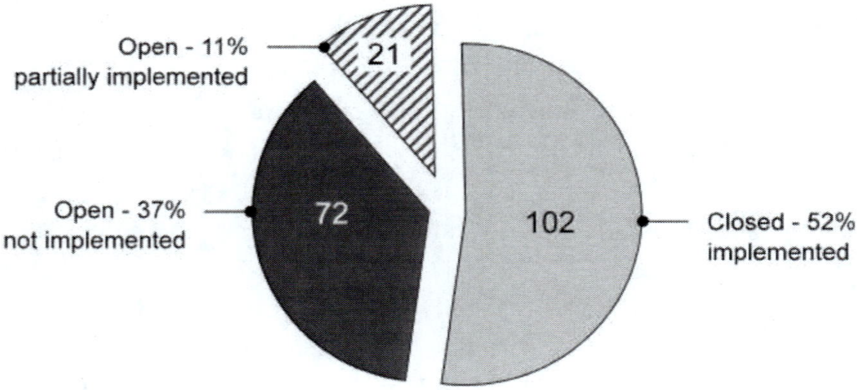


Source: GAO analysis of CDC data. | GAO-19-70.

Status of GAO Recommendations to the Centers for Disease Control and Prevention.

Additionally, CDC has created remedial action plans to implement the majority of the remaining open recommendations by September 2019. Until CDC implements these recommendations and resolves the associated deficiencies, its information systems and information will remain at increased risk of misuse, improper disclosure or modification, and destruction.

December 20, 2018

The Honorable Greg Walden
Chairman
Committee on Energy and Commerce
House of Representatives

The Honorable Trey Gowdy
Chairman

The Honorable Elijah E. Cummings
Ranking Member
Committee on Oversight and Government Reform
House of Representatives

The Honorable Fred Upton
House of Representatives

The Centers for Disease Control and Prevention (CDC) is responsible for protecting America from both foreign and domestic health, safety, and security threats. Its roles include detecting and responding to new and emerging health threats, tackling the biggest health problems causing death and disability for Americans, putting science and advanced technology into action to prevent disease, and controlling dangerous and exotic substances that can cause incurable and deadly diseases. Performing these roles may involve tracking diseases and finding out what is making people sick and the most effective ways to prevent diseases.

CDC confronts global disease threats through advanced computing and laboratory analysis of large amounts of data to find solutions, making use of computer systems critical to the process. However, cyber incidents at federal agencies demonstrate the damage that increasingly sophisticated threats can cause and underscore the importance of effectively protecting federal systems, including those used by CDC to achieve its mission.

Since 1997, we have designated the security of information on federal systems (i.e., information security) to be a government-wide high-risk area. In 2003, we expanded the area to include securing the computerized systems supporting the nation's critical infrastructure and, in 2015, we included protecting the privacy of personally identifiable information.[1]

Given the critical role that CDC performs and concerns over the security of federal information systems, you requested that we examine the security controls over key CDC systems. Accordingly, our specific objective was to assess the extent to which CDC had effectively implemented an information security program and controls to protect the confidentiality, integrity, and availability of its information on selected information systems.

---

[1] For our latest high-risk report, see GAO, *High-Risk Series: Progress on Many High-Risk Areas, While Substantial Efforts Needed on Others*, GAO-17-317 (Washington, D.C.: Feb. 15, 2017).

In June 2018, we issued a report that addressed the extent to which CDC had effectively implemented an information security program and controls to protect the confidentiality, integrity, and availability of its information on selected information systems.[2] In the report, we made 184 recommendations to CDC to resolve the technical security control deficiencies in the information systems we reviewed and 11 additional recommendations to improve its information security program. We designated that report as "limited official use only" (LOUO) and did not release it to the general public because of the sensitive information it contained.

This subsequent report publishes the findings discussed in our June 2018 report, but we have removed all references to the sensitive information. Specifically, we deleted the names of the information systems and computer networks that we examined, disassociated identified control deficiencies from named systems, deleted certain details about information security controls and control deficiencies, and omitted an appendix that was contained in the LOUO report. The appendix contained sensitive details about the technical security control deficiencies in CDC's information systems and computer networks that we reviewed, and the 184 recommendations we made to mitigate those deficiencies. We also provided a draft of this chapter to CDC officials to review and comment on the sensitivity of the information contained herein and to affirm that the report can be made available to the public without jeopardizing the security of CDC's information systems and networks.

In addition, this chapter addresses a second objective that was not included in the June 2018 report. Specifically, this objective was to determine the extent to which CDC has taken corrective actions to address the previously identified security program and technical control deficiencies and related recommendations for improvement that we identified in the earlier report.

As noted in our LOUO report, to accomplish the first objective—to determine the extent to which CDC had effectively implemented an

[2] GAO, *Information Security: CDC Needs to Improve Its Program and Resolve Control Deficiencies*, GAO-18-437SU (Washington, D.C.: June 20, 2018).

information security program and controls—we had examined the agency's security policies, procedures, and practices, and evaluated the technical security controls over 24 CDC systems. These included 10 key systems, 8 of which were mission-essential, that (1) collect, process, and maintain private or potentially sensitive proprietary business, medical, and personally identifiable information; (2) are essential to CDC's mission; (3) could have a catastrophic or severe impact on operations if compromised; or (4) could be of particular interest to potential adversaries. We also selected 14 general support systems that were part of the network infrastructure supporting the 10 systems.

To review CDC's information security program, we had examined security policies, procedures, and other documents; analyzed risk assessments, security plans, security control assessments, remedial action plans, and contingency plans for 8 selected mission-essential systems; and interviewed personnel at CDC headquarters. To review controls over the 10 key systems and 14 general support systems, we had examined the agency's network infrastructure and assessed the controls associated with system access, encryption, configuration management, and logging and monitoring. We conducted site visits to two CDC facilities located in Atlanta, Georgia.

To accomplish our second objective—on CDC's actions to address the previously identified security program and technical control deficiencies and related recommendations—we requested that the agency provide a status report of its actions to implement each recommendation we made in the June 2018 report. For each recommendation that CDC indicated it had implemented as of August 3, 2018, we examined supporting documents, observed or tested the associated security control or procedure, and/or interviewed the responsible agency officials to assess the effectiveness of the actions taken to implement the recommendation or otherwise resolve the underlying control deficiency. Based on this assessment and CDC status reports, we categorized the status of each recommendation as being closed-implemented, open-partially implemented, or open-not implemented. Additional details on our objectives, scope, and methodology are provided in appendix I.

We conducted this performance audit from December 2016 to December 2018 in accordance with generally accepted government auditing standards. Those standards require that we plan and perform the audit to obtain sufficient, appropriate evidence to provide a reasonable basis for our findings and conclusions based on our audit objectives. We believe that the evidence obtained provides a reasonable basis for our findings and conclusions based on our audit objectives.

## BACKGROUND

CDC—an operating division of the Department of Health and Human Services (HHS)—serves as the national focal point for disease prevention and control, environmental health, and promotion and education activities designed to improve the health of Americans. The agency is also responsible for leading national efforts to detect, respond to, and prevent illnesses and injuries that result from natural causes or the release of biological, chemical, or radiological agents.

To achieve its mission and goals, the agency relies on an array of partners, including public health associations and state and local public health agencies. It collaborates with these partners on initiatives such as monitoring the public's health, investigating disease outbreaks, and implementing prevention strategies. The agency also uses its staff located in foreign countries to aid in international efforts, such as guarding against global diseases. Table 1 describes the organization of CDC.

CDC is staffed by approximately 20,000 employees across the United States and around the world. For fiscal year 2017, according to agency officials, the agency's total appropriation was approximately $12 billion, of which it reported spending approximately $424 million on information technology. In addition, the officials stated that approximately $31 million (or about 7.3 percent of the amount spent on information technology) was for information security across all CDC information technology investments.

**Table 1. Organization of the Centers for Disease Control and Prevention (CDC)**

| CDC Organization | Description |
|---|---|
| Office of the Director | Guides agency priorities and activities; coordinates program, science, policy, and communications across CDC; and coordinates administrative management activities. |
| Deputy Director for Infectious Diseases | Leads, promotes, and facilitates science, programs, and policies to reduce the burden of infectious diseases, both domestically and globally. This office includes the National Center for Emerging and Zoonotic Infectious Diseases; the National Center for HIV/AIDS, Viral Hepatitis, Sexually Transmitted Diseases, and Tuberculosis Prevention; and the National Center for Immunization and Respiratory Diseases. |
| Deputy Director for Non-Infectious Diseases | Reduces the burden of non-infectious diseases, injuries, birth defects, disabilities, and environmental health hazards. This office includes the National Center on Birth Defects and Developmental Disabilities, the National Center for Chronic Disease Prevention and Health Promotion, the National Center for Environmental Health/Agency for Toxic Substances and Disease Registry, and the National Center for Injury Prevention and Control. |
| Deputy Director for Public Health Science and Surveillance | Leads, promotes, and facilitates science, surveillance, standards, and policies to reduce the burden of diseases, both domestically and globally. This office includes the Office of Science; the Office of Laboratory Science and Safety; the Center for Surveillance, Epidemiology, and Laboratory Services; and the National Center for Health Statistics. |
| Deputy Director for Public Health Service and Implementation Science | Leads, promotes, and facilitates science, programs and policies to identify and respond to public health threats, both domestically and internationally. It includes the Office of Minority Health and Health Equity; the Center for Global Health; the Center for Preparedness and Response; and the Center for State, Tribal, Local, and Territorial Support. |
| National Institute for Occupational Safety and Health | Provides leadership to prevent workplace injuries and illness by conducting scientific research, developing guidance and recommendations, sharing information, and responding to requests for workplace health hazard evaluations. |

Source: CDC. | GAO-19-70.

## CDC Relies on Information Systems to Help Achieve Its Mission

CDC relies extensively on information technology to fulfill its mission and support related administrative needs. Among the approximately 750 systems reported in its inventory, the agency has systems dedicated to supporting public health science, practice, and administration. All of these systems rely on an information technology infrastructure that includes network components, critical servers, and data centers.

## CDC Has Defined Organizational Security Roles and Responsibilities

At CDC, the chief information officer (CIO) is responsible for establishing and enforcing policies and procedures protecting information resources. The CIO is to lead the efforts to protect the confidentiality, integrity, and availability of the information and systems that support the agency and its operations, and is to report quarterly to the HHS CIO on the overall effectiveness of CDC's information security and privacy program, including the progress of remedial actions.

The CIO designated a chief information security officer (CISO), who is to oversee compliance with applicable information security and privacy requirements of the agency. The CISO, among other things, is responsible for providing information security protections commensurate with the risk and magnitude of the harm resulting from unauthorized access, use, disclosure, and disruption of information and information systems that support the operations and assets of the agency.

To further ensure information security compliance, information systems security officers (ISSO) are responsible for managing the information security program within their respective organizations and report on security program matters to the CISO, including computer security-related incidents. ISSO responsibilities include ensuring that vendor-issued security patches are expeditiously installed and that system owners establish processes for timely removal of access privileges when a user's system access is no longer necessary. In addition, security stewards are to perform operational security analyses supporting the efforts of the ISSO. Further, business stewards serve as program managers, accepting full accountability for the operations of the systems and ensuring that security is planned, documented, and properly resourced for each aspect of the information security program.

## Federal Laws and Guidance Establish Security Requirements to Protect Federal Information and Systems

The *Federal Information Security Modernization Act* (FISMA) of 2014[3] provides a comprehensive framework for ensuring the effectiveness of information security controls over information resources that support federal operations and assets. FISMA assigns responsibility to the head of each agency for providing information security protections commensurate with the risk and magnitude of the harm resulting from unauthorized access, use, disclosure, disruption, modification, or destruction of information systems used or operated by an agency or by a contractor of an agency or other organization on behalf of an agency. The law also delegates to the agency CIO (or comparable official) the authority to ensure compliance with FISMA requirements. The CIO is responsible for designating a senior agency information security officer whose primary duty is information security.

The law also requires each agency to develop, document, and implement an agency-wide information security program to provide risk-based protections for the information and information systems that support the operations and assets of the agency. In addition, FISMA requires agencies to comply with National Institute of Standards and Technology (NIST) standards, and the Office of Management and Budget (OMB) requires agencies to comply with NIST guidelines.

[3] The *Federal Information Security Modernization Act of 2014* (FISMA 2014) (Pub. L. No. 113-283, Dec. 18, 2014) largely superseded the *Federal Information Security Management Act of 2002* (FISMA 2002), enacted as *Title III, E-Government Act of 2002*, Pub. L. No. 107-347, 116 Stat. 2899, 2946 (Dec. 17, 2002). As used in this report, FISMA refers both to FISMA 2014 and to those provisions of FISMA 2002 that were either incorporated into FISMA 2014 or were unchanged and continue in full force and effect.

NIST *Federal Information Processing Standards* (FIPS) Publication 199 requires agencies to categorize systems based on an assessment of the potential impact that a loss of confidentiality, integrity, or availability of such information or information system would have on organizational operations, organizational assets, individuals, other organizations, and the nation.[4] NIST FIPS 200[5] requires agencies to meet minimum security requirements by selecting the appropriate security controls, as described in NIST Special Publication (SP) 800-53.[6] This NIST publication provides a catalog of security and privacy controls for federal information systems and a process for selecting controls to protect organizational operations and assets.[7] The publication provides baseline security controls for low-, moderate-, and high-impact systems, and agencies have the ability to tailor or supplement their security requirements and policies based on agency mission, business requirements, and operating environment.

Further, in May 2017, the President issued an executive order[8] requiring agencies to immediately begin using NIST's Cybersecurity Framework[9] for managing their cybersecurity risks. The framework, which

---

[4] The potential impact of a loss is categorized as one of three impact levels: 1) low – limited impact; 2) moderate – serious impact; and 3) high – severe or catastrophic impact. National Institute of Standards and Technology, *Standards for Security Categorization of Federal Information and Information Systems*, Federal Information Processing Standards Publication 199 (Gaithersburg, MD: February 2004).

[5] National Institute of Standards and Technology, *Minimum Security Requirements for Federal Information and Information Systems*, Federal Information Processing Standards Publication 200 (Gaithersburg, MD: March 2006).

[6] National Institute of Standards and Technology, *Security and Privacy Controls for Federal Information Systems and Organizations*, Special Publication 800-53, Revision 4 (Gaithersburg, MD: April 2013).

[7] Security control topics, referred to as families of security controls, covered by Special Publication 800-53 include access control, awareness and training, audit and accountability, security assessment and authorization, configuration management, contingency planning, identification and authentication, incident response, maintenance, media protection, physical and environmental protection, planning, personnel security, risk assessment, system and services acquisition, system and communications protection, system and information integrity, and program management.

[8] The White House, *Strengthening the Cybersecurity of Federal Networks and Critical Infrastructure*, Executive Order 13800 (Washington, D.C.: May 11, 2017).

[9] National Institute of Standards and Technology, *Framework for Improving Critical Infrastructure Cybersecurity* Version 1.1 (Gaithersburg, MD: Apr. 16, 2018). The framework was developed in response to an executive order issued by the prior administration, *Improving Critical Infrastructure Cybersecurity*, Executive Order 13636 (Washington, D.C.: Feb. 12, 2013). It was originally intended for use in protection of

provides guidance for cybersecurity activities, is based on five core security functions:

- Identify: Develop the organizational understanding to manage cybersecurity risk to systems, assets, data, and capabilities.
- Protect: Develop and implement the appropriate safeguards to ensure delivery of critical infrastructure services.
- Detect: Develop and implement the appropriate activities to identify the occurrence of a cybersecurity event.[10]
- Respond: Develop and implement the appropriate activities to take action regarding a detected cybersecurity event.
- Recover: Develop and implement the appropriate activities to maintain plans for resilience and to restore any capabilities or services that were impaired due to a cybersecurity event.

According to NIST, these 5 functions occur concurrently and continuously, and provide a strategic view of the life cycle of an organization's management of cybersecurity risk. Within the 5 functions are 23 categories and 108 subcategories that include controls for achieving the intent of each function.[11] Appendix II provides a description of the framework categories and subcategories of controls.

---

critical infrastructure. NIST initially issued guidance in February 2014 and has since revised the framework.

[10] According to the National Institute of Standards and Technology, a cybersecurity event is defined as a cybersecurity change that may have an impact on organizational operations (including mission, capabilities, or reputation).

[11] For example, "risk assessment" is one of five categories that comprise the "identify" function. The risk assessment category is divided into six subcategories that involve activities such as identifying and documenting internal and external threats; identifying potential business impacts and likelihoods; and determining risk based on threats, vulnerabilities, likelihoods, and impacts. Each subcategory activity cross-references information system controls from various information security publications, including the National Institute of Standards and Technology's Special Publication 800-53.

## Security Control Deficiencies Placed Selected CDC Systems at Risk

We reported in June 2018 that CDC had implemented numerous controls over the 24 systems we reviewed, but had not always effectively implemented controls to protect the confidentiality, integrity, and availability of these systems and the information maintained on them.

**Table 2. Number of GAO-Identified Technical Control and Information Security Program Deficiencies at the Centers for Disease Control and Prevention and Associated Recommendations by Core Security Function**

| Core security function | Number of technical control deficiencies | Number of technical control recommendations | Number of information security program deficiencies | Number of information security program recommendations |
|---|---|---|---|---|
| Identify | 0 | 0 | 5 | 5 |
| Protect | 85 | 161 | 1 | 1 |
| Detect | 8 | 18 | 3 | 3 |
| Respond | 1 | 5 | 1 | 1 |
| Recover | 0 | 0 | 1 | 1 |
| Total | 94 | 184 | 11 | 11 |

Source: GAO. | GAO-19-70.

Deficiencies existed in the technical controls[12] and agency-wide information security program[13] that were intended to (1) identify risk, (2) protect systems from threats and vulnerabilities, (3) detect cybersecurity events, (4) respond to these events, and (5) recover system operations. These deficiencies increased the risk that sensitive personally identifiable and health-related information, including information regarding the

[12] According to the National Institute of Standards and Technology, the technical controls (i.e., safeguards or countermeasures) for an information system are primarily implemented and executed by the information system through mechanisms contained in the hardware, software, or firmware components of the system. We also included physical security at data processing facilities as technical controls.

[13] The information security program includes processes, procedures, and practices used to manage the security of information systems.

transfer of biological agents and toxins dangerous to public health, could be disclosed or modified without authorization. As shown in table 2, deficiencies existed in all 5 core security function areas for the selected systems we reviewed.

## CDC Had Identified Risk and Developed Policies and Plans, but Shortcomings Existed

Controls associated with the *identify* core security function are intended to help an agency develop an understanding of its resources and related cybersecurity risks to its systems, assets, data, and capabilities. These controls include identifying and assessing cybersecurity risk and establishing information security policies, procedures, and plans. We reported in June 2018 that, although CDC had taken steps to implement these controls, it had not (1) categorized the risk-related impact of a key system, identified threats, or reassessed risk for systems or facilities when needed; (2) sufficiently documented technical requirements in policies, procedures, and standards; and (3) described intended controls in facility security plans.

### *CDC Did Not Appropriately Categorize at Least One Key System, but Assessed Risk to Some Extent at System and Entity-Wide Levels*

#### CDC Categorized Systems Based on Potential Impact of Compromise, but Did Not Appropriately Categorize a Key General Support System

As discussed earlier, FIPS Publication 199 requires agencies to categorize systems based on an assessment of the potential impact that a loss of confidentiality, integrity, or availability of such information or information system would have on organizational operations, organizational assets, individuals, other organizations, and the nation. For networks and other general support systems, NIST SP 800-60[14] notes that the categorization should be based on the high water mark[15] of supported information systems, and on the information types processed, transmitted across the network, or stored on the network or support system. Further, CDC's architecture design principles state that high-impact systems are to be maintained on dedicated machinery and be physically and logically secured from lower-risk systems.

CDC had categorized the 24 systems we reviewed, but the assigned impact level was not always appropriate. In this regard, the agency did not ensure that high-impact systems were logically secured from a lower-risk system. Specifically, seven selected high-impact systems relied on a general support system that the agency had categorized as a moderate-impact system (i.e., a lower-risk system). As a result, the high-impact systems were relying on controls in a less secure environment. Officials from the Office of the Chief Information Officer (OCIO) explained that the categorization of the supporting system was outdated based on changes to the agency's operating environment and that they planned to reevaluate the assigned impact level.

## CDC Assessed Risk at the System Level, but Did Not Assess Threats, Document Risk-based Decisions, or Reassess Risk When Needed

According to NIST SP 800-30,[16] risk is determined by identifying potential threats to an organization and vulnerabilities in its systems, determining the likelihood that a particular threat may exploit vulnerabilities, and assessing the resulting impact on the organization's

---

[14] National Institute of Standards and Technology, Volume 1: *Guide for Mapping Types of Information and Information Systems to Security Categories*, Special Publication 800-60, Revision 1 (Gaithersburg, MD: August 2008).

[15] For an information system, the potential security impact levels assigned to each of the respective security objectives (confidentiality, integrity, availability) are the highest level (i.e., high water mark) for any one of these objectives that has been determined for the types of information resident on the information system. For example, if confidentiality is considered high impact, integrity moderate impact, and availability low impact, the system should be categorized as a high-impact system based on confidentiality being the highest level of the three objectives.

[16] National Institute of Standards and Technology, *Guide for Conducting Risk Assessments*, Special Publication 800-30, Revision 1 (Gaithersburg, MD: September 2012).

mission, including the effect on sensitive and critical systems and data. NIST also states that assessments should be monitored on an ongoing basis to keep current on risk-impacting changes to the operating environment.

CDC had developed system-level risk assessments for the 8 selected mission-essential systems, and had summarized its risks in a risk assessment report. However, only two of the eight risk assessments had identified potential threats, and only one of these assessments determined the likelihood and impact of threats to that system.

Further, CDC had not always documented risks associated with less secure configuration settings or monitored its assessments to address changes to the operating environment. For example, among the 94 technical control deficiencies that we identified for the 24 systems we reviewed, OCIO officials stated that the agency had not implemented controls for 20 deficiencies due to technical constraints.[17] However, CDC did not address risks associated with decisions not to implement controls for these reasons in the system risk assessments.

OCIO officials also partially attributed 5 of the 94 technical control deficiencies to new cybersecurity threats and to threat vectors that turned initially sound architecture decisions into vulnerabilities. However, CDC had not addressed such changes in the risk assessments for the affected systems. By not assessing threats or the likelihood of their occurrence and impact and by not documenting the risks, CDC cannot have assurance that appropriate controls are in place commensurate with the level of risk.

### CDC Had a Process in Place to Assess Risk to Systems from an Entity-Wide Perspective

Beyond the system level, newly discovered threats or vulnerabilities may require an agency to make risk decisions from an entity-wide perspective. An entity-wide perspective is needed because the threats and vulnerabilities may affect more than specific systems.

CDC had a process in place to assess risk from an entity-wide perspective. This process included regular meetings among OCIO and

[17] A technical constraint could include, for example, implementing a control potentially causing functionality problems with legacy applications.

program office staff to discuss policy, threats, and incidents. Specifically, ISSOs held monthly meetings as a continuous monitoring working group to discuss policy updates. In addition, an OCIO official held quarterly briefings that included presentations on incident response tools, incident statistics, and potential threats. OCIO officials also held ad hoc meetings, as necessary, regarding vulnerability and threat concerns when the agency received email alerts from the Federal Bureau of Investigation, the Department of Homeland Security (DHS), or HHS.

**CDC Had Not Updated Facility Risk Assessments**

In addition to assessing risks for systems, agencies are to assess the risk to their facilities. The Interagency Security Committee (ISC)[18] requires agencies to determine the security level for federal facilities, and to conduct risk assessments at least once every 5 years for Level I and Level II facilities and at least once every 3 years for Level III, Level IV, and Level V facilities.[19]

However, the two facility risk assessments that we reviewed had not been updated in a timely manner.[20] Specifically, the risk assessments, covering Level III and Level IV facilities that house the 24 reviewed systems, had been last updated in January 2009 and March 2014—8 years earlier and just over 3 years earlier, at the time of our review in July 2017.

According to a CDC physical security official, the agency had previously relied on a third-party assessor to perform the assessments. The official also said that the agency planned to conduct its own facility risk

---

[18] The Interagency Security Committee, an interagency organization chaired by the Department of Homeland Security, was established by Executive Order No. 12977, 60 Fed. Reg. 54411 (October 1995), to enhance the quality and effectiveness of security and the protection of buildings and facilities in the United States occupied by federal employees for nonmilitary activities. Executive Order No. 12977 was later amended by Executive Order No. 13286, 68 Fed. Reg. 10619 (March 2003). The organization is comprised of senior level executives from federal agencies and departments.

[19] The facility security level is a categorization that ranges from Level I (lowest risk) to Level V (highest risk) based on the analysis of security-related factors, such as symbolism, population (e.g., employees and visitors), and size. The facility security level serves as the basis for identifying countermeasures that should be implemented at federal facilities to reduce the level of risk to an acceptable level.

[20] We reviewed two facility risk assessments because these two assessments covered facilities housing resources for the eight selected systems.

assessments and had recently developed procedures for conducting these assessments. Until it performs these assessments, CDC may not be aware of new risks to its facilities or the controls needed to mitigate the risks.

## CDC Had Documented Controls in Policies, Procedures, and Standards, but Had Not Included Certain Technical Requirements

FISMA requires each agency to develop, document, and implement an information security program that, among other things, includes policies and procedures that (1) are based on a risk assessment, (2) cost-effectively reduce information security risks to an acceptable level, (3) ensure that information security is addressed throughout the life cycle of each system, and (4) ensure compliance with applicable requirements. According to NIST SP 800-53, an agency should develop policies and procedures for each of the 18 NIST families of security controls to facilitate the implementation of the controls.

CDC had documented numerous policies, procedures, and standards that addressed each of the 18 control families identified in NIST SP 800-53.

For example, the agency had developed policies and procedures governing physical access to CDC facilities, role-based training of personnel with significant security responsibilities, security assessment and authorization of systems, and continuity of operations, in addition to standard operating procedures that covered numerous other controls.

The agency had also developed the *CDC IT Security Program Implementation Standards*, which describes the agency's security program requirements and minimum mandatory standards for the implementation of information security and privacy controls. In addition, the agency had documented configuration standards, which specified minimum configuration settings, for devices such as firewalls, routers, switches, as well as Unix and Windows servers.

However, these policies and standards sometimes lacked the technical specificity needed to ensure controls were in place. To illustrate, the agency had not sufficiently documented detailed guidance or instructions to address numerous technical control deficiencies we identified, such as insecure network devices, insecure database configurations, not blocking certain email attachments, and not deploying a data loss prevention capability.

According to OCIO officials, the agency's periodic reviews and updates to existing cybersecurity policies and standards did not reveal and address these issues. Nevertheless, without clear and specific guidance or instructions for implementing technical controls, the agency had less assurance that controls were in place and operating as intended.

## CDC Had Identified and Updated Controls in System Security Plans Annually, but Had Not Developed Facility Security Plans

FISMA requires each agency to develop, document, and implement an information security program that, among other things, includes subordinate plans for providing adequate information security for networks, facilities, and systems or a group of information systems, as appropriate. NIST states that plans should be reviewed and updated to ensure that they continue to reflect the correct information about the systems, such as changes in system owners, interconnections, and authorization status, among other things.

HHS and CDC policies require that such plans be reviewed annually. In addition, the ISC requires that agencies develop and implement an operable and effective facility security plan. CDC standards require the organization to prepare a facility security plan (or similar document).

CDC had developed security plans for the 8 selected mission-essential systems. With a few exceptions, the plans addressed the applicable security controls for those systems.[21] The agency also had reviewed and updated the plans annually.

However, CDC had not developed security plans for the facilities housing resources for the selected systems. Physical security officials stated that they had not developed security plans because they did not have a sufficient number of staff to develop them. Without comprehensive security plans for the facilities, CDC's information and systems would be at an increased risk that controls to address emergency situations would not be in place and personnel at the facilities would not be aware of their roles and responsibilities for implementing sound security practices to protect systems housed at these CDC locations.

## CDC Had Implemented Controls Intended to Protect Its Systems, but Deficiencies Existed

The *protect* core security function is intended to help agencies develop and implement the appropriate safeguards for their systems to ensure achieving the agency's mission and to support the ability to limit or contain the impact of a potential cybersecurity event. Controls associated with this function include implementing controls to limit access to authorized users, processes or devices; encrypting data to protect its confidentiality and integrity; configuring devices securely and updating software to protect systems from known vulnerabilities; and providing training for cybersecurity awareness and performing security-related duties. Although CDC had implemented controls that were intended to protect its operating environment, we reported in June 2018 that the agency did not consistently (1) implement access controls effectively, (2) encrypt sensitive data, (3) configure devices securely or apply patches in a timely manner, or (4) ensure staff with significant security responsibilities received role-based training.

---

[21] We determined that, of the approximately 2,800 total controls listed in the security plans for the 8 selected mission-essential systems, CDC had not provided detailed implementation information for 57 of the controls (or about 2 percent).

***CDC Did Not Consistently Implement Effective Access Controls***

A basic management objective for any agency is to protect the resources that support its critical operations from unauthorized access. Agencies accomplish this objective by designing and implementing controls that are intended to prevent, limit, and detect unauthorized access to computing resources, programs, information, and facilities. Access controls include those related to identifying and authenticating users, authorizing access needed to perform job duties, protecting system boundaries, and physically protecting information system assets. However, CDC had not consistently implemented these controls.

**CDC Implemented Enterprise-Wide Identification and Authentication Controls, but Did Not Consistently and Securely Configure Password Controls for Certain Accounts on Devices and Systems**

NIST SP 800-53 states that agencies should implement multi-factor authentication for their users of information systems. Multi-factor authentication involves using two or more factors to achieve authentication. A factor is something you know (password or personal identification number), something you have (token and personal identity verification (PIV) card), or something you are (biometric). Also, NIST and CDC policy state that information systems shall have password management controls established to include minimum password complexity requirements, password lifetime restrictions, prohibitions on password reuse, and user accounts temporarily locked out after a certain number of failed login attempts during a specified period of time.

CDC had applied enterprise-wide solutions to ensure appropriate identification and multi-factor authentication of its general user community through, for example, the use of PIV cards. However, instances of weak password management controls existed for certain accounts on network devices, servers, and database systems. According to OCIO officials, password control deficiencies existed primarily due to technical constraints, administrators not being aware of technical requirements, or administrators not adequately monitoring configuration settings. Without more secure password settings, CDC's information and systems are at an increased risk that unauthorized individuals could have guessed passwords and used them to obtain unauthorized access to agency systems and databases.

**CDC Authorized Users More Access than Needed to Perform Their Jobs**

NIST SP 800-53 states that agencies should employ the principle of least privilege, allowing only authorized access for users (or processes acting on behalf of users) that are necessary to accomplish assigned tasks. It also states that privileged accounts—those with elevated access permissions—should be strictly controlled and used only for their intended administrative purposes.

CDC had implemented controls intended to ensure that users were granted the minimum level of access permissions necessary to perform their legitimate job-related functions. However, the agency had granted certain users more access than needed for their job functions, including excessive access permissions on a key server.

According to OCIO officials, CDC systems had deficiencies related to restricting access primarily due to technical constraints or administrators not adequately monitoring configuration settings. By not appropriately restricting access, CDC's information and systems are at an increased risk that individuals could deliberately or inadvertently compromise database systems or gain inappropriate access to information resources.

**CDC Did Not Effectively Implement Boundary Controls to Ensure Network Integrity**

NIST SP 800-53 states that agencies should control communications at information systems' external boundaries. It states that, to manage risks, agencies should use boundary protection mechanisms to separate or partition computing systems and network infrastructures containing higher-risk systems from lower-risk systems.[22]

---

[22] Boundary protection controls logical connectivity into and out of networks and controls connectivity to and from devices connected to a network. Implementing multiple layers of security to protect an information system's boundaries can reduce the risk of a successful

Although CDC had implemented multiple controls that were designed to protect system boundaries, the agency had not sufficiently separated higher-risk systems from lower-risk systems. According to OCIO officials, deficiencies in boundary protection controls existed due to new cybersecurity threats turning initially sound architecture decisions into vulnerabilities, technical constraints, and administrators not being aware of technical requirements or adequately monitoring configuration settings. Without stronger boundary controls, CDC's information and systems are at an increased risk that an attacker could have exploited these boundary deficiencies and leveraged them to compromise CDC's internal network.

**CDC Physically Protected Information System Assets, but Did Not Consistently Ensure Access Remained Appropriate**

NIST SP 800-53 states that agencies should implement physical access controls to protect employees and visitors, information systems, and the facilities in which they are located. In addition, NIST states that agencies should review access lists detailing authorized facility access by individuals at the agency-defined frequency. In its standards, CDC requires implementation of the NIST special publication and requires that access lists detailing authorized facility access by individuals be reviewed at least every 365 days.

CDC had implemented physical security controls. The agency had implemented physical security measures to control access to certain areas and to ensure the safety and security of its employees, contractors, and visitors to CDC facilities. For example, CDC had issued PIV cards and Cardkey Proximity Cards to its employees and contractors, and had limited physical access to restricted areas based on the permissions it granted via these cards.

However, the agency had not consistently reviewed authorized access lists. In this regard, CDC did not have a process in place for periodically reviewing the lists of individuals with access to rooms containing sensitive

---

cyberattack. For example, multiple firewalls can be deployed to prevent both outsiders and trusted insiders from gaining unauthorized access to systems, and intrusion detection technologies can be deployed to defend against attacks from the Internet.

resources to ensure that such access remained appropriate. Without reviewing authorized access lists, CDC has reduced assurance that individual access to its computing resources and sensitive information is appropriate.

***CDC Had Not Consistently Encrypted Sensitive Authentication Data***

NIST SP 800-53 states that agencies should encrypt passwords both while stored and transmitted, and configure information systems to establish a trusted communication path between the user and the system.

Additionally, NIST requires that, when agencies use encryption, they use an encryption algorithm that complies with FIPS 140-2.[23]

CDC had used FIPS-compliant encryption for its PIV card implementation, but had not effectively implemented encryption controls in other areas. According to OCIO officials, encryption control deficiencies existed primarily due to technical constraints, administrators not being aware of a technical solution, or configuration settings not being adequately monitored. By not using encryption effectively, CDC limits its ability to protect the confidentiality of sensitive information, such as passwords.

***CDC Had Not Consistently Configured Servers Securely or Applied Patches in a Timely Manner***

NIST SP 800-53 states that agencies should disable certain services with known security vulnerabilities. This includes configuring security control settings on operating systems in accordance with publicly available security checklists (or benchmarks) promulgated by NIST's National Checklist Program repository. This repository contains, for example, the security configuration benchmarks established by the Center for Internet Security (CIS) for Windows servers.

NIST also states that agencies should test and install newly-released security patches, service packs, and hot fixes in a timely manner. In

---

[23] National Institute of Standards and Technology, *Security Requirements for Cryptographic Modules*, Federal Information Processing Standards Publication 140-2 (Gaithersburg, MD: May 25, 2001).

addition, CDC policy required that software patches for remediating vulnerabilities designated as critical or high risk be applied to servers within 45 days of being notified that a patch is available or within 7 days of when an exploit is known to exist. Further, agency policy specified that administrators configure Windows servers in accordance with the CDC-approved security benchmarks.

CDC had documented security configuration baselines, but had not always securely configured its systems or applied patches. In addition, the agency had not consistently configured security settings in accordance with prescribed security benchmarks or applied patches in a timely manner. For example:

- CDC had configured Windows servers to run unnecessary services.
- CDC had configured only about 62 percent of the security settings in accordance with prescribed benchmark criteria on the Windows and infrastructure servers supporting five systems that we reviewed.
- During our site visit in April 2017, CDC had not installed 21 updates on about 20 percent of the network devices, including 17 updates that the vendor considered to be critical or high-risk. The oldest of the missing updates dated back to January 2015.
- CDC had not updated database software supporting two selected systems to a more recent version that addressed vulnerabilities with a medium severity rating.

According to OCIO officials, CDC had deficiencies in configuration and patching primarily due to administrators not being aware that there was a technical solution or did not adequately monitor configuration settings. By not securely configuring devices and installing updates and patches in a timely manner, the agency is at increased risk that individuals could have exploited known vulnerabilities to gain unauthorized access to agency computing resources.

***Staff Received Security Awareness Training, but at Least 15 Percent of Those with Significant Security Responsibilities Did Not Receive Role-Based Training***

According to NIST SP 800-53, agencies should provide adequate security training to individuals in a role such as system/network administrator and to personnel conducting configuration management and auditing activities, tailoring the training to their specific roles. In addition, one of the cybersecurity cross-agency priority goals requires that agencies implement training that reduces the risk that individuals will introduce malware through email and malicious or compromised web sites.[24]

Consistent with NIST SP 800-53, CDC policy required network users to receive annual security awareness training. Accordingly, for fiscal year 2017, all CDC staff completed the required annual security awareness training.

CDC policy also required that those staff identified as having significant security responsibilities receive role-based training every 3 years. However, not all staff with significant security responsibilities received role-based training within the defined time frames. The agency used a tracking system to monitor the status of role-based training for 377 individuals who had been identified as having significant security responsibilities. As of May 2017, 56 (about 15 percent) of the 377 individuals had not completed the training within the last 3 years, and 246 (about 65 percent) of them had not taken training within the last year.

In addition, CDC had not identified at least 30 other staff with significant security responsibilities who required role-based training. Specifically, none of the 18 security and database administrators for four selected systems were included among the individuals being tracked, although these administrators had significant security responsibilities. Further, the agency provided us with a list of 42 individuals whose job series indicated that they required role-based training. However, 12 of the

[24] Cybersecurity cross-agency priority goals were established by the prior administration as part of implementing the requirement in the *Government Performance and Results Act Modernization Act of 2010* to develop federal government priority goals for information technology management. Sec. 5, Pub. L. No. 111-352 (Jan. 4, 2011); 124 Stat. 3866, 3873; 31 U.S.C. § 1120(a)(1)(B).

42 were not included among the tracked individuals. Furthermore, given the number of deficiencies identified and the rapidly evolving nature of cyber threats, CDC's requirement that staff take role-based training only once every 3 years is not sufficient for individuals with significant cybersecurity responsibilities.

According to OCIO officials, managers are responsible for identifying those individuals with significant security responsibilities. The process used to track training was manual and required an individual's manager to specify training requirements. The officials noted that the agency plans to implement a new HHS annual role-based training requirement in fiscal year 2018 and that they intend to work to enhance oversight as the new requirement is implemented.[25]

The officials also stated that at least 10 of the 94 technical control-related deficiencies identified in our June 2018 report had resulted, at least in part, from staff not being aware of control requirements or solutions to address the deficiencies. As a result, CDC's information and systems are at increased risk that staff may not have the knowledge or skills needed to appropriately protect them.

## CDC Had Not Effectively Implemented Controls Intended to Detect Incidents or Deficiencies

The *detect* core security function is intended to allow for the timely discovery of cybersecurity events. Controls associated with this function include logging and monitoring system activities and configurations, assessing security controls in place, and implementing continuous monitoring. In June 2018, we reported that, although CDC had implemented controls intended to detect the occurrence of a cybersecurity event, it had not sufficiently implemented logging and monitoring capabilities or effectively assessed security controls.

[25] Since the issuance of the June 2018 report, CDC has updated their role-based training requirement from once every three years to annually.

### *CDC Had Implemented Limited Logging and Monitoring Capabilities*

NIST SP 800-53 states that agencies should enable system logging features and retain sufficient audit logs to support the investigations of security incidents and the monitoring of select activities for significant security-related events. In addition, National Archives and Records Administration records retention guidance states that system files containing information requiring special accountability[26] that may be needed for audit or investigative purposes should be retained for 6 years after user accounts have been terminated or passwords altered, or when an account is no longer needed for investigative or security purposes, whichever is later.[27] NIST also states that agencies should monitor physical access to facilities where their information systems reside to detect physical security incidents. Further, NIST SP 800-53 states that agencies should monitor and control changes to configuration settings.

Although CDC had implemented centralized logging and network traffic monitoring capabilities, the capabilities were limited. For example, the agency's centralized logging system used for security monitoring had a limited storage capacity and did not meet the National Archives and Records Administration requirements. In addition, CDC had not centrally collected and monitored security event data for many key assets connected to the network. As a result, increased risk existed that CDC would not have been able to detect anomalous activities that may have occurred from malware attacks over time. OCIO officials stated that, as a compensating measure, the agency prevents direct communications between workstations. However, such a measure does not allow the agency to detect potentially inconsistent activities that may have occurred from malware attacks within the same data center.

CDC also had not consistently reviewed physical access logs to detect suspicious physical access activities, such as access outside of normal work hours and repeated access to areas not normally accessed. Program

---

26 Files containing information requiring special accountability are user identification records associated with systems which are highly sensitive and potentially vulnerable.

27 National Archives and Records Administration, *General Records Schedule 3.2: Information Systems Security Records*, Transmittal 26 (Washington D.C.: September 2016).

offices responsible for 7 of the 8 selected mission-essential systems did not conduct such a review. According to OCIO officials, the offices were not aware of the need for a review. However, without reviewing physical access logs, CDC has reduced assurance that the agency would detect suspicious physical access activities.

Further, CDC had not routinely monitored the configuration settings of its systems to ensure that the configurations were securely set. For example, for at least 41 of 94 technical control deficiencies we identified, OCIO officials cited quality control gaps where the change management process or system administrators had not discovered deficiencies resulting from insecure configuration settings. Without an effective monitoring process in place for system configurations, the agency was not aware of insecure system configurations.

### *CDC Did Not Effectively Test or Assess Controls to Detect Deficiencies*

FISMA requires each agency to periodically test and evaluate the effectiveness of its information security policies, procedures, and practices. The law also requires agencies to test the management, operational, and technical controls for every system identified in the agency's required inventory of major information systems at a frequency depending on risk, but no less than annually. In addition, NIST SP 800- 53A identifies three assessment methods—interview, examine, and test—and describes the potential depth and coverage for each.[28] Assessing a control's effectiveness based on an interview is likely less rigorous than examining a control; similarly, examining a control is likely less rigorous than testing the control's functionality.

---

[28] According to NIST, the interview method is the process of holding discussions with individuals or groups of individuals within an organization to facilitate assessor understanding, achieve clarification, or obtain evidence. The examine method is the process of reviewing, inspecting, observing, studying, or analyzing one or more assessment objects (i.e., specifications, mechanisms, or activities) to facilitate assessor understanding, achieve clarification, or obtain evidence. The test method is the process of exercising one or more assessment objects (i.e., activities or mechanisms) under specified conditions to compare actual with expected behavior.

CDC had not sufficiently tested or assessed the effectiveness of the security controls for the 8 mission-essential systems that we reviewed. Although CDC annually assessed security controls of selected systems, the agency had only examined control descriptions in security plans to ensure accuracy. At least once every 3 years, the agency selected controls for a more in-depth assessment of the 8 mission-essential systems we reviewed. However, CDC had assessed only 191 (about 7 percent) of 2,818 controls described in the security plans for the selected systems. In addition, the agency used methods for assessing controls that were often not rigorous enough to identify the control deficiencies that we identified. For example, as depicted in Figure 1, CDC relied exclusively on interviews—a less rigorous method—to assess 20 percent of the 191 controls it assessed for the selected systems.

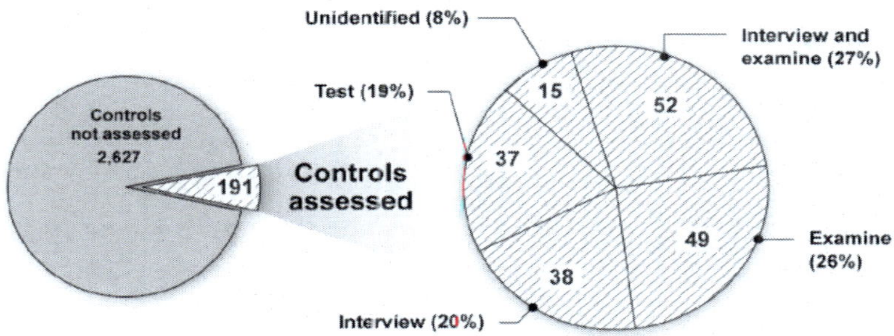


Source: GAO analysis of selected system assessments. | GAO-19-70.

Figure 1. Methods Used by the Centers for Disease Control and Prevention to Assess Security Controls.

The security control tests and assessments were insufficient in part because CDC had not developed comprehensive security assessment plans or had not consistently implemented the plans for the 8 selected mission-essential systems we reviewed. For example, one system's assessment plan indicated that five controls should be assessed using a testing methodology; instead, however, the assessor conducted interviews to determine whether controls were effective or not.

OCIO officials stated that the security control test and assessment process is manual and staffing is limited. They stated that the agency intends to rely increasingly on automated tools—such as the tools implemented by the Continuous Diagnostics and Mitigation program—for performing the assessments. Nevertheless, by not assessing controls in an in-depth and comprehensive manner, CDC has limited assurance that the security controls are in place and operating as intended. Further, without developing and implementing comprehensive assessment plans, assessments may not be performed with sufficient rigor to identify control deficiencies.

## CDC Had Implemented Processes for Responding to Incidents or Identified Deficiencies, but Did Not Always Take Timely Corrective Actions

The *respond* core security function is intended to support the ability to contain the impact of a potential cybersecurity event. Controls associated with this function include implementing an incident response capability and remediating newly-identified deficiencies. Although CDC had implemented controls for incident response to detect cybersecurity events, we reported in June 2018 that the agency had not maintained adequate information to support its incident response capability or taken timely corrective actions to remediate identified control deficiencies.

### *CDC Had Implemented Incident Response Capabilities, but Did Not Maintain Adequate Information*

NIST SP 800-53 and SP 800-61 state that agencies should develop and document an incident response policy with corresponding implementation procedures and an incident response plan, and keep them updated according to agency requirements. NIST also states that agencies should implement an incident handling capability, including an incident response team that consists of forensic/malicious code analysts. In addition, agencies are to provide incident response training for the team and test the incident response capability to determine the effectiveness of the response.

Further, NIST states that agencies are to monitor incidents by tracking and documenting them and maintain records about each incident, including forensic analysis. Finally, National Archives and Records Administration guidance states that records and data relevant to security incident investigations should be retained for 3 years.

CDC had implemented an incident response capability. The agency had developed policy, procedures, and a plan that addressed incident response, and updated them annually. CDC had an incident response team that managed all of the incident handling and response efforts for the agency, and conducted forensic analyses for reported security incidents. Team members had undergone training, such as an advanced network forensic and analysis course offered by a private firm. In addition, the agency had periodically tested its incident handling capability by conducting penetration testing exercises. These exercises allowed the team to test its real-time response capabilities.

CDC's incident response procedures state that incident tickets should include a description of actions taken, response time, and whether actions have been completed or not. The agency's procedures also require that computers affected by an incident be removed from the network immediately.

Nevertheless, CDC had shortcomings in implementing its incident response capability and monitoring procedures. For the 11 security incidents CDC considered most significant over a 19-month period ending in March 2017,[29] the agency had not consistently described the actions taken, the response times, or whether remedial actions had been completed. The agency also had not maintained audit log records for its security incidents. For example, the agency described recommended actions for 10 of the 11 incidents, but did not describe the actions that had been taken.

In addition, although incident response team officials told us that all incident ticket records had been saved, CDC had not retained system log data that supported incident resolution for at least five of the incidents. The agency's policy did not address record retention in accordance with

[29] We conducted our initial site visit to assess incident response capabilities during the week of March 7, 2017.

National Archives and Records Administration guidance. Further, for two of the security incidents, the security incident tickets did not clearly indicate when two compromised workstations had been removed from the network. According to OCIO officials, shortcomings in fully documenting incidents resulted from the organization being understaffed, primarily due to budget limitations and the inability to hire qualified personnel. Without effectively tracking and documenting information system security incidents, CDC's systems are at increased risk that the impact of security incidents would not be fully addressed.

### *CDC Had Remedial Action Plans to Address Identified Deficiencies for Selected Systems, but Did Not Always Take Timely Corrective Actions or Have Plans for Other Needed Corrective Actions*

FISMA requires each agency to develop, document, and implement an information security program that, among other things, includes a process for planning, implementing, evaluating, and documenting remedial actions to address any deficiencies in information security policies, procedures, or practices. NIST SP 800-53 states that agencies are to develop a plan of action and milestones (POA&M) for an information system to document the agency's planned remedial actions to correct identified deficiencies. CDC policy was consistent with the NIST guidelines.

CDC had developed POA&Ms for deficiencies identified by its security control assessments, but had not remediated the deficiencies in a timely manner. For each of the 8 selected mission-essential systems, the agency had created plans for correcting control deficiencies. However, the agency did not implement several remedial actions by their due date. For example, expected completion dates had passed for correcting deficiencies associated with 4 of the 8 selected mission-essential systems. For these 4 systems, the completion dates were 1 to 8 months beyond the due dates at the time of our review in September 2017.

According to Office of the Chief Information Security Officer officials, program offices that own the systems did not always communicate updates on the status of remedial actions for their respective systems, noting that deficiencies may have been corrected. Without effective communication to update its POA&Ms, CDC was not in a position to effectively manage its remedial actions and correct known deficiencies in a timely manner.

## CDC Had Developed and Tested Plans for System Recovery, but Had Not Assessed the Risk Associated with the Close Proximity of an Alternate Processing Site

The *recover* core security function is intended to support timely recovery of normal operations to reduce the impact from a cybersecurity event. Controls associated with this function include developing and testing contingency plans to ensure that, when unexpected events occur, critical operations can continue without interruption or can be promptly resumed, and that information resources are protected. Losing the capability to process, retrieve, and protect electronically maintained information can significantly affect an agency's ability to accomplish its mission. If contingency planning is inadequate, even relatively minor interruptions can result in lost or incorrectly processed data, which can cause financial losses, expensive recovery efforts, and inaccurate or incomplete information.

NIST SP 800-53 states that agency systems should have a contingency plan that includes the identification of key personnel and the systems' essential mission functions and addresses full information system restoration. For high-impact systems, NIST specifies that agencies test contingency plans at an alternate processing site that is separated from the primary processing site to reduce susceptibility to the same threats. In addition, NIST states that organizations should initiate corrective actions based on testing if they are needed.

As we reported in June 2018, CDC had developed and fully tested contingency plans for each of the 8 selected mission-essential systems that we reviewed. Each plan identified key personnel and their contact information, essential mission functions of the systems, and instructions on how to fully restore the systems in the event of a disruption. Additionally, between January 2015 and May 2017, CDC had tested whether the 8 systems could be recovered at their respective alternate sites, and had initiated corrective actions based on the results of the tests.

However, the alternate site for 6 of the 8 selected mission-essential systems was located in relatively close proximity to the main processing site. Although 2 systems had alternate sites located in another state, the alternate site for the other 6 systems was within the same metropolitan area. As a result, an event such as a natural disaster or substantial power outage could affect both the main and alternate sites for these systems, potentially rendering CDC unable to complete functions associated with its mission. Prompt restoration of service is necessary because the required recovery time for these systems ranged from 4 to 24 hours.

Security plans for 3 of the systems recognized the hazards of having the sites within the same geographical region, but stated that CDC had accepted this risk. According to OCIO officials, having a site further away was cost prohibitive; however, the officials had not documented this analysis or the associated risk of having the agency's processing sites located within the same geographical area. Without documenting the analysis and associated risk, CDC had less assurance that senior leadership was aware of the risk of agency systems being unavailable. As a consequence, senior leadership may not agree whether acceptance of the risk was warranted.

## CDC Had Not Consistently or Effectively Implemented Elements of Its Information Security Program

An underlying reason for the information security deficiencies in selected systems was that, although the agency had developed and documented an agency-wide information security program, it had not consistently or effectively implemented elements of the program. FISMA requires each agency to develop, document, and implement an information security program that, among other things, includes the following elements:

- periodic assessments of the risk and magnitude of the harm that could result from the unauthorized access, use, disclosure, disruption, modification, or destruction of information and information systems that support the operations and assets of the agency;
- policies and procedures that (1) are based on risk assessments, (2) cost-effectively reduce information security risks to an acceptable level, (3) ensure that information security is addressed throughout the life cycle of each system, and (4) ensure compliance with applicable requirements;
- plans for providing adequate information security for networks, facilities, and systems or group of information systems, as appropriate;
- security awareness training to inform personnel of information security risks and of their responsibilities in complying with agency policies and procedures, as well as training personnel with significant security responsibilities for information security;
- periodic testing and evaluation of the effectiveness of information security policies, procedures, and practices, to be performed with a frequency depending on risk, but no less than annually, and that includes testing of management, operational, and technical controls for every system identified in the agency's required inventory of major information systems;
- a process for planning, implementing, evaluating, and documenting remedial actions to address any deficiencies in the information security policies, procedures, or practices of the agency; and

- plans and procedures to ensure continuity of operations for information systems.

As discussed previously in this chapter, CDC had implemented aspects of each of these elements. For example, the agency had conducted risk assessments, developed security plans, assessed security controls, developed remedial action plans, and developed and tested contingency plans for each of the 8 selected mission-essential systems. In addition, the agency had documented numerous policies and procedures and ensured that staff had completed annual security awareness training.

However, CDC's program had shortcomings. For example, as discussed earlier in this chapter, CDC had not consistently or effectively:

- addressed threats, technical constraints, and the changing threat environment in its system risk assessments, or assessed the risk of having alternate processing sites within close proximity to each other;
- documented detailed technical requirements in policies and procedures, or facility controls in facility security plans;
- tracked and trained staff with significant security responsibilities;
- monitored configuration settings and comprehensively assessed system controls;
- remediated deficiencies in a timely manner; or
- documented its cost analysis and associated risk of having an alternate processing site within the same geographical region as its primary processing site.

Until CDC addresses these shortcomings and consistently and effectively implements all elements of its information security program, the agency will lack reasonable assurance that its computing resources are protected from inadvertent or deliberate misuse.

# CDC Has Implemented Many of the Recommendations in Our June 2018 Report and Plans to Implement the Rest

In our June 2018 report,[30] we made 195 recommendations to CDC to strengthen its technical security controls and bolster its agency-wide information security program. Specifically, we recommended that the agency take 184 actions to resolve technical control deficiencies by implementing stronger access controls, encrypting sensitive data, configuring devices securely, applying patches in a timely manner, strengthening firewall rules, and implementing logging and monitoring controls more effectively, among other actions. We also made 11 recommendations for CDC to improve its information security program by, among other things, assessing risks as needed, documenting more detailed technical requirements, monitoring and assessing controls more comprehensively, and remediating deficiencies in a timely manner.

Since the issuance of our June 2018 report, CDC has made significant progress in implementing the recommendations we made to resolve the technical security control deficiencies in the information systems we reviewed and to improve its information security program. In this regard, the agency has implemented many of the recommendations for improving technical security controls for the systems we reviewed and has developed plans to implement recommendations for enhancing its information security program.

Specifically, as of August 3, 2018, CDC had fully implemented 102 (55 percent) of the 184 recommendations we made to fortify the technical security controls over the systems we reviewed. In addition, the agency had partially implemented 20 (11 percent) of the 184 recommendations. In these instances, CDC had made progress toward implementing the recommendations, but had not completed all of the necessary corrective actions for us to close the recommendations. Therefore, these recommendations remain open. Further, CDC did not provide any evidence

---

[30] GAO-18-437SU.

that it had implemented the remaining 62 technical control-related recommendations.

Table 3 summarizes the status of CDC's efforts to implement the 184 recommendations that we made to resolve the technical control deficiencies, as of August 3, 2018.[31]

**Table 3. Status of Efforts by the Centers for Disease Control and Prevention to Implement GAO's Technical Control-Related Recommendations by Core Security Function, as of August 3, 2018**

| Core security function | Number of technical control-related recommendations | Status of Technical Control-related Recommendations | | |
|---|---|---|---|---|
| n/a | n/a | Closed–implemented | Open–partially implemented | Open–not implemented |
| Identify | 0 | 0 | 0 | 0 |
| Protect | 161 | 89 | 18 | 54 |
| Detect | 18 | 9 | 2 | 7 |
| Respond | 5 | 4 | 0 | 1 |
| Recover | 0 | 0 | 0 | 0 |
| Totals | 184 | 102 | 20 | 62 |

Legend:

Closed-implemented (CDC successfully completed actions to implement the recommendation)

Open-partially implemented (CDC had made progress toward—but has not completed—implementing the recommendation) Open-not implemented (CDC has not acted to implement the recommendation)

Source: GAO analysis of CDC data. | GAO-19-70.

By implementing 102 recommendations, CDC (as of August 3, 2018) reduced some of the risks associated with certain key activities. Specifically, these efforts included protecting network boundaries and logging and monitoring security events for indications of inappropriate or unusual activity on systems—that we highlighted in our June 2018 report as being particularly vulnerable and requiring the agency's greater priority

[31] We determined that 14 of the implemented, and 9 of the partially-implemented recommendations were either fully or partially addressed due to the decommissioning of one of the mission-essential systems, a key application process, and certain servers selected for this review. In August 2018, while onsite, we reviewed configuration settings—to include the authorization to operate, and change management procedures— to ensure the vulnerabilities were addressed in the new systems and servers.

and attention. In addition, the agency had implemented several of our recommendations to rectify a number of the security control deficiencies. These efforts included strengthening firewall rules, implementing stronger access controls, configuring devices securely, and expanding its audit monitoring capabilities.

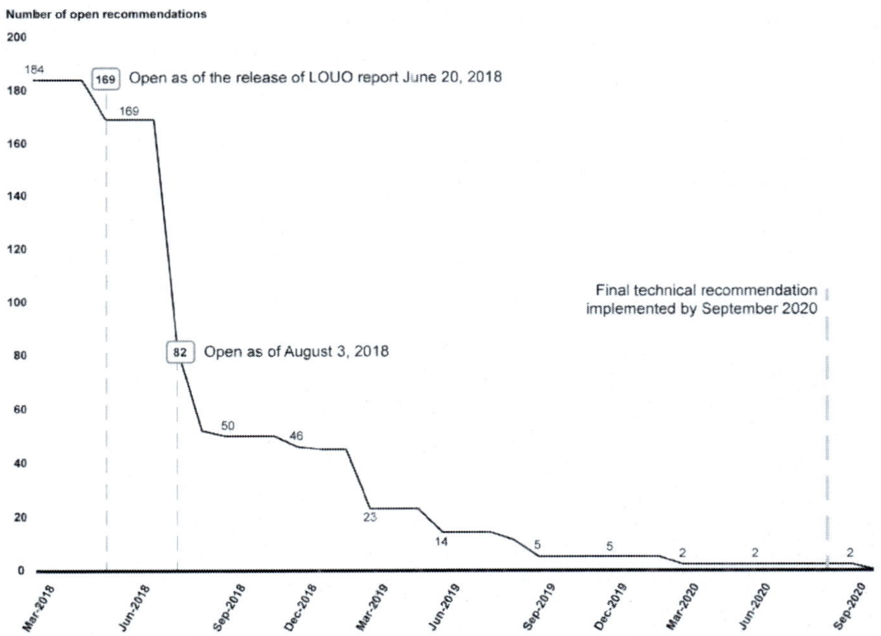


Source: GAO analysis of Centers for Disease Control and Prevention data. | GAO-19-70.

Figure 2. The Centers for Disease Control and Prevention's Planned Timeline for Fully Implementing GAO's Technical Control-Related Recommendations.

In addition, CDC had developed a plan of action and milestones (POA&M) for each of the identified technical control deficiencies and related recommendations that remained open as of August 3, 2018. The POA&Ms assigned organization responsibilities, identified estimated costs, identified points of contact, and established time frames for resolving the deficiencies and closing the related recommendations. The agency's plans called for it to implement the majority of the remaining open technical control-related recommendations by September 2019, and all recommendations by September 2020, as shown in Figure 2.

Our June 2018 report also included 11 recommendations to CDC to improve its information security program. In particular, we recommended that the agency, among other things, evaluate system impact level categorizations to ensure they reflect the current operating environment; update risk assessments to identify threats and the likelihood of impact of the threat on the environment; and update the facility risk assessments. In addition, we recommended that the agency take the necessary steps to make sure staff with significant security roles and responsibilities are appropriately identified and receive role-based training; monitor the configuration settings of agency systems to ensure the settings are set as intended; update security control assessments to include an assessment of controls using an appropriate level of rigor; and remediate POA&Ms in a timely manner. Further, we recommended that the agency document the cost-benefit analysis with associated risk of having an alternate site within the same geographical region as the main site.

As of August 3, 2018, the agency had partially implemented 1 of the 11 information security program-related recommendations, but had not provided any evidence that it had implemented the remaining 10 recommendations. Regarding the partially implemented recommendation, CDC had provided role-based training to all personnel performing significant security responsibilities. However, the agency still needed to establish and automate the identification process and the tracking of training records for individuals needing specialized security role-based training. CDC had developed plans to fully implement this recommendation and each of the remaining 10 information security program-related recommendations by July 2019. Fully implementing the open recommendations is essential to ensuring that the agency's systems and sensitive information are not at increased and unnecessary risk of unauthorized use, disclosure, modification, or disruption.

## AGENCY COMMENTS

We received written comments on a draft of this chapter from CDC. In its comments, which are reprinted in appendix III, the agency stated that it recognizes the risks associated with operating a large, global information technology enterprise and has implemented processes, procedures, and tools to better ensure the prevention, detection, and correction of potential incidents. CDC also said cybersecurity remains a high priority and that it takes the responsibilities for protecting public health information and data entrusted to it seriously. To strengthen its cybersecurity program, the agency stated that it is restructuring and streamlining the cyber program and IT infrastructure of its Office of the Chief Information Officer.

Further, CDC stated that it has leveraged GAO's limited official use only report, issued in June 2018, to accelerate its implementation, infrastructure, and software deployments to complete phrases one and two of DHS's Continuous Diagnostics and Mitigation program. The agency also said it concurred with, and highlighted a number of actions that it had planned or begun taking to remediate, the 11 security program recommendations that we made to CDC in our June 2018 report.

Gregory C. Wilshusen
Director, Information Security Issues

Nabajyoti Barkakati
Chief Technologist

## APPENDIX I: OBJECTIVES, SCOPE, AND METHODOLOGY

Our objective was to assess the extent to which CDC had effectively implemented an information security program and controls to protect the confidentiality, integrity, and availability of its information on selected information systems. In June 2018, we issued a report which detailed the findings from our work in response to this objective.[32] In the report, we made 184 recommendations to CDC to resolve the technical security control deficiencies in the information systems we reviewed and 11 additional recommendations to improve its information security program. We designated that report as "limited official use only" (LOUO) and did not release it to the general public because of the sensitive information it contained.

This chapter publishes the findings discussed in our June 2018 report, but we have removed all references to the sensitive information. Specifically, we deleted the names of the information systems and computer networks that we examined, disassociated identified control deficiencies from named systems, deleted certain details about information security controls and control deficiencies, and omitted an appendix that was contained in the LOUO report. The appendix contained sensitive details about the technical security control deficiencies in the CDC's information systems and computer networks that we reviewed, and the 184 recommendations we made to mitigate those deficiencies. We also provided a draft of this chapter to CDC officials to review and comment on the sensitivity of the information contained herein and to affirm that the report can be made available to the public without jeopardizing the security of CDC's information systems and networks.

In addition, this chapter addresses a second objective that was not included in the June 2018 report. Specifically, this objective was to determine the extent to which CDC had taken corrective actions to address the previously identified security program and technical control deficiencies and related recommendations for improvement that we identified in the earlier report.

As noted in our June 2018 report, we determined the extent to which CDC had effectively implemented an information security program and controls to protect the confidentiality, integrity, and availability of its information on selected information systems. To do this, we initially gained an understanding of the overall network environment, identified

[32] GAO, *Information Security: CDC Needs to Improve Its Program and Resolve Control Deficiencies*, GAO-18-437SU (Washington, D.C.: June 20, 2018).

interconnectivity and control points, and examined controls for the agency's networks and facilities. We conducted site visits at two CDC facilities in Atlanta, Georgia.

To evaluate CDC's controls over its information systems, we used our Federal Information System Controls Audit Manual,[33] which contains guidance for reviewing information system controls that affect the confidentiality, integrity, and availability of computerized information. We based our assessment of controls on requirements identified by the Federal Information Security Modernization Act of 2014 (FISMA),[34] which establishes key elements for an effective agency-wide information security program; NIST guidelines and standards;[35] Department of Health and Human Services and CDC policies, procedures, and standards; and standards and guidelines from relevant security organizations, such as the National Security Agency, the Center for Internet Security,[36] and the Interagency Security Committee.[37]

We had reviewed a non-generalizable sample of the agency's information systems, focusing on those systems that (1) collect, process, and maintain private or potentially-sensitive proprietary business, medical,

---

[33] GAO, *Federal Information System Controls Audit Manual* (FISCAM), GAO-09-232G (Washington, D.C.: February 2009).

[34] *The Federal Information Security Modernization Act of 2014* (FISMA 2014) (Pub. L. No. 113-283, Dec. 18, 2014) largely superseded the *Federal Information Security Management Act of 2002* (FISMA 2002), enacted as Title III, *E-Government Act of 2002*, Pub. L. No. 107-347, 116 Stat. 2899, 2946 (Dec. 17, 2002). As used in this report, FISMA refers both to FISMA 2014 and to those provisions of FISMA 2002 that were either incorporated into FISMA 2014 or were unchanged and continue in full force and effect.

[35] For example, see National Institute of Standards and Technology, *Minimum Security Requirements for Federal Information and Information Systems*, Federal Information Processing Standards Publication 200 (Gaithersburg, MD: March 2006), and National Institute of Standards and Technology, *Security and Privacy Controls for Federal Information Systems and Organizations*, Special Publication 800-53, Revision 4 (Gaithersburg, MD: April 2013).

[36] The Center for Internet Security is a nonprofit entity that uses a global information technology community to safeguard private and public organizations against cyber threat. We used the Center for Internet Security tool to assess CDC's information systems.

[37] The Interagency Security Committee, an interagency organization chaired by the Department of Homeland Security, was established by Executive Order No. 12977, 60 Fed. Reg. 54411 (October 1995), to enhance the quality and effectiveness of security and the protection of buildings and facilities in the United States occupied by federal employees for nonmilitary activities. Executive Order No. 12977 was later amended by Executive Order No. 13286, 68 Fed. Reg. 10619 (March 2003). The organization is comprised of senior level executives from federal agencies and departments.

and personally identifiable information; (2) are essential to CDC's mission; and (3) were assigned a Federal Information Processing Standard rating of moderate or high impact.[38] Based on these criteria, we had selected eight mission-essential systems for our review.

Of these systems, the agency had categorized 7 as high-impact systems and 1 as a moderate-impact system. For these 8 selected mission-essential systems, we had reviewed information security program-related controls associated with risk assessments, security plans, security control assessments, remedial action plans, and contingency plans.

To assess the safeguards CDC implemented for its systems, we had examined technical security controls for 24 CDC systems,[39] including systems the agency designated as high-value assets.[40] These included 10 key systems, 8 of which were high- and moderate-impact mission-essential systems just described, 1 additional high-impact system, 1 additional moderate-impact system, and 14 general support systems. We selected the additional high-impact system because the agency re-categorized it as a high-impact system during our review. We selected the additional moderate-impact system because the agency used it to control physical access to highly sensitive CDC biologic lab facilities, including facilities that handle dangerous and exotic substances that cause incurable and deadly diseases.

---

[38] National Institute of Standards and Technology, *Standards for Security Categorization of Federal Information and Information Systems*, FIPS Publication 199 (Gaithersburg, MD: February 2004). The standard requires agencies to categorize each information system according to the magnitude of harm or impact should the system or its information be compromised. The standard defines three impact levels where the loss of confidentiality, integrity, or availability could be expected to have a limited adverse effect (low), a serious adverse effect (moderate), or a severe or catastrophic adverse effect (high) on organizational operations, organizational assets, or individuals.

[39] Because we examined only 24 of the more than 750 systems CDC reported in its FISMA inventory with FIPS 199 categorizations, the results of our review of system-level controls cannot be generalized to the entire CDC environment.

[40] High-value assets refer to those assets, systems, facilities, data and datasets that are of particular interest to potential adversaries. These assets, systems, and datasets may contain sensitive controls, instructions or data used in critical federal operations, or house unique collections of data (by size or content), making them of particular interest to criminal, politically-motivated, or state-sponsored actors for either direct exploitation of the data or to cause a loss of confidence in the U.S. government.

We selected 10 key systems, 8 of which were mission-essential systems, for review that (1) collect, process, and maintain private or potentially sensitive proprietary business, medical, and personally identifiable information; (2) are essential to CDC's mission; (3) could have a catastrophic or severe impact on operations if compromised; or (4) could be of particular interest to potential adversaries. We also selected 14 general support systems that were part of the agency's network infrastructure supporting the 10 key systems.[41]

To review controls over the 10 key systems and 14 general support systems, we had examined the agency's network infrastructure and assessed the controls associated with system access, encryption, configuration management, and logging and monitoring. For reporting purposes, we had categorized the security controls that we assessed into the five core security functions described in the National Institute of Standards and Technology's (NIST) cybersecurity framework.[42] The five core security functions are:

- Identify: Develop the organizational understanding to manage cybersecurity risk to systems, assets, data, and capabilities.
- Protect: Develop and implement the appropriate safeguards to ensure delivery of critical infrastructure services.
- Detect: Develop and implement the appropriate activities to identify the occurrence of a cybersecurity event.
- Respond: Develop and implement the appropriate activities to take action regarding a detected cybersecurity event.

[41] The 14 general support systems included network devices such as routers, switches, and firewalls; workstations; and servers.

[42] National Institute of Standards and Technology, *Framework for Improving Critical Infrastructure Cybersecurity* Version 1.1 (Gaithersburg, MD: Apr. 16, 2018). The framework was developed in response to an executive order issued by the prior administration, *Improving Critical Infrastructure Cybersecurity*, Executive Order 13636 (Washington, D.C.: Feb. 12, 2013). It was originally intended for use in protection of critical infrastructure. NIST initially issued guidance in February 2014 and has since revised the framework.

- Recover: Develop and implement the appropriate activities to maintain plans for resilience and to restore any capabilities or services that were impaired due to a cybersecurity event.

These core security functions are described in more detail in appendix II. For the *identify* core security function, we had examined CDC's reporting for its hardware and software assets; analyzed risk assessments for the eight selected mission-essential systems to determine whether threats and vulnerabilities were being identified; reviewed risk assessments for two facilities; analyzed CDC policies, procedures, and practices to determine their effectiveness in providing guidance to personnel responsible for securing information and information systems; and analyzed security plans for the eight selected systems to determine if those plans had been documented and updated according to federal guidance. We also evaluated the risk assessments for two facilities that housed the 8 mission-essential selected systems.

For the *protect* core security function, we had examined access controls for the 24 systems. These controls included the complexity and expiration of password settings to determine if password management was being enforced; administrative users' system access permissions to determine whether their authorizations exceeded the access necessary to perform their assigned duties; firewall configurations, among other things, to determine whether system boundaries had been adequately protected; and physical security controls to determine if computer facilities and resources were being protected from espionage, sabotage, damage, and theft.

We also had examined configurations for providing secure data transmissions across the network to determine whether sensitive data were being encrypted. In addition, we had examined configuration settings for routers, network management servers, switches, firewalls, and workstations to determine if settings adhered to configuration standards, and inspected key servers and workstations to determine if critical patches had been installed and/or were up-to-date. Further, we had examined training records to determine if employees and contractors had received security awareness training according to federal requirements, and whether personnel who have significant security responsibilities had received training commensurate with those responsibilities.

For the *detect* core security function, we had analyzed centralized logging and network traffic monitoring capabilities for key assets connected to the network; analyzed CDC's procedures and results for assessing security controls to determine whether controls for the eight selected mission-essential systems had been sufficiently tested at least annually and based on risk. We also had reviewed the agency's implementation of continuous monitoring practices to determine whether the agency had developed and implemented a continuous monitoring strategy to manage its information technology assets and monitor the security configurations and vulnerabilities for those assets.

For the *respond* core security function, we had reviewed CDC's implementation of incident response practices, including an examination of incident tickets for 11 incidents; and had examined the agency's process for correcting identified deficiencies for the eight selected mission-essential systems.

For the *recover* core security function, we had examined contingency plans for eight selected mission-essential systems to determine whether those plans had been developed and tested. In assessing CDC's controls associated with this function, as well as the other four core functions, we had interviewed Office of the Chief Information Officer officials, as needed.

Within the core security functions, as appropriate, we had evaluated the elements of CDC's information security program based on elements required by FISMA. For example, we analyzed risk assessments, security plans, security control assessments, and remedial action plans for each of the 8 selected mission-essential systems. In addition, we had assessed whether the agency had ensured staff had completed security awareness training and whether those with significant security responsibilities received commensurate training. We also had evaluated CDC's security policies and procedures.

To determine the reliability of CDC's computer-processed data for training and incident response records, we had evaluated the materiality of the data to our audit objective and assessed the data by various means, including reviewing related documents, interviewing knowledgeable agency officials, and reviewing internal controls. Through a combination of methods, we concluded that the data were sufficiently reliable for the purposes of our work.

To accomplish our second objective—on CDC's actions to address the previously identified security program and technical control deficiencies and related recommendations[43]—we requested that the agency provide a status report of its actions to implement each of the recommendations. For each recommendation that CDC indicated it had implemented as of August 3, 2018, we examined supporting documents, observed or tested the associated security control or procedure, and/or interviewed the responsible agency officials to assess the effectiveness of the actions taken to implement the recommendation or otherwise resolve the underlying control deficiency. Based on this assessment and CDC status reports, we defined the status of each recommendation into the following 3 categories:

- closed-implemented—CDC had implemented the recommendation;
- open-partially implemented—CDC had made progress toward, but had not completed, implementing the recommendation; and
- open-not implemented—CDC had not provided evidence that it had acted to implement the recommendation.

We conducted this performance audit from December 2016 to December 2018 in accordance with generally accepted government auditing standards. Those standards require that we plan and perform the audit to obtain sufficient, appropriate evidence to provide a reasonable basis for our findings and conclusions based on our audit objectives. We

[43] GAO-18-437SU.

believe that the evidence obtained provides a reasonable basis for our findings and conclusions based on our audit objectives.

# APPENDIX II: THE NATIONAL INSTITUTE OF STANDARDS AND TECHNOLOGY CYBERSECURITY FRAMEWORK

The National Institute of Standards and Technology's cybersecurity framework consists of five core functions: identify, protect, detect, respond, and recover.[44] Within the five functions are 23 categories and 108 subcategories, as described in the table.

**Table 4. National Institute of Standards and Technology Framework for Improving Critical Infrastructure Cybersecurity**

| Category | Subcategory |
|---|---|
| **Identify (ID) core function: Asset Management (ID.AM)**: The data, personnel, devices, systems, and facilities that enable the organization to achieve business purposes are identified and managed consistent with their relative importance to organizational objectives and the organization's risk strategy. | ID.AM-1: Physical devices and systems within the organization are inventoried. |
| **Identify (ID) core function: Asset Management (ID.AM)**: The data, personnel, devices, systems, and facilities that enable the organization to achieve business purposes are identified and managed consistent with their relative importance to organizational objectives and the organization's risk strategy. | ID.AM-2: Software platforms and applications within the organization are inventoried. |
| **Identify (ID) core function: Asset Management (ID.AM)**: The data, personnel, devices, systems, and facilities that enable the organization to achieve business purposes are identified and managed consistent with their relative importance to organizational objectives and the organization's risk strategy. | ID.AM-3: Organizational communication and data flows are mapped. |

[44] National Institute of Standards and Technology, *Framework for Improving Critical Infrastructure Cybersecurity* Version 1.1 (Gaithersburg, MD: Apr. 16, 2018). The framework was developed in response to an executive order issued by the prior administration, *Improving Critical Infrastructure Cybersecurity*, Executive Order 13636 (Washington, D.C.: Feb. 12, 2013). It was originally intended for use in protection of critical infrastructure. NIST initially issued guidance in February 2014 and has since revised the framework.

**Table 4. (Continued)**

| Category | Subcategory |
|---|---|
| **Identify (ID) core function: Asset Management (ID.AM)**: The data, personnel, devices, systems, and facilities that enable the organization to achieve business purposes are identified and managed consistent with their relative importance to organizational objectives and the organization's risk strategy. | ID.AM-4: External information systems are catalogued. |
| **Identify (ID) core function: Asset Management (ID.AM)**: The data, personnel, devices, systems, and facilities that enable the organization to achieve business purposes are identified and managed consistent with their relative importance to organizational objectives and the organization's risk strategy. | ID.AM-5: Resources (e.g., hardware, devices, data, time, personnel, and software) are prioritized based on their classification, criticality, and business value. |
| **Identify (ID) core function: Asset Management (ID.AM)**: The data, personnel, devices, systems, and facilities that enable the organization to achieve business purposes are identified and managed consistent with their relative importance to organizational objectives and the organization's risk strategy. | ID.AM-6: Cybersecurity roles and responsibilities for the entire workforce and third-party stakeholders (e.g., suppliers, customers, and partners) are established. |
| **Identify (ID) core function: Business Environment (ID.BE)**: The organization's mission, objectives, stakeholders, and activities are understood and prioritized; this information is used to inform cybersecurity roles, responsibilities, and risk management decisions. | ID.BE-1: The organization's role in the supply chain is identified and communicated. |
| **Identify (ID) core function: Business Environment (ID.BE)**: The organization's mission, objectives, stakeholders, and activities are understood and prioritized; this information is used to inform cybersecurity roles, responsibilities, and risk management decisions. | ID.BE-2: The organization's place in critical infrastructure and its industry sector is identified and communicated. |
| **Identify (ID) core function: Business Environment (ID.BE)**: The organization's mission, objectives, stakeholders, and activities are understood and prioritized; this information is used to inform cybersecurity roles, responsibilities, and risk management decisions. | ID.BE-3: Priorities for organizational mission, objectives, and activities are established and communicated. |
| **Identify (ID) core function: Business Environment (ID.BE)**: The organization's mission, objectives, stakeholders, and activities are understood and prioritized; this information is used to inform cybersecurity roles, responsibilities, and risk management decisions. | ID.BE-4: Dependencies and critical functions for delivery of critical services are established. |
| **Identify (ID) core function: Business Environment (ID.BE)**: The organization's mission, objectives, stakeholders, and activities are understood and prioritized; this information is used to inform cybersecurity roles, responsibilities, and risk management decisions. | ID.BE-5: Resilience requirements to support delivery of critical services are established for all operating states (e.g., under duress/attack, during recovery, normal operations). |

| Category | Subcategory |
|---|---|
| **Identify (ID) core function: Governance (ID.GV)**: The policies, procedures, and processes to manage and monitor the organization's regulatory, legal, risk, environmental, and operational requirements are understood and inform the management of cybersecurity risk. | ID.GV-1: Organizational cybersecurity policy is established and communicated. |
| **Identify (ID) core function: Governance (ID.GV)**: The policies, procedures, and processes to manage and monitor the organization's regulatory, legal, risk, environmental, and operational requirements are understood and inform the management of cybersecurity risk. | ID.GV-2: Cybersecurity roles and responsibilities are coordinated and aligned with internal roles and external partners. |
| **Identify (ID) core function: Governance (ID.GV)**: The policies, procedures, and processes to manage and monitor the organization's regulatory, legal, risk, environmental, and operational requirements are understood and inform the management of cybersecurity risk. | ID.GV-3: Legal and regulatory requirements regarding cybersecurity, including privacy and civil liberties obligations, are understood and managed. |
| **Identify (ID) core function: Governance (ID.GV)**: The policies, procedures, and processes to manage and monitor the organization's regulatory, legal, risk, environmental, and operational requirements are understood and inform the management of cybersecurity risk. | ID.GV-4: Governance and risk management processes address cybersecurity risks. |
| **Identify (ID) core function: Risk Assessment (ID.RA)**: The organization understands the cybersecurity risk to organizational operations (including mission, functions, image, or reputation), organizational assets, and individuals. | ID.RA-1: Asset vulnerabilities are identified and documented. |
| **Identify (ID) core function: Risk Assessment (ID.RA)**: The organization understands the cybersecurity risk to organizational operations (including mission, functions, image, or reputation), organizational assets, and individuals. | ID.RA-2: Cyber threat intelligence is received from information sharing forums and sources. |
| **Identify (ID) core function: Risk Assessment (ID.RA)**: The organization understands the cybersecurity risk to organizational operations (including mission, functions, image, or reputation), organizational assets, and individuals. | ID.RA-3: Threats, both internal and external, are identified and documented. |
| **Identify (ID) core function: Risk Assessment (ID.RA)**: The organization understands the cybersecurity risk to organizational operations (including mission, functions, image, or reputation), organizational assets, and individuals. | ID.RA-4: Potential business impacts and likelihoods are identified. |
| **Identify (ID) core function: Risk Assessment (ID.RA)**: The organization understands the cybersecurity risk to organizational operations (including mission, functions, image, or reputation), organizational assets, and individuals. | ID.RA-5: Threats, vulnerabilities, likelihoods, and impacts are used to determine risk. |
| **Identify (ID) core function: Risk Assessment (ID.RA)**: The organization understands the cybersecurity risk to organizational operations (including mission, functions, image, or reputation), organizational assets, and individuals. | ID.RA-6: Risk responses are identified and prioritized. |

## Table 4. (Continued)

| Category | Subcategory |
|---|---|
| **Identify (ID) core function: Risk Management Strategy (ID.RM)**: The organization's priorities, constraints, risk tolerances, and assumptions are established and used to support operational risk decisions. | ID.RM-1: Risk management processes are established, managed, and agreed to by organizational stakeholders. |
| **Identify (ID) core function: Risk Management Strategy (ID.RM)**: The organization's priorities, constraints, risk tolerances, and assumptions are established and used to support operational risk decisions. | ID.RM-2: Organizational risk tolerance is determined and clearly expressed. |
| **Identify (ID) core function: Risk Management Strategy (ID.RM)**: The organization's priorities, constraints, risk tolerances, and assumptions are established and used to support operational risk decisions. | ID.RM-3: The organization's determination of risk tolerance is informed by its role in critical infrastructure and sector specific risk analysis. |
| **Identify (ID) core function: Supply Chain Risk Management (ID.SC):** The organization's priorities, constraints, risk tolerances, and assumptions are established and used to support risk decisions associated with managing supply chain risk. The organization has established and implemented the processes to identify, assess and manage supply chain risks. | ID.SC-1: Cyber supply chain risk management processes are identified, established, assessed, managed, and agreed to by organizational stakeholders. |
| **Identify (ID) core function: Supply Chain Risk Management (ID.SC):** The organization's priorities, constraints, risk tolerances, and assumptions are established and used to support risk decisions associated with managing supply chain risk. The organization has established and implemented the processes to identify, assess and manage supply chain risks. | ID.SC-2: Suppliers and third party partners of information systems, components, and services are identified, prioritized, and assessed using a cyber supply chain risk assessment process. |
| **Identify (ID) core function: Supply Chain Risk Management (ID.SC):** The organization's priorities, constraints, risk tolerances, and assumptions are established and used to support risk decisions associated with managing supply chain risk. The organization has established and implemented the processes to identify, assess and manage supply chain risks. | ID.SC-3: Contracts with suppliers and third-party partners are used to implement appropriate measures designed to meet the objectives of an organization's cybersecurity program and Cyber Supply Chain Risk Management Plan. |
| **Identify (ID) core function: Supply Chain Risk Management (ID.SC):** The organization's priorities, constraints, risk tolerances, and assumptions are established and used to support risk decisions associated with managing supply chain risk. The organization has established and implemented the processes to identify, assess and manage supply chain risks. | ID.SC-4: Suppliers and third-party partners are routinely assessed using audits, test results, or other forms of evaluations to confirm they are meeting their contractual obligations. |

| Category | Subcategory |
|---|---|
| **Identify (ID) core function: Supply Chain Risk Management (ID.SC):** The organization's priorities, constraints, risk tolerances, and assumptions are established and used to support risk decisions associated with managing supply chain risk. The organization has established and implemented the processes to identify, assess and manage supply chain risks. | ID.SC-5: Response and recovery planning and testing are conducted with suppliers and third-party providers. |
| **Protect (PR) core function: Identity Management, Authentication and Access Control (PR.AC)**: Access to physical and logical assets and associated facilities is limited to authorized users, processes, and devices, and is managed consistent with the assessed risk of unauthorized access to authorized activities and transactions. | PR.AC-1: Identities and credentials are issued, managed, verified, revoked, and audited for authorized devices, users and processes. |
| **Protect (PR) core function: Identity Management, Authentication and Access Control (PR.AC)**: Access to physical and logical assets and associated facilities is limited to authorized users, processes, and devices, and is managed consistent with the assessed risk of unauthorized access to authorized activities and transactions. | PR.AC-2: Physical access to assets is managed and protected. |
| **Protect (PR) core function: Identity Management, Authentication and Access Control (PR.AC)**: Access to physical and logical assets and associated facilities is limited to authorized users, processes, and devices, and is managed consistent with the assessed risk of unauthorized access to authorized activities and transactions. | PR.AC-3: Remote access is managed. |
| **Protect (PR) core function: Identity Management, Authentication and Access Control (PR.AC)**: Access to physical and logical assets and associated facilities is limited to authorized users, processes, and devices, and is managed consistent with the assessed risk of unauthorized access to authorized activities and transactions. | PR.AC-4: Access permissions and authorizations are managed, incorporating the principles of least privilege and separation of duties. |
| **Protect (PR) core function: Identity Management, Authentication and Access Control (PR.AC)**: Access to physical and logical assets and associated facilities is limited to authorized users, processes, and devices, and is managed consistent with the assessed risk of unauthorized access to authorized activities and transactions. | PR.AC-5: Network integrity is protected (e.g., network segregation and network segmentation). |
| **Protect (PR) core function: Identity Management, Authentication and Access Control (PR.AC)**: Access to physical and logical assets and associated facilities is limited to authorized users, processes, and devices, and is managed consistent with the assessed risk of unauthorized access to authorized activities and transactions. | PR.AC-6: Identities are proofed and bound to credentials and asserted in interactions. |

## Table 4. (Continued)

| Category | Subcategory |
|---|---|
| **Protect (PR) core function: Identity Management, Authentication and Access Control (PR.AC)**: Access to physical and logical assets and associated facilities is limited to authorized users, processes, and devices, and is managed consistent with the assessed risk of unauthorized access to authorized activities and transactions. | PR.AC-7: Users, devices, and other assets are authenticated (e.g., single-factor and multi-factor) commensurate with the risk of the transaction (e.g., individuals' security and privacy risks and other organizational risks). |
| **Protect (PR) core function: Awareness and Training (PR.AT)**: The organization's personnel and partners are provided cybersecurity awareness education and are trained to perform their cybersecurity duties and responsibilities consistent with related policies, procedures, and agreements. | PR.AT-1: All users are informed and trained. |
| **Protect (PR) core function: Awareness and Training (PR.AT)**: The organization's personnel and partners are provided cybersecurity awareness education and are trained to perform their cybersecurity duties and responsibilities consistent with related policies, procedures, and agreements. | PR.AT-2: Privileged users understand their roles and responsibilities. |
| **Protect (PR) core function: Awareness and Training (PR.AT)**: The organization's personnel and partners are provided cybersecurity awareness education and are trained to perform their cybersecurity duties and responsibilities consistent with related policies, procedures, and agreements. | PR.AT-3: Third-party stakeholders (e.g., suppliers, customers, partners) understand their roles and responsibilities. |
| **Protect (PR) core function: Awareness and Training (PR.AT)**: The organization's personnel and partners are provided cybersecurity awareness education and are trained to perform their cybersecurity duties and responsibilities consistent with related policies, procedures, and agreements. | PR.AT-4: Senior executives understand their roles and responsibilities. |
| **Protect (PR) core function: Awareness and Training (PR.AT)**: The organization's personnel and partners are provided cybersecurity awareness education and are trained to perform their cybersecurity duties and responsibilities consistent with related policies, procedures, and agreements. | PR.AT-5: Physical and cybersecurity personnel understand their roles and responsibilities. |
| **Protect (PR) core function: Data Security (PR.DS)**: Information and records (data) are managed consistent with the organization's risk strategy to protect the confidentiality, integrity, and availability of information. | PR.DS-1: Data-at-rest is protected. |
| **Protect (PR) core function: Data Security (PR.DS)**: Information and records (data) are managed consistent with the organization's risk strategy to protect the confidentiality, integrity, and availability of information. | PR.DS-2: Data-in-transit is protected. |

| **Category** | **Subcategory** |
|---|---|
| **Protect (PR) core function: Data Security (PR.DS)**: Information and records (data) are managed consistent with the organization's risk strategy to protect the confidentiality, integrity, and availability of information. | PR.DS-3: Assets are formally managed throughout removal, transfers, and disposition. |
| **Protect (PR) core function: Data Security (PR.DS)**: Information and records (data) are managed consistent with the organization's risk strategy to protect the confidentiality, integrity, and availability of information. | PR.DS-4: Adequate capacity to ensure availability is maintained. |
| **Protect (PR) core function: Data Security (PR.DS)**: Information and records (data) are managed consistent with the organization's risk strategy to protect the confidentiality, integrity, and availability of information. | PR.DS-5: Protections against data leaks are implemented. |
| **Protect (PR) core function: Data Security (PR.DS)**: Information and records (data) are managed consistent with the organization's risk strategy to protect the confidentiality, integrity, and availability of information. | PR.DS-6: Integrity checking mechanisms are used to verify software, firmware, and information integrity. |
| **Protect (PR) core function: Data Security (PR.DS)**: Information and records (data) are managed consistent with the organization's risk strategy to protect the confidentiality, integrity, and availability of information. | PR.DS-7: The development and testing environment(s) are separate from the production environment. |
| **Protect (PR) core function: Data Security (PR.DS)**: Information and records (data) are managed consistent with the organization's risk strategy to protect the confidentiality, integrity, and availability of information. | PR.DS-8: Integrity checking mechanisms are used to verify hardware integrity. |
| **Protect (PR) core function: Information Protection Processes and Procedures (PR.IP)**: Security policies (that address purpose, scope, roles, responsibilities, management commitment, and coordination among organizational entities), processes, and procedures are maintained and used to manage protection of information systems and assets. | PR.IP-1: A baseline configuration of information technology/industrial control systems is created and maintained incorporating security principles (e.g., concept of least functionality). |
| **Protect (PR) core function: Information Protection Processes and Procedures (PR.IP)**: Security policies (that address purpose, scope, roles, responsibilities, management commitment, and coordination among organizational entities), processes, and procedures are maintained and used to manage protection of information systems and assets. | PR.IP-2: A System Development Life Cycle to manage systems is implemented. |
| **Protect (PR) core function: Information Protection Processes and Procedures (PR.IP)**: Security policies (that address purpose, scope, roles, responsibilities, management commitment, and coordination among organizational entities), processes, and procedures are maintained and used to manage protection of information systems and assets. | PR.IP-3: Configuration change control processes are in place. |

## Table 4. (Continued)

| Category | Subcategory |
|---|---|
| **Protect (PR) core function: Information Protection Processes and Procedures (PR.IP)**: Security policies (that address purpose, scope, roles, responsibilities, management commitment, and coordination among organizational entities), processes, and procedures are maintained and used to manage protection of information systems and assets. | PR.IP-4: Backups of information are conducted, maintained, and tested. |
| **Protect (PR) core function: Information Protection Processes and Procedures (PR.IP)**: Security policies (that address purpose, scope, roles, responsibilities, management commitment, and coordination among organizational entities), processes, and procedures are maintained and used to manage protection of information systems and assets. | PR.IP-5: Policy and regulations regarding the physical operating environment for organizational assets are met. |
| **Protect (PR) core function: Information Protection Processes and Procedures (PR.IP)**: Security policies (that address purpose, scope, roles, responsibilities, management commitment, and coordination among organizational entities), processes, and procedures are maintained and used to manage protection of information systems and assets. | PR.IP-6: Data are destroyed according to policy. |
| **Protect (PR) core function: Information Protection Processes and Procedures (PR.IP)**: Security policies (that address purpose, scope, roles, responsibilities, management commitment, and coordination among organizational entities), processes, and procedures are maintained and used to manage protection of information systems and assets. | PR.IP-7: Protection processes are improved |
| **Protect (PR) core function: Information Protection Processes and Procedures (PR.IP)**: Security policies (that address purpose, scope, roles, responsibilities, management commitment, and coordination among organizational entities), processes, and procedures are maintained and used to manage protection of information systems and assets. | PR.IP-8: Effectiveness of protection technologies is shared. |
| **Protect (PR) core function: Information Protection Processes and Procedures (PR.IP)**: Security policies (that address purpose, scope, roles, responsibilities, management commitment, and coordination among organizational entities), processes, and procedures are maintained and used to manage protection of information systems and assets. | PR.IP-9: Response plans (Incident Response and Business Continuity) and recovery plans (Incident Recovery and Disaster Recovery) are in place and managed. |
| **Protect (PR) core function: Information Protection Processes and Procedures (PR.IP)**: Security policies (that address purpose, scope, roles, responsibilities, management commitment, and coordination among organizational entities), processes, and procedures are maintained and used to manage protection of information systems and assets. | PR.IP-10: Response and recovery plans are tested. |

| Category | Subcategory |
|---|---|
| **Protect (PR) core function: Information Protection Processes and Procedures (PR.IP)**: Security policies (that address purpose, scope, roles, responsibilities, management commitment, and coordination among organizational entities), processes, and procedures are maintained and used to manage protection of information systems and assets. | PR.IP-11: Cybersecurity is included in human resources practices (e.g., deprovisioning and personnel screening). |
| **Protect (PR) core function: Information Protection Processes and Procedures (PR.IP)**: Security policies (that address purpose, scope, roles, responsibilities, management commitment, and coordination among organizational entities), processes, and procedures are maintained and used to manage protection of information systems and assets. | PR.IP-12: A vulnerability management plan is developed and implemented **Protect (PR) core function:**. |
| **Protect (PR) core function: Protect (PR) core function: Maintenance (PR.MA)**: Maintenance and repairs of industrial control and information system components are performed consistent with policies and procedures. | PR.MA-1: Maintenance and repair of organizational assets are performed and logged, with approved and controlled tools. |
| **Protect (PR) core function: Maintenance (PR.MA)**: Maintenance and repairs of industrial control and information system components are performed consistent with policies and procedures. | PR.MA-2: Remote maintenance of organizational assets is approved, logged, and performed in a manner that prevents unauthorized access. |
| **Prot Protect (PR) core function: ective Technology (PR.PT)**: Technical security solutions are managed to ensure the security and resilience of systems and assets, consistent with related policies, procedures, and agreements. | PR.PT-1: Audit/log records are determined, documented, implemented, and reviewed in accordance with policy. |
| **Protect (PR) core function: Protective Technology (PR.PT)**: Technical security solutions are managed to ensure the security and resilience of systems and assets, consistent with related policies, procedures, and agreements. | PR.PT-2: Removable media is protected and its use restricted according to policy. |
| **Protect (PR) core function: Protective Technology (PR.PT)**: Technical security solutions are managed to ensure the security and resilience of systems and assets, consistent with related policies, procedures, and agreements. | PR.PT-3: The principle of least functionality is incorporated by configuring systems to provide only essential capabilities. |
| **Protect (PR) core function: Protective Technology (PR.PT)**: Technical security solutions are managed to ensure the security and resilience of systems and assets, consistent with related policies, procedures, and agreements. | PR.PT-4: Communications and control networks are protected. |
| **Protect (PR) core function: Protective Technology (PR.PT)**: Technical security solutions are managed to ensure the security and resilience of systems and assets, consistent with related policies, procedures, and agreements. | PR.PT-5: Mechanisms (e.g., failsafe, load balancing, hot swap) are implemented to achieve resilience requirements in normal and adverse situations. |

**Table 4. (Continued)**

| Category | Subcategory |
|---|---|
| **Detect (DE) core function: Anomalies and Events (DE.AE):** Anomalous activity is detected and the potential impact of events is understood. | DE.AE-1: A baseline of network operations and expected data flows for users and systems is established and managed. |
| **Detect (DE) core function: Anomalies and Events (DE.AE):** Anomalous activity is detected and the potential impact of events is understood. | DE.AE-2: Detected events are analyzed to understand attack targets and methods. |
| **Detect (DE) core function: Anomalies and Events (DE.AE):** Anomalous activity is detected and the potential impact of events is understood. | DE.AE-3: Event data are collected and correlated from multiple sources and sensors. |
| **Detect (DE) core function: Anomalies and Events (DE.AE):** Anomalous activity is detected and the potential impact of events is understood. | DE.AE-4: Impact of events is determined. |
| **Detect (DE) core function: Anomalies and Events (DE.AE):** Anomalous activity is detected and the potential impact of events is understood. | DE.AE-5: Incident alert thresholds are established. |
| **Detect (DE) core function: Security Continuous Monitoring (DE.CM)**: The information system and assets are monitored to identify cybersecurity events and verify the effectiveness of protective measures. | DE.CM-1: The network is monitored to detect potential cybersecurity events. |
| **Detect (DE) core function: Security Continuous Monitoring (DE.CM)**: The information system and assets are monitored to identify cybersecurity events and verify the effectiveness of protective measures | DE.CM-2: The physical environment is monitored to detect potential cybersecurity events. |
| **Detect (DE) core function: Security Continuous Monitoring (DE.CM)**: The information system and assets are monitored to identify cybersecurity events and verify the effectiveness of protective measures | DE.CM-3: Personnel activity is monitored to detect potential cybersecurity events. |
| **Detect (DE) core function: Security Continuous Monitoring (DE.CM)**: The information system and assets are monitored to identify cybersecurity events and verify the effectiveness of protective measures | DE.CM-4: Malicious code is detected. |
| **Detect (DE) core function: Security Continuous Monitoring (DE.CM)**: The information system and assets are monitored to identify cybersecurity events and verify the effectiveness of protective measures | DE.CM-5: Unauthorized mobile code is detected. |
| **Detect (DE) core function: Security Continuous Monitoring (DE.CM)**: The information system and assets are monitored to identify cybersecurity events and verify the effectiveness of protective measures | DE.CM-6: External service provider activity is monitored to detect potential cybersecurity events. |

| Category | Subcategory |
|---|---|
| **Detect (DE) core function: Security Continuous Monitoring (DE.CM)**: The information system and assets are monitored to identify cybersecurity events and verify the effectiveness of protective measures | DE.CM-7: Monitoring for unauthorized personnel, connections, devices, and software is performed. |
| **Detect (DE) core function: Security Continuous Monitoring (DE.CM)**: The information system and assets are monitored to identify cybersecurity events and verify the effectiveness of protective measures | DE.CM-8: Vulnerability scans are performed. |
| **Detect (DE) core function: Detection Processes (DE.DP):** Detection processes and procedures are maintained and tested to ensure awareness of anomalous events. | DE.DP-1: Roles and responsibilities for detection are well defined to ensure accountability. |
| **Detect (DE) core function: Detection Processes (DE.DP):** Detection processes and procedures are maintained and tested to ensure awareness of anomalous events. | DE.DP-2: Detection activities comply with all applicable requirements. |
| **Detect (DE) core function: Detection Processes (DE.DP):** Detection processes and procedures are maintained and tested to ensure awareness of anomalous events. | DE.DP-3: Detection processes are tested. |
| **Detect (DE) core function: Detection Processes (DE.DP):** Detection processes and procedures are maintained and tested to ensure awareness of anomalous events. | DE.DP-4: Event detection information is communicated. |
| **Detect (DE) core function: Detection Processes (DE.DP):** Detection processes and procedures are maintained and tested to ensure awareness of anomalous events. | DE.DP-5: Detection processes are continuously improved. |
| **Respond (RS) core function: Response Planning (RS.RP):** Response processes and procedures are executed and maintained, to ensure response to detected cybersecurity incidents. | RS.RP-1: Response plan is executed during or after an incident. |
| **Respond (RS) core function: Communications (RS.CO):** Response activities are coordinated with internal and external stakeholders (e.g., external support from law enforcement agencies). | RS.CO-1: Personnel know their roles and order of operations when a response is needed. |
| **Respond (RS) core function: Communications (RS.CO):** Response activities are coordinated with internal and external stakeholders (e.g., external support from law enforcement agencies). | RS.CO-2: Incidents are reported consistent with established criteria. |
| **Respond (RS) core function: Communications (RS.CO):** Response activities are coordinated with internal and external stakeholders (e.g., external support from law enforcement agencies). | RS.CO-3: Information is shared consistent with response plans. |
| **Respond (RS) core function: Communications (RS.CO):** Response activities are coordinated with internal and external stakeholders (e.g., external support from law enforcement agencies). | RS.CO-4: Coordination with stakeholders occurs consistent with response plans. |

**Table 4. (Continued)**

| Category | Subcategory |
|---|---|
| **Respond (RS) core function: Communications (RS.CO):** Response activities are coordinated with internal and external stakeholders (e.g., external support from law enforcement agencies). | RS.CO-5: Voluntary information sharing occurs with external stakeholders to achieve broader cybersecurity situational awareness. |
| **Respond (RS) core function: Analysis (RS.AN):** Analysis is conducted to ensure effective response and support recovery activities. | RS.AN-1: Notifications from detection systems are investigated. |
| **Respond (RS) core function: Analysis (RS.AN):** Analysis is conducted to ensure effective response and support recovery activities. | RS.AN-2: The impact of the incident is understood. |
| **Respond (RS) core function: Analysis (RS.AN):** Analysis is conducted to ensure effective response and support recovery activities. | RS.AN-3: Forensics are performed. |
| **Respond (RS) core function: Analysis (RS.AN):** Analysis is conducted to ensure effective response and support recovery activities. | RS.AN-4: Incidents are categorized consistent with response plans. |
| **Respond (RS) core function: Analysis (RS.AN):** Analysis is conducted to ensure effective response and support recovery activities. | RS-AN-5: Processes are established to receive, analyze and respond to vulnerabilities disclosed to the organization from internal and external sources (e.g. internal testing, security bulletins, or security researchers). |
| **Respond (RS) core function: Mitigation (RS.MI):** Activities are performed to prevent expansion of an event, mitigate its effects, and eradicate the incident. | RS.MI-1: Incidents are contained. |
| **Respond (RS) core function: Mitigation (RS.MI):** Activities are performed to prevent expansion of an event, mitigate its effects, and eradicate the incident. | RS.MI-2: Incidents are mitigated. |
| **Respond (RS) core function: Mitigation (RS.MI):** Activities are performed to prevent expansion of an event, mitigate its effects, and eradicate the incident. | RS.MI-3: Newly identified vulnerabilities are mitigated or documented as accepted risks. |
| **Respond (RS) core function: Improvements (RS.IM):** Organizational response activities are improved by incorporating lessons learned from current and previous detection/response activities. | RS.IM-1: Response plans incorporate lessons learned. |
| **Respond (RS) core function: Improvements (RS.IM):** Organizational response activities are improved by incorporating lessons learned from current and previous detection/response activities. | RS.IM-2: Response strategies are updated. |

| Category | Subcategory |
| --- | --- |
| **Recover (RC) core function: Recovery Planning (RC.RP):** Recovery processes and procedures are executed and maintained to ensure restoration of systems or assets affected by cybersecurity events. | RC.RP-1: Recovery plan is executed during or after a cybersecurity incident. |
| **Recover (RC) core function: Improvements (RC.IM):** Recovery planning and processes are improved by incorporating lessons learned into future activities. | RC.IM-1: Recovery plans incorporate lessons learned. |
| **Recover (RC) core function: Improvements (RS.IM):** Organizational response activities are improved by incorporating lessons learned from current and previous detection/response activities. | RC.IM-2: Recovery strategies are updated. |
| **Recover (RC) core function: Communications (RC.CO):** Restoration activities are coordinated with internal and external parties (e.g., coordinating centers, Internet Service Providers, owners of attacking systems, victims, other CSIRTs, and vendors). | RC.CO-1: Public relations are managed. |
| **Recover (RC) core function: Communications (RC.CO):** Restoration activities are coordinated with internal and external parties (e.g., coordinating centers, Internet Service Providers, owners of attacking systems, victims, other CSIRTs, and vendors). | RC.CO-2: Reputation is repaired after an incident. |
| **Recover (RC) core function: Communications (RC.CO):** Restoration activities are coordinated with internal and external parties (e.g., coordinating centers, Internet Service Providers, owners of attacking systems, victims, other CSIRTs, and vendors). | RC.CO-3: Recovery activities are communicated to internal and external stakeholders as well as executive and management teams. |

Source: National Institute of Standards and Technology. | GAO-19-70.

# APPENDIX III: COMMENTS FROM DEPARTMENT OF HEALTH AND HUMAN SERVICES

DEPARTMENT OF HEALTH & HUMAN SERVICES | OFFICE OF THE SECRETARY

Assistant Secretary for Legislation
Washington, DC 20201

DEC 0 6 2018

Gregory C. Wilshusen
Director, Information Security Issues
U.S. Government Accountability Office
441 G Street NW
Washington, DC 20548

Dear Mr. Wilshusen:

Attached are comments on the U.S. Government Accountability Office's (GAO) report entitled, "*Information Security: Significant Progress Made, but CDC Needs to Take Further Action to Resolve Control Deficiencies and Improve Its Program*" (GAO-19-70).

The Department appreciates the opportunity to review this report prior to publication.

Sincerely,

Matthew D. Bassett
Assistant Secretary for Legislation

**GENERAL COMMENTS FROM THE DEPARTMENT OF HEALTH & HUMAN SERVICES ON THE GOVERNMENT ACCOUNTABILITY OFFICE'S DRAFT REPORT ENTITLED - INFORMATION SECURITY: SIGNIFICANT PROGRESS MADE, BUT CDC NEEDS TO TAKE FURTHER ACTION TO RESOLVE CONTROL DEFICIENCIES AND IMPROVE ITS PROGRAM (GAO-19-70)**

CDC greatly appreciates the opportunity to review and comment on this report. CDC recognizes the risks associated with operating a large, global information technology (IT) enterprise and has implemented processes, procedures, and tools to better ensure the prevention, detection, and correction of potential incidents.

Cybersecurity remains a high priority at CDC, and the agency continues to take the responsibility to protect the public health information and data entrusted to it seriously. With a history of operating a robust cybersecurity program, CDC continues to provide sophisticated preventive, detective, and responsive controls to reduce risk to programs, systems, and data. As cyber-threats continue to evolve, the agency recognizes the need for, and remains committed to, protecting public health information and strengthening our cybersecurity posture. CDC has not experienced a major cybersecurity breach that exposed public health information.

CDC appreciates the collaborative interaction with the GAO audit team. Since receiving GAO's report in June 2018, 68 percent of GAO's recommendations have been implemented and work is underway on the remaining 32 percent. As evidenced by these figures, CDC is aggressively working to address all identified deficiencies as quickly and completely as possible.

To further strengthen the agency's cybersecurity program, CDC is restructuring and streamlining the Office of the Chief Information Officer, which includes both the cyber program and IT infrastructure. These changes will increase the agility and resilience of the agency's cybersecurity program. Furthermore, CDC has completed the implementation of phase one and two of the Department of Homeland Security's (DHS) mandatory three-phrase Continuous Diagnostics and Mitigation (CDM) program. CDC leveraged GAO's report to accelerate its implementation, infrastructure, and software deployments for CDM. CDC is actively engaging in phase three, now referred to as CDM DEFEND, and closely following the timeline established by DHS and HHS for completion.

CDC has undertaken unprecedented action through increased investment, dedicated resources, and project management rigor to ensure the protection of CDC information. As a result, tremendous progress has been made on a significant proportion of GAO's recommendations. According to the GAO team, CDC's aggressive and successful approach to recommendation implementation has not been seen in recent audits.

Highlighted below are examples of CDC's efforts and accomplishments:

- Categorized all 184 GAO technical recommendations and 11 program recommendations based on system type, impact level, and level of effort and identified those associated with CDC mission-critical systems to prioritize focus and rapidly reduce risk;
- Used an industry standard and recognized approach to determining risk and applied National Institute of Standards and Technology's (NIST) risk ratings and methodology to all 195 recommendations. This included threat sources maintained by CDC on a routine

**GENERAL COMMENTS FROM THE DEPARTMENT OF HEALTH & HUMAN SERVICES ON THE GOVERNMENT ACCOUNTABILITY OFFICE'S DRAFT REPORT ENTITLED - INFORMATION SECURITY: SIGNIFICANT PROGRESS MADE, BUT CDC NEEDS TO TAKE FURTHER ACTION TO RESOLVE CONTROL DEFICIENCIES AND IMPROVE ITS PROGRAM (GAO-19-70)**

basis, the likelihood of an adverse event based on previous ability to thwart attacks and current cyber capabilities, and the potential adverse impact to CDC's mission;

- Actively engaged the House Energy and Commerce Committee, initially reporting progress on a bi-weekly basis. Based on significant progress by CDC, this was reduced to monthly at the request of the Committee.
- Provided implementation evidence to GAO for 105 (54 percent) of the technical recommendations by August 8, 2018, of which GAO validated 102 during the initial review of the submissions;
- Provided implementation evidence to GAO for 28 (68 percent) of the high-risk technical recommendations by September 30, 2018;
- Provided implementation evidence to GAO for one of the 11 program recommendations, as of November 1, 2018, and completed significant progress on the remaining ten (10) program recommendations; and
- Executing plans for the remaining, more complex, high-risk recommendations with minimal disruption to CDC's operations, while submitting evidence for an additional 23 recommendations as of November 26, 2018, moving the overall completion rate to 68 percent.

In support of these efforts and accomplishments, CDC:

- Established a Cybersecurity Task Force to strengthen and protect public health computing capabilities to meet program needs;
- Coordinated with all points of contact to verify ownership and track remediation progress;
- Coordinated with key Information Systems Security Officers to verify accountability and responsibility for groups if GAO provided recommendations common to systems, infrastructure, or security domains;
- Developed a plan of action and milestones for all remaining actions not validated by GAO, as of July 23, 2018, to monitor progress for remediation tracking and reporting purposes;
- Provided recurring status updates to CDC leadership in order to communicate remediation progress;
- Created real-time dashboards to track and monitor remediation status in terms of risk, NIST cybersecurity framework categories, and organizational ownership;
- Made critical and appropriate investments to support implementation of necessary IT infrastructure changes and security improvements; and
- Acquired industry-leading expertise to provide support and advisory internal control services necessary to develop actions plans to immediately address GAO audit findings and recommendations. Support also includes execution and program/project management activities to implement the 195 recommendations for improving the cybersecurity program.

**GENERAL COMMENTS FROM THE DEPARTMENT OF HEALTH & HUMAN SERVICES ON THE GOVERNMENT ACCOUNTABILITY OFFICE'S DRAFT REPORT ENTITLED - INFORMATION SECURITY: SIGNIFICANT PROGRESS MADE, BUT CDC NEEDS TO TAKE FURTHER ACTION TO RESOLVE CONTROL DEFICIENCIES AND IMPROVE ITS PROGRAM (GAO-19-70)**

These efforts, along with other ongoing remediation activities, reinforce CDC's commitment to continuously improve its cybersecurity program to protect its information technology resources and data. Addressing the weaknesses and recommendations identified will strengthen the agency's ability to conduct highly effective incident response, insider threat detection, operational situational awareness, and decrease the overall security risks to sensitive information and IT infrastructure.

CDC is in the midst of remediation activities for all the Program recommendations, and progress to date includes:

Recommendation 1. The Director of CDC should take steps to evaluate system impact level categorizations to ensure that they reflect the current operating environment, particularly for the selected mission essential systems currently categorized as high impact that are interfacing with systems currently categorized at lower impact levels.

*CDC concurs with this recommendation and is strengthening processes to ensure that risk assessments for the systems reviewed by GAO reflect the current operating environment, as well as the likelihood and impact of threats to the agency.*

Recommendation 2. The Director of CDC should take steps to update risk assessments for selected systems to identify threats, including the likelihood and impact of threats, as well as to address technical constraints and new threats and threat vectors that affect the implementation of controls.

*CDC concurs with this recommendation and is strengthening processes to ensure that risk assessments for the systems reviewed by GAO appropriately evaluate the likelihood and impact of threats to the agency, as well as address technical constraints and new threats and threat vectors that affect the implementation of controls.*

Recommendation 3. The Director of CDC should take steps to update facility risk assessments for the facilities housing selected systems.

*CDC concurs with this recommendation and has updated facility risk assessments for the facilities housing selected systems, which were reviewed by GAO. Evidence for this Program Recommendation is being prepared for submission to GAO for validation.*

Recommendation 4. The Director of CDC should take steps to update policies, procedures, and standards with more detailed requirements, to include topics such as (1) configuring and restricting services on network devices and regulating certain connections on firewalls; (2) securely configuring database parameters; and (3) blocking email attachments and deploying a data loss prevention solution.

*CDC concurs with this recommendation and is revising the policies, procedures, and standards identified by GAO.*

**GENERAL COMMENTS FROM THE DEPARTMENT OF HEALTH & HUMAN SERVICES ON THE GOVERNMENT ACCOUNTABILITY OFFICE'S DRAFT REPORT ENTITLED - INFORMATION SECURITY: SIGNIFICANT PROGRESS MADE, BUT CDC NEEDS TO TAKE FURTHER ACTION TO RESOLVE CONTROL DEFICIENCIES AND IMPROVE ITS PROGRAM (GAO-19-70)**

Recommendation 5. The Director of CDC should take steps to develop [facility] security plans for the facilities housing resources for the selected systems.

*CDC concurs with this recommendation and has developed security plans for the facilities housing selected systems, which were reviewed by GAO, to include all aspects of security for space and equipment, including access control mechanisms, visitor control, and maintenance of records, as well as the process for equipment/inventory control. Evidence for this Program Recommendation is being prepared for submission to GAO for validation.*

Recommendation 6. The Director of CDC should take steps to review staff roles and responsibilities to ensure that those with significant security responsibilities are appropriately identified and receive role-based training.

*CDC concurs with this recommendation and has implemented a formal process in accordance with National and Departmental standards to monitor and track training requirements for personnel with significant security roles and responsibilities. CDC completed the training requirements by ensuring that all CDC staff with significant security roles and responsibilities have completed role-based training for fiscal year 2018. Evidence for this Program Recommendation has been provided to GAO for validation.*

Recommendation 7. The Director of CDC should take steps to routinely monitor the configuration settings of agency systems to ensure that the configurations are set as intended.

*CDC concurs with this recommendation and is assessing and enhancing procedures to ensure the monitoring of configuration setting of agency systems are set as intended.*

Recommendation 8. The Director of CDC should take steps to update security control assessments for the selected mission essential systems to include an assessment of controls described in system security plans, using an appropriate level of rigor.

*CDC concurs with this recommendation and is enhancing processes to increase the rigor with which it performs security assessments on controls of the selected systems reviewed by GAO.*

Recommendation 9. The Director of CDC should take steps to update and follow security control assessment plans for the selected mission essential systems, including ensuring the plans have sufficient detail for procedures to be performed and identify assessment team roles and responsibilities.

*CDC concurs with this recommendation and is updating and following modified security assessment plans on controls of the selected systems reviewed by GAO, while also ensuring the procedures to be performed and assessment team's roles and responsibilities are clearly defined.*

**GENERAL COMMENTS FROM THE DEPARTMENT OF HEALTH & HUMAN SERVICES ON THE GOVERNMENT ACCOUNTABILITY OFFICE'S DRAFT REPORT ENTITLED - INFORMATION SECURITY: SIGNIFICANT PROGRESS MADE, BUT CDC NEEDS TO TAKE FURTHER ACTION TO RESOLVE CONTROL DEFICIENCIES AND IMPROVE ITS PROGRAM (GAO-19-70)**

Recommendation 10. The Director of CDC should take steps to improve office communication for updating plans of action and milestones for selected systems and act to monitor and support timely completion of corrective actions.

*CDC concurs with this recommendation and has partnered with an industry leader to provide support and advisory internal control services necessary to develop actions plans to immediately address GAO audit findings and recommendations. Support also includes execution and program/project management activities to implement the eleven recommendations for improving the cybersecurity program.*

Recommendation 11. The Director of CDC should take steps to document the cost-benefit analysis and associated risk of having an alternate processing site within the same geographical region as the main site.

*CDC concurs with this recommendation and has developed a cost-benefit analysis, along with all associated risks, of the same geographical region placement of an alternate processing site in relation to the main processing site. Evidence for this recommendation is being prepared for submission to GAO for validation.*

CDC appreciates the opportunity to review and comment on our progress associated with this report prior to publication.

# APPENDIX IV: ACCESSIBLE DATA

## Data Tables

### Accessible Data for Status of GAO Recommendations to the Centers for Disease Control and Prevention

| Open | No Evidence | Open-Partial |
|---|---|---|
| 72 | 21 | 102 |

### Accessible Data for Figure 1: Methods Used by the Centers for Disease Control and Prevention to Assess Security Controls

| Interview and examine | Examine | Interview | Test | Unidentified |
|---|---|---|---|---|
| 52 | 49 | 38 | 37 | 15 |

## Accessible Data for Figure 2: The Centers for Disease Control and Prevention's Planned Timeline for Fully Implementing GAO's Technical Control-Related Recommendations

| Month | Number of open recommendations |
|---|---|
| Mar-2018 | 184 |
| Apr-2018 | 184 |
| May-2018 | 184 |
| Jun-2018 | 169 |
| Jun-2018 | 169 |
| Jul-2018 | 169 |
| Aug-2018 | 82 |
| Aug-2018 | 52 |
| Sep-2018 | 50 |
| Oct-2018 | 50 |
| Nov-2018 | 50 |
| Dec-2018 | 46 |
| Jan-2019 | 45 |
| Feb-2019 | 45 |
| Mar-2019 | 23 |
| Apr-2019 | 23 |
| May-2019 | 23 |
| Jun-2019 | 14 |
| Jul-2019 | 14 |
| Jul-2019 | 14 |
| Aug-2019 | 11 |
| Sep-2019 | 5 |
| Oct-2019 | 5 |
| Nov-2019 | 5 |
| Dec-2019 | 5 |
| Jan-2020 | 5 |
| Feb-2020 | 5 |
| Mar-2020 | 2 |
| Apr-2020 | 2 |
| May-2020 | 2 |
| Jun-2020 | 2 |
| Jul-2020 | 2 |
| Aug-2020 | 2 |
| Sep-2020 | 2 |
| Sep-2020 | 2 |

In: Information Security …
Editor: Lauren Van Raalte
ISBN: 978-1-53615-621-8


*Chapter 5*

# INFORMATION TECHNOLOGY: AGENCIES NEED BETTER INFORMATION ON THE USE OF NONCOMPETITIVE AND BRIDGE CONTRACTS*

***United States Government Accountability Office***

## ABBREVIATIONS

| | |
|---|---|
| CBP | Customs and Border Protection |
| DOD | Department of Defense |
| DHS | Department of Homeland Security |
| DISA | Defense Information Systems Agency |
| DLA | Defense Logistics Agency |
| FAR | Federal Acquisition Regulation |
| FDA | Food and Drug Administration |

* This is an edited, reformatted and augmented version of United States Government Accountability Office; Report to Congressional Requesters, Accessible Version, Publication No. GAO-19-63, dated December 2018.

| | |
|---|---|
| FPDS-NG | Federal Procurement Data System-Next Generation |
| FSS | Federal Supply Schedule |
| GSA | General Services Administration |
| HHS | Department of Health and Human Services |
| IDIQ | Indefinite Delivery / Indefinite Quantity |
| IT | Information Technology |
| J&A | Justification and Approval |
| JETS | J6 Enterprise Technology Services |
| MGT | Modernizing Government Technology Act |
| OFPP | Office of Federal Procurement Policy |
| OMB | Office of Management and Budget |
| SBA | Small Business Administration |
| SOCOM | U.S. Special Operations Command |

## WHY GAO DID THIS STUDY

The federal government spends tens of billions of dollars each year on IT products and services. Competition is a key component to achieving the best return on investment for taxpayers. Federal acquisition regulations allow for noncompetitive contracts in certain circumstances. Some noncompetitive contracts act as "bridge contracts"— which can be a useful tool to avoid a lapse in service but can also increase the risk of the government overpaying. There is currently no government-wide definition of bridge contracts.

GAO was asked to review the federal government's use of noncompetitive contracts for IT. This chapter examines (1) the extent that agencies used noncompetitive contracts for IT, (2) the reasons for using noncompetitive contracts for selected IT procurements, (3) the extent to which IT procurements at selected agencies were bridge contracts, and (4) the extent to which IT procurements were in support of legacy systems. GAO analyzed FPDSNG data from fiscal years 2013 through 2017 (the most recent and complete data available). GAO developed a generalizable sample of 171 fiscal year 2016 noncompetitive IT contracts and orders awarded by DOD, DHS, and HHS—the agencies with the most spending on IT, to determine the reasons for using noncompetitive contracts and orders, and the extent to which these were bridge contracts or supported legacy systems.

## What GAO Recommends

GAO recommended DOD and HHS identify the reasons why competition data for certain orders in FPDS-NG were misreported and take corrective action. DOD and HHS concurred.

## What GAO Found

From fiscal years 2013 through 2017, federal agencies reported obligating more than $15 billion per year, or about 30 percent, of information technology (IT) contract spending on a noncompetitive basis (see Figure).

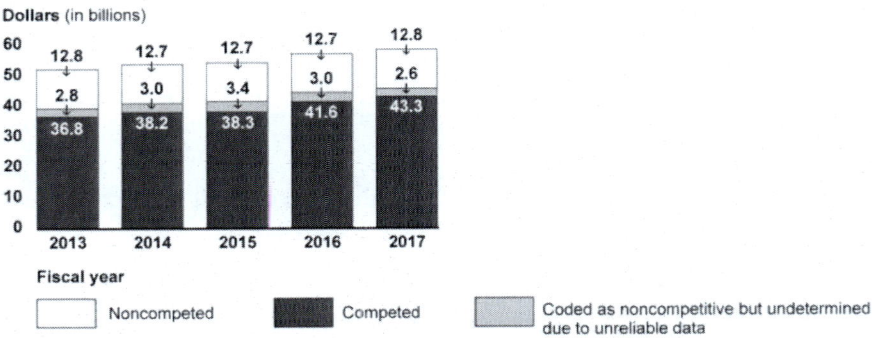


Source: GAO analysis of Federal Procurement Data System - Next generation data | GAO-19-63.

Reported Competition on Information Technology Contract Obligations, Fiscal Years 2013- 2017 (fiscal year 2017 dollars).

GAO found, however, that Departments of Defense (DOD), Homeland Security (DHS), and Health and Human Services (HHS) contracting officials misreported competition data in the Federal Procurement Data System-Next Generation (FPDS-NG) for 22 of the 41 orders GAO reviewed. GAO's findings call into question competition data associated with nearly $3 billion in annual obligations for IT-related orders. DHS identified underlying issues resulting in the errors for its orders and took corrective action. DOD and HHS, however, had limited insight into why the errors occurred. Without identifying the issues contributing to the errors, DOD and HHS are unable to take action to ensure that competition data are accurately recorded in the future, and are at risk of using inaccurate information to assess whether they are achieving their competition objectives.

GAO found that DOD, DHS, and HHS primarily cited two reasons for awarding a noncompetitive contract or order: (1) only one source could meet the need (for example, the contractor owned proprietary technical or data rights) or (2) the agency awarded the contract to a small business to help meet agency goals.

GAO estimates that about 8 percent of 2016 noncompetitive IT contracts and orders at DOD, DS, and HHS were bridge contracts, awarded in part because of acquisition planning challenges. GAO previously recommended that the Office of Federal Procurement Policy define bridge contracts and provide guidance on their use, but it has not yet done so. GAO believes that addressing this recommendation will help agencies better manage their use of bridge contracts.

Additionally, GAO estimates that about 7 percent of noncompetitive IT contracts and orders were used to support outdated or obsolete legacy IT systems. Officials from the agencies GAO reviewed stated these systems are needed for their mission or that they are in the process of modernizing the legacy systems or buying new systems.

December 11, 2018
Congressional Requesters

The federal government obligates tens of billions of dollars for products and services related to information technology (IT) each year. Meeting the federal government's IT needs is critical to the health, economy, and security of the nation. Competition for these IT products and services is a key component to fostering IT innovation and achieving the best return on investment for taxpayers. Federal agencies are generally required to award contracts competitively but are permitted to award noncompetitive contracts under certain circumstances, such as when only one contractor can meet the need or to eligible small businesses in order to meet agencies' small business goals.

In some cases, noncompetitive contracts act as "bridge contracts." While there is no government-wide definition for bridge contracts, GAO has defined it as an extension to an existing contract beyond the period of performance (including base and option years), or a new, short-term contract awarded on a sole-source basis to an incumbent contractor to avoid a lapse in service caused by a delay in awarding a follow-on contract.[1] Bridge contracts can be a useful tool to avoid a gap in services and are typically envisioned as short-term. However, in October 2015, we found that some bridge contracts spanned multiple years, potentially undetected by approving officials. When noncompetitive bridge contracts are used frequently or for prolonged periods, the government is at risk of paying more than it should for products and services. In addition, our past work found that agencies are investing most of their IT dollars on maintaining legacy IT systems, which are becoming increasingly obsolete. For example, in May 2016, we found that many systems use outdated software languages and hardware parts that are no longer supported by their vendors. The government, in these instances, runs the risk of maintaining systems that have outlived their effectiveness.[2]

You asked us to review the federal government's use of noncompetitive contracts for IT, including the use of bridge contracts. This chapter examines (1) the extent to which agencies used noncompetitive

[1] GAO, *Sole-source Contracting: Defining and Tracking Bridge Contracts Would Help Agencies Manage Their Use*, GAO-16-15 (Washington, D.C.: Oct.14, 2015).

[2] GAO, *Information Technology: Federal Agencies Need To Address Aging Legacy Systems*, GAO-16-696T (Washington, D.C.: May 25, 2016).

contracts to procure IT products and services for fiscal years 2013 through 2017; (2) the reasons for using noncompetitive contracts for selected IT procurements; (3) the extent to which IT procurements at selected agencies were bridge contracts; and (4) the extent to which noncompetitive IT procurements at selected agencies were in support of legacy systems. For the last objective, you requested that we ascertain the extent to which our generalizable sample of contracts and orders were in support of legacy systems as defined by the Modernizing Government Technology Act (MGT), which was enacted in December 2017, after our work was underway.[3]

To examine the extent to which agencies used noncompetitive contracts and orders to procure IT products and services, we analyzed government-wide Federal Procurement Data System-Next Generation (FPDS-NG) data on IT obligations from fiscal years 2013 through 2017 (the most recent and complete data available).[4] To define IT, we used the Office of Management and Budget's (OMB) Category Management Leadership Council list of IT product and service codes to identify IT-related products and services.[5] To assess the reliability of the FPDS-NG data, we electronically tested for missing data, outliers, and inconsistent coding, and compared data on selected noncompetitive contracts to contract documentation we obtained. Based on these steps, we determined that FPDS-NG data were sufficiently reliable for describing general trends in government-wide and IT contract obligations data for fiscal years 2013 through 2017. We determined, however, that a subset of noncompetitive

---

[3] The MGT Act was enacted as part of the Fiscal Year 2018 National Defense Authorization Act on December 12, 2017. National Defense Authorization Act for Fiscal Year 2018, Pub. L. No. 115-91, div. A. title X, subtitle G, 131 Stat. 1283, 1586-94 (Dec. 12, 2017).

[4] For the purposes of our report, we are considering noncompetitive contracts and orders to be those that use the exceptions to full and open competition listed in Federal Acquisition Regulation (FAR) § 6.302, orders awarded in accordance with FAR § 8.405-6 and FAR § 13.106-1, contracts and orders awarded on a sole-source basis in accordance with FAR subpart 19.8 under the 8(a) small business program, and orders awarded under multiple award contracts that use the exceptions to fair opportunity listed in FAR § 16.505.

[5] OMB's category management leadership council identified 79 related codes for IT services and products. Under IT, there are six subcategories—consulting, hardware, software, outsourcing, telecommunications, and security.

obligations were inaccurately coded as noncompetitive and thus not reliable. We explore this issue further in the body of this chapter.

To determine the reasons for using noncompetitive contracts and orders for selected IT procurements, we selected the three agencies with the highest reported obligations on IT noncompetitive contracts for fiscal years 2012 through 2016 (the most recent year of data available at the time we began our review)—the Departments of Defense (DOD), Homeland Security (DHS), and Health and Human Services (HHS). These three agencies collectively accounted for 70 percent of all noncompetitively awarded contracts for IT during this period. From these agencies, we selected a generalizable stratified random sample of 171 fiscal year 2016 noncompetitive contracts and orders for IT above the simplified acquisition threshold of $150,000 to determine the reasons for using noncompetitive contracts and orders.[6] The sample was proportionate to the amount of noncompetitive contracts and orders for IT at each agency. For each of the contracts and orders in our generalizable sample, we analyzed selected contract documentation, such as justification and approval documents (J&A), exception to fair opportunity documents, and small business coordination records. Based on our review of documentation, we excluded 29 contracts and orders because they were awarded competitively, but had been miscoded as noncompetitive or as having an exception to fair opportunity. As a result, our sample consisted of 142 contracts and orders. See Table 1 for a breakdown by agency.

---

[6] For the purposes of this report, contracts include definitive contracts, purchase orders, and blanket purchase agreements; single-award contracts include an indefinite-delivery vehicle or blanket purchase agreement to one vendor; multiple-award contracts include indefinite-delivery vehicles or blanket purchase agreements to two or more vendors. Orders refer to task or delivery orders as defined in FAR 2.101. Since all our contracts and orders were awarded in fiscal year (FY) 2016, the prior simplified acquisition threshold of $150,000 applies to our generalizable sample. In 2016, the simplified acquisition threshold was generally $150,000. See 80 FR 38293 (Oct. 1, 2015). In December 2017, the simplified acquisition threshold increased to $250,000. See 41 U.S.C. § 134 (2018). Although DOD and DHS issued class deviations implementing this increase, and the Civilian Agency Advisory Council issued guidance permitting civilian agencies to issue class deviations to implement the increased threshold, this change has not yet been implemented in the FAR. FAR Case 2018-004, Increased Micro-Purchase and Simplified Acquisition Thresholds (open as of Nov. 26, 2018).

**Table 1. Number of Noncompetitively Awarded Contracts and Orders GAO Reviewed**

| Agency | Number of contracts | Number of orders on single award contracts | Number of orders on multiple award contracts | Total number of contracts and orders initially reviewed | Excluded due to miscoding in the Federal Procurement Data System | Revised total |
|---|---|---|---|---|---|---|
| Department of Defense | 36 | 54 | 21 | 111 | 16 | 95 |
| Department of Homeland Security | 10 | 10 | 10 | 30 | 6 | 24 |
| Department of Health and Human Services | 10 | 10 | 10 | 30 | 7 | 23 |
| Total | 56 | 74 | 41 | 171 | 29 | 142 |

Source: GAO analysis of Federal Procurement Data System-Next Generation data and agency documentation.| GAO-19-63.

Note: Contracts include definitive contracts, purchase orders, and blanket purchase agreements; noncompetitive orders refer to task and delivery orders as defined in FAR § 2.101 and orders off of blanket purchase agreements. Single award describes indefinite-delivery vehicles or blanket purchase agreements awarded to one vendor and those awarded to more than one vendor are referred to as multiple award.

To determine the extent to which IT procurements at selected agencies were bridge contracts or in support of legacy systems, we leveraged the generalizable sample described above to estimate the percentage of bridge contracts and legacy IT systems at DOD, DHS, and HHS. Agencies provided information as to whether the contracts and orders within the generalizable sample met GAO's definition of a bridge contract and whether the systems they supported met the definition of legacy IT systems in OMB's draft IT Modernization Initiative or the definition provided under the Modernizing Government Technology Act (MGT).[7] OMB's draft IT Modernization Initiative defined legacy systems as spending dedicated to maintaining the existing IT portfolio excluding provisioned services

[7] Pub. L. No. 115-91, div. A. title X, subtitle G.

such as cloud, while the MGT Act defined them as an outdated or obsolete IT system.[8] We verified the agencies' determinations of bridge contracts by reviewing documentation for the contracts and orders in our generalizable sample. To obtain additional insights into the bridge contracts and legacy systems, we selected a nonprobability sample of 26 contracts and orders from our generalizable sample of 142 contracts and orders for in-depth review. Our selection was based on factors such as obtaining a mix of bridge contracts and contracts used in support of legacy IT systems.

For our in-depth review, we collected and analyzed contract file documentation for the selected contracts and orders. In cases where we selected a potential bridge contract, we also reviewed the contract preceding it, additional bridge contracts (if any), and, if awarded at the time of our review, the follow-on contract. We interviewed contracting and program officials to gain insights into the facts and circumstances surrounding the awards of IT noncompetitive contracts and orders. For bridge contracts and orders, we asked about the reasons why bridge contracts were needed and status of follow-on contracts; for legacy contracts, we asked about the nature of the requirement and plans to move to newer technologies or systems. For more information on our scope and methodology, see Appendix I.

We conducted this performance audit from April 2017 to December 2018 in accordance with generally accepted government auditing standards. Those standards require that we plan and perform the audit to obtain sufficient, appropriate evidence to provide a reasonable basis for our findings and conclusions based on our audit objectives. We believe the evidence obtained provides a reasonable basis for our findings and conclusions based on our audit objectives.

---

[8] OMB's definition of legacy system was in place at the time we began our review. In December 2017, the MGT was enacted and we requested that each agency reassess how they would characterize the nature of the IT systems using the revised definition provided under the MGT Act.

## BACKGROUND

The federal government obligates tens of billions annually on IT. Prior IT expenditures, however, have too often produced failed projects—that is, projects with multimillion dollar cost overruns and schedule delays and with questionable mission-related achievements.[9] In our 2017 high risk series update, we reported that improving the management of IT acquisitions and operations remains a high risk area because the federal government has spent billions of dollars on failed IT investments.[10]

### Awarding Contracts and Orders Noncompetitively

Agencies are generally required to use full and open competition—meaning all responsible sources are permitted to compete—when awarding contracts.[11] However, the Competition in Contracting Act of 1984 recognizes that full and open competition is not feasible in all circumstances and authorizes contracting without full and open competition under certain conditions.[12] In addition, there are competition-related requirements for other types of contract vehicles, including multiple award indefinite-delivery/indefinite-quantity (IDIQ) contracts and the General Services Administration's (GSA) Federal Supply Schedule (FSS).[13] The rules regarding exceptions to full and open competition and

---

[9] GAO, Information Technology: Agencies Need to Involve Chief Information Officers in Reviewing Billions of Dollars in Acquisitions, GAO-18-42 (Washington, D.C.: Jan. 10, 2018).

[10] GAO, High Risk Series: Progress on Many High-Risk Areas, While Substantial Efforts Needed on Others, GAO 17-317 (Washington, D.C.: Feb. 15, 2017).

[11] See FAR § 2.101; FAR subpart 6.1.

[12] See Deficit Reduction Act of 1984, Pub. L. No. 98-369, div. B, title VII ("Competition in Contracting Act of 1984") (July 18, 1984); 10 U.S.C. § 2304, et seq.; 41 U.S.C. § 3301, et seq. See also FAR part 6 ("Competition Requirements").

[13] An IDIQ contract provides for an indefinite quantity, within stated limits, of supplies or services during a fixed period. The government places orders for individual requirements. FAR § 16.504(a). If multiple awards are made, awardees are generally given a fair opportunity to be considered for each order. See FAR §§ 16.504(a), 16.505(b). The FSS program managed by GSA provides agencies a simplified method of purchasing commercial products and services at prices associated with volume buying. A schedule is a

other competition-related requirements are outlined in various parts of the Federal Acquisition Regulation (FAR). For example:

- Contracting officers may award a contract without providing for full and open competition if one of seven exceptions listed in FAR Subpart 6.3 apply. Examples of allowable exceptions include circumstances when products or services required by the agency are available from only one source, when disclosure of the agency's need would compromise national security, or when the need for products and services is of such an unusual and compelling urgency that the federal government faces the risk of serious financial or other injury.[14] Generally, exceptions to full and open competition under FAR subpart 6.3 must be supported by written justifications that contain sufficient facts and rationale to justify use of the specific exception.[15] Depending on the proposed value of the contract, the justifications require review and approval at successively higher approval levels within the agency.[16]
- Contracting officers are also authorized to issue orders under multiple award IDIQ contracts noncompetitively. Generally contracting officers must provide each IDIQ contract holder with a fair opportunity to be considered for each order unless exceptions apply.[17] Contracting officers who issue orders over certain thresholds under an exception to fair opportunity are required to provide written justification for doing so.[18] In April 2017 we found

---

set of contracts awarded to multiple vendors that provide similar products and services. Certain FSS orders may require competitive procedures under FAR § 8.405.

[14] See FAR § 6.302. The other four exceptions to the requirement for full and open competition in FAR subpart 6.3 may be based on the following circumstances, as detailed in the FAR: (1) industrial mobilization; engineering, developmental or research capability; or expert services; (2) international agreement; (3) authorized or required by statute; and (4) public interest.

[15] See FAR §§ 6.302, 6.303.

[16] See FAR § 6.304. Under the FAR, generally for a proposed contract not exceeding $700,000, the contracting officers' certification is sufficient, and no higher level review is needed.

[17] See FAR § 16.505(b)(2).

[18] See FAR § 16.505 (b)(2)(ii). Orders over $3,500 but less than the simplified acquisition threshold require the contracting officer to document the basis for using the exception in accordance with FAR § 16.505(b)(2)(ii)(A). Orders in excess of the simplified acquisition

that government-wide, more than 85 percent of all order obligations under multiple-award IDIQ contracts were competed from fiscal years 2011 through 2015.[19]

- Orders placed under GSA's FSS program are also exempt from FAR part 6 requirements.[20] However, ordering procedures require certain FSS orders exceeding the simplified acquisition threshold to be placed on a "competitive basis," which includes requesting proposals from as many schedule contractors as practicable.[21] If a contracting officer decides not to provide opportunity to all contract holders when placing an FSS order over the simplified acquisition threshold, that decision must be documented and approved.[22] The FAR allows for orders to be placed under these circumstances based on the following justifications: when an urgent and compelling need exists; when only one source is capable of providing the supplies or services because they are unique or highly specialized; when in the interest of economy and efficiency, the new work is a logical follow-on to an original FSS order that was placed on a "competitive basis;" and when an item is "peculiar to one manufacturer."[23]
- Agencies may also award contracts on a sole-source basis in coordination with the Small Business Administration (SBA) to eligible 8(a) program participants.[24] While agencies are generally

---

threshold require additional information in accordance with FAR § 16.505(b)(2)(ii)(B), and are approved in accordance with FAR § 16.505 (b)(2)(ii)(C). Generally, under the FAR, for proposed orders exceeding the simplified acquisition threshold, but not exceeding $700,000, the contracting officer's certification will serve as the approval with no additional higher level review necessary.

[19] GAO, *Federal Contracts: Agencies Widely Used Indefinite Contracts to Provide Flexibility to Meet Mission Needs*, GAO 17-329 (Washington, D.C.: Apr. 13, 2017).

[20] See FAR § 8.405-6; FAR § 6.102(d)(3) ("Use of multiple award schedules issued under the procedures established by the Administrator of General Services consistent with the requirement of 41 U.S.C. 152(3)(A) for the multiple award schedule program of the General Services Administration is a competitive procedure.").

[21] FAR §§ 8.405-1(d), 8.405-2(c)(3).

[22] See FAR § 8.405-6(a)(1)(ii), (c).

[23] FAR § 8.405-6(c)(2)(iv) (referring to FAR § 8.405-6(a)(1)(i) and (b)(1)).

[24] As GAO previously reported, the 8(a) program was designed to assist small, disadvantaged businesses in competing in the American economy through business development. Over the course of the program, qualified small, disadvantaged businesses can receive business

not required to justify these sole-source awards, contracts that exceed a total value of $22 million require a written justification in accordance with FAR Subpart 6.3.[25]

## Bridge Contracts

In certain situations, it may become evident that services could lapse before a subsequent contract can be awarded. In these cases, because of time constraints, contracting officers generally use one of two options: (1) extend the existing contract or (2) award a short-term stand-alone contract to the incumbent contractor on a sole-source basis to avoid a lapse in services.[26] While no government-wide definition of bridge contracts exists, we developed the following definitions related to bridge contracts that we used for our October 2015 report:

- *Bridge contract.* An extension to an existing contract beyond the period of performance (including base and option years), or a new, short-term contract awarded on a sole-source basis to an incumbent contractor to avoid a lapse in service caused by a delay in awarding a follow-on contract.
- *Predecessor contract*. The contract in place prior to the award of a bridge contract.
- *Follow-on contract.* A longer-term contract that follows a bridge contract for the same or similar services. This contract can be competitively awarded or awarded on a sole-source basis.[27]

development support from SBA. One of the key areas of support is eligibility for set-aside competitive and sole-source federal contracts for 8(a) businesses, which can be an important factor in their financial development. See GAO, *Alaska Native Corporations: Oversight Weaknesses Continue to Limit SBA's Ability to Monitor Compliance with 8(a) Program Requirements,* GAO-16-113 (Washington, D.C.: Mar. 21, 2016).

[25]. See FAR §§ 19.805-1(b) and 19.808-1(a).

[26] See FAR § 52.217-8; FAR subpart 6.3.

[27] GAO-16-15.

Contracts, orders, and extensions (both competitive and noncompetitive) are included in our definition of a "bridge contract" because the focus of the definition is on the intent of the contract, order, or extension.[28] DOD and some of its components, including the Navy, the Defense Logistics Agency (DLA), and the Defense Information Systems Agency (DISA), have established their own bridge contract definitions and policies. Congress enacted legislation in 2017 that established a definition of "bridge contracts" for DOD and its components.[29]

For the purposes of this chapter, we use the same definition as we used in our October 2015 report to define bridge contracts, unless otherwise specified. We acknowledge that in the absence of a government-wide definition, agencies may have differing views of what constitutes a bridge contract. We discuss these views further in the body of this chapter.

In our October 2015 report on bridge contracts, we found that the agencies included in our review—DOD, HHS, and the Department of Justice—had limited or no insight into their use of bridge contracts. In addition, we found that while bridge contracts are typically envisioned as short term, some bridge contracts included in our review involved one or more bridges that spanned multiple years—potentially undetected by approving officials. The fact that the full length of a bridge contract, or multiple bridge contracts for the same requirement, is not readily apparent from documents that may require review and approval, such as an individual J&A, presents a challenge for those agency officials responsible for approving the use of bridge contracts. Approving officials signing off on individual J&As may not have insight into the total number of bridge contracts that may be put in place by looking at individual J&As alone.

In October 2015, we recommended that the Administrator of the Office of Federal Procurement Policy (OFPP) take the following two actions: (1)

---

[28] GAO's definition includes all types of contract extensions, both those that may be considered "competitive", e.g. the use of FAR 52.217-8 when it was evaluated at award, and those that are "noncompetitive", e.g. those that are used to extend the period of performance beyond that of the original contract and require a J&A, when the intention is to bridge a gap in services. When collectively referring to all of these subsets, we refer to them as "bridge contracts", when we are describing specific examples, we specifically use "bridge contract", "bridge order", or "extensions".

[29] See Pub. L. No. 115-91, § 851.

take appropriate steps to develop a standard definition for bridge contracts and incorporate it as appropriate into relevant FAR sections; and (2) as an interim measure until the FAR is amended, provide guidance to agencies on:

- a definition of bridge contracts, with consideration of contract extensions as well as stand-alone bridge contracts; and
- suggestions for agencies to track and manage their use of these contracts, such as identifying a contract as a bridge in a J&A when it meets the definition, and listing the history of previous extensions and stand-alone bridge contracts.

OFPP concurred with our recommendation to provide guidance to agencies on bridge contracts, and stated its intention is to work with members of the FAR Council to explore the value of incorporating a definition of bridge contracts in the FAR. As of November 2018, OFPP had not yet implemented our recommendations but has taken steps to develop guidance on bridge contracts. Specifically, OFPP staff told us they have drafted management guidance, which includes a definition of bridge contracts, and provided it to agencies' Chief Acquisition Officers and Senior Procurement Executives for review. OFPP staff told us they received many comments on the draft guidance and were in the process of addressing those comments.

## AGENCIES OBLIGATED MORE THAN $10 BILLION ANNUALLY FOR INFORMATION TECHNOLOGY ON NONCOMPETITIVELY AWARDED CONTRACTS AND ORDERS, BUT UNRELIABLE DATA OBSCURES FULL PICTURE

Federal agencies reported annually obligating between $53 billion in fiscal year 2013 to $59 billion in fiscal year 2017 on IT-related products and services. Of that amount, agencies reported that more than $15 billion each year—or about 30 percent of all obligations for IT products and services—were awarded noncompetitively. However, in a generalizable sample of contracts and orders, we found significant errors in certain types of orders, which call into question the reliability of competition data associated with roughly $3 billion per year in obligations. As a result, the actual amount agencies obligated on noncompetitive contract awards for IT products and services is unknown.

## IT Contract Obligations Totaled More than $50 Billion Annually

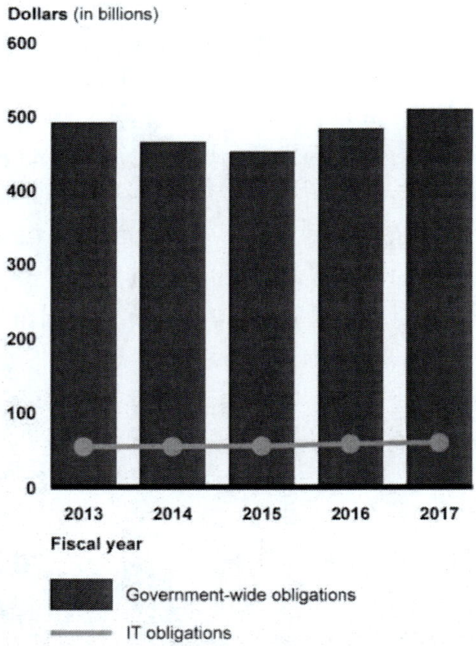


Source: GAO analysis of Federal Procurement Data System – Next Generation data GAO-19-63. Note: Obligation amounts obtained from Federal Procurement Data System-Next Generation were adjusted for inflation using the fiscal year 2017 Gross Domestic Product Index.

Figure 1. Government-wide Information Technology (IT) Contract Obligations in Comparison with Total Contract Obligations, Fiscal Years 2013-2017 (fiscal year 2017 dollars).

From fiscal years 2013 through 2017, we found that total IT obligations reported by federal agencies ranged from nearly $53 billion in fiscal year 2013 to $59 billion in fiscal year 2017. The amount obligated on IT products and services generally accounted for about one-tenth of total federal contract spending (see Figure 1).

For fiscal years 2013 through 2017, the three agencies we reviewed in more depth—DOD, DHS and HHS—collectively accounted for about two-thirds of federal IT spending (see Figure 2).

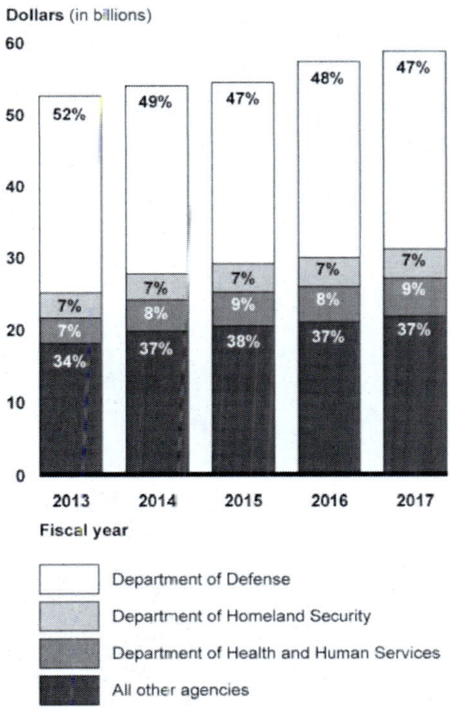


Source: GAO analysis of Federal Procurement Data System – Next Generation data GAO-19-63.

Note: Obligation amounts obtained from Federal Procurement Data System-Next Generation were adjusted for inflation using the fiscal year 2017 Gross Domestic Product Index.

Figure 2. Comparison of Information Technology Contract Obligations by Agency, Fiscal Years 2013 through 2017 (fiscal year 2017 dollars).

## Agencies Reported Obligating More than $15 Billion on Noncompetitive Contracts for IT Annually, but Full Extent of Noncompetitive Dollars Is Not Known Due to Unreliable Data

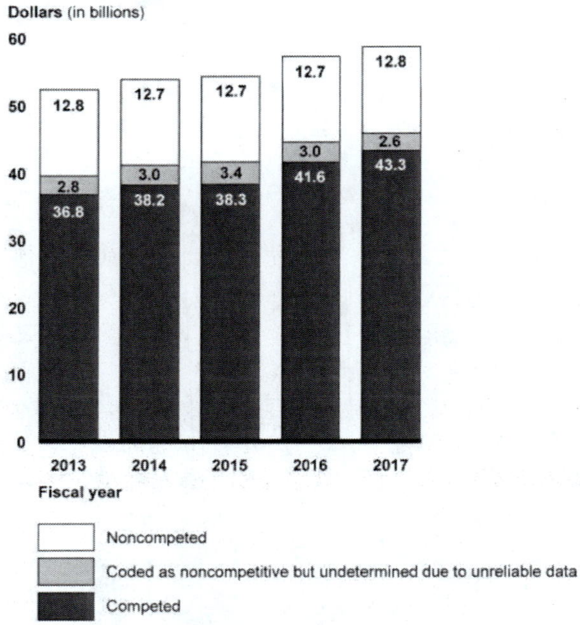


Source: GAO analysis of Federal Procurement Data System – Next Generation data GAO-19-63.

Note: Obligation data obtained from Federal Procurement Data System-Next Generation were adjusted for inflation using the fiscal year 2017 Gross Domestic Product Index. These data include about $3 billion in annual obligations on certain multiple award orders for which we determined the reported competition data were unreliable. Between $10 million and $148 million annually did not include a code for competition. Therefore, these dollars are excluded from the figure.

Figure 3. Reported Competition on Information Technology Contract Obligations, Fiscal Years 2013-2017 (fiscal year 2017 dollars).

From fiscal years 2013 through 2017, agencies reported in FPDS-NG obligating more than $15 billion—about 30 percent of all annual IT obligations—each year on noncompetitively awarded contracts and orders.

We determined, however, that the agencies' reporting of certain competition data was unreliable (see Figure 3).

Specifically, we found that contracting officers miscoded 22 out of 41 orders in our sample, of which 21 cited "follow-on action following competitive initial action" or "other statutory authority" as the legal authority for using an exception to fair opportunity.[30] DOD contracting officers had miscoded 11 of the 21 orders, while DHS and HHS contracting officers had miscoded 4 and 6 orders, respectively. This miscoding occurred at such a high rate that it put into question the reliability of the competition data on orders totaling roughly $3 billion per year in annual obligations. In each of these cases, contracting officers identified these orders as being noncompetitively awarded when they were, in fact, competitively awarded. As an assessment of the extent to which contracts and orders that were identified as being competitively awarded were properly coded was outside the scope of our review, we are not in a position to assess the overall reliability of competition information of IT-related contracts.

For these 21 orders, we found that DHS was aware of issues surrounding most of their miscodings and had taken actions to fix the problems, while DOD and HHS generally had limited insights as to why these errors occurred.

DHS miscoded 4 orders, 3 of which were orders awarded under single award contracts. DHS officials told us that orders issued from single award contracts should inherit the competition characteristics of the parent contract.[31] However, as FPDS-NG currently operates, contracting officers have the ability to input a different competition code for these orders. In this case, each of the single award contracts was competitively awarded and therefore all the subsequent orders issued from these contracts should be considered competitively awarded, as there are no additional opportunities for competition. DHS has taken actions to address this issue.

---

[30] The remaining miscoded order was awarded by DHS and was coded as "only one source."

[31] Single award describes indefinite-delivery vehicles or blanket purchase agreements awarded to one vendor and those awarded to more than one vendor are referred to as multiple award.

DHS officials stated that in conjunction with DOD they have asked GSA, which manages the FPDS-NG data system, to modify FPDS-NG to automatically prefill competition codes for orders awarded under single award contracts. DHS officials noted that GSA expects to correct the issue in the first quarter of fiscal year 2019, which should mitigate the risks of agencies miscoding orders issued under single award contracts in the future. DHS officials have also provided training to their contracting personnel that single award orders must inherit the characteristics of the parent contract.

DOD and HHS officials, on the other hand, had limited insights as to why their orders were miscoded. For example, DOD miscoded a total of 11 orders (5 orders awarded under single award contracts and 6 awarded under multiple award contracts). For 8 of these orders, contracting officers did not provide the reasons as to why these errors occurred. For the remaining 3 orders awarded—each of which were issued under single award contracts—contracting officials told us that they had used the "follow-on action following competitive initial action" because the underlying contract had been competed. Similarly, at HHS, which miscoded a total of 6 orders (4 awarded under single award contracts and 2 awarded under multiple award contracts), component officials told us that these errors were accidental and could not provide any additional insight as to why these errors were made.

While GSA's changes in the FPDS-NG system, when implemented, may help address the issue of miscoding competition data on orders issued from single award contracts, it will not address errors in coding for multiple award orders that cited exceptions to competition even when they were competed.

The FAR notes that FPDS-NG data are used in a variety of ways, including assessing the effects of policies and management initiatives, yet we have previously reported on the shortcomings of the FPDS-NG system, including issues with the accuracy of the data.[32] Miscoding of competition requirements may hinder the accomplishment of certain statutory, policy, and regulatory requirements. For example,

- The FAR requires agency competition advocates, among other duties and responsibilities, to prepare and submit an annual report to their agencies' senior procurement executive and chief acquisition officer on actions taken to achieve full and open competition in the agency and recommend goals and plans for increasing competition.[33]
- OMB required agencies to reduce their reliance on noncompetitive contracts, which it categorized as high-risk, because, absent competition, agencies must negotiate contracts without a direct market mechanism to help determine price.[34]

Federal internal control standards state that management should use quality information to achieve an entity's objectives. Without identifying the reasons why contracting officers are miscoding these orders in FPDS-NG, DOD and HHS are unable to take action to ensure that competition data are accurately recorded, and are at risk of using inaccurate information to assess whether they are achieving their competition objectives.

After excluding the $3 billion in annual obligations we determined was not sufficiently reliable, we found that from fiscal years 2013 through 2017 about 90 percent of noncompetitive IT obligations reported in FPDS-NG were used to buy services, hardware, and software (see Figure 4).[35]

---

[32] GAO, *Federal Contracting: Improvements Needed in How Some Agencies Report Personal Services Contracts*, GAO-17-610 (Washington, D.C.: July 27, 2017); and GAO, *Improvements Needed to the Federal Procurement Data System-Next Generation*, GAO-05-960R (Washington D.C.: Sept. 27, 2005); FAR subpart 4.6.

[33] FAR § 6.502(b).

[34] OMB, *Memorandum for the Head of Departments and Agencies: Improving Government Acquisition,* M-09-25 (July 29, 2009.)

[35] For the purposes of this report, we are referring to the category management leadership council's outsourcing category as services, as this category is predominantly for services.

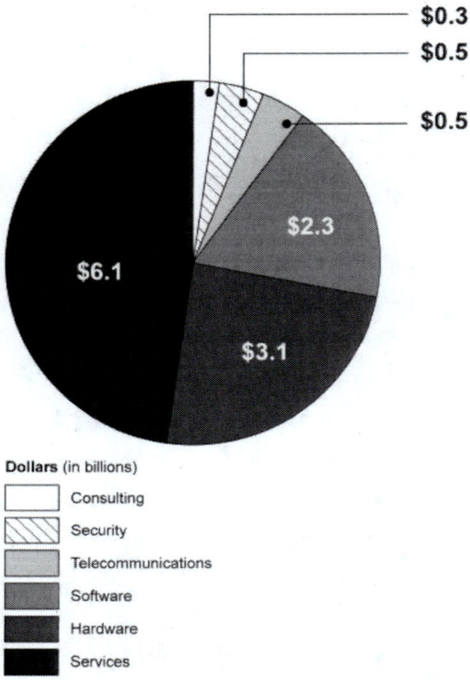


Source: GAO analysis of Federal Procurement Data System – Next Generation data GAO-19-63.

Note: Obligation amounts obtained from FPDS-NG were adjusted for inflation, using the fiscal year 2017 Gross Domestic Product Index, and exclude about $3 billion in multiple award orders that cited "follow-on action following competitive initial action" and "other statutory authority" as exceptions to fair opportunity," which we determined were unreliable.

Figure 4. Fiscal Year 2017 Information Technology Noncompetitive Obligations by Spending Category.

Services include the maintenance and repair of IT equipment as well as professional technology support. Hardware includes products such as fiber optic cables and computers, and software includes items such as information technology software and maintenance service plans.

## Agencies Cited That Only One Contractor Could Meet the Need or Small Business Requirements as Most Common Reasons for Awarding Noncompetitive Contracts

The documentation for the contracts and orders at the three agencies we reviewed generally cited either that only one source could meet their needs or that they were awarding the contract sole-source to an 8(a) small business participant when noncompetitively awarding IT contracts or orders.[36] Specifically, based on our generalizable sample, we estimate that nearly 60 percent of fiscal year 2016 noncompetitive contracts and orders at DOD, DHS, and HHS were awarded noncompetitively because agencies cited that only one contractor could meet the need, and approximately 26 percent of contracts and orders were awarded sole-source to an 8(a) small business participant.[37] We estimate that agencies cited a variety of other reasons for not competing approximately 16 percent of noncompetitive contracts and orders, such as unusual and compelling urgency, international agreement, and national security.[38]

Within our sample of 142 contracts and orders, we analyzed J&As or similar documents to obtain additional detail as to why the contracts and orders were awarded noncompetitively. See Table 2 for a breakdown of the overall reasons cited for awarding contracts noncompetitively within our sample.

---

[36] Generally, documentation accompanying noncompetitive contacts and orders cited only one source could meet the agency's need pursuant to FAR § 6.302-1, FAR § 16.505 or FAR § 8.405-6. Noncompetitive contracts and orders awarded to a small business participant in the 8(a) program were awarded pursuant to FAR subpart 19.8 and FAR § 6.302-5(b)(4).

[37] Estimates are based on the results of our generalizable stratified random sample of contracts and orders. All percentage estimates in this report have a margin of error of plus or minus 9 percentage points or fewer, unless otherwise noted. See appendix I for more details.

[38] Estimated percentages do not add to 100 because a contract or order could have more than one reason for not competing. The noncompetitive contacts and orders cited other reasons such as unusual and compelling urgency, international agreement, authorized or required by statute, or national security. See FAR §§ 6.302-2, 6.302-4, 6.302-5, or 6.302- 6.

## Table 2. Reasons Cited for Awarding 142 Noncompetitive Contracts and Orders We Reviewed

| Reasons cited | Number of times cited |
|---|---|
| Only one source could meet the need | 79 |
| Sole-source to 8(a) small business participants | 42 |
| Other reasons[a] | 23 |
| Total | 144[b] |

Source: GAO analysis of contract documentation. | GAO-19-63.

[a]Other reasons include international agreement, authorized by statute, and national security.

[b]Although our sample included 142 contracts, 2 contracts we reviewed cited more than one reason for award in their contract documentation.

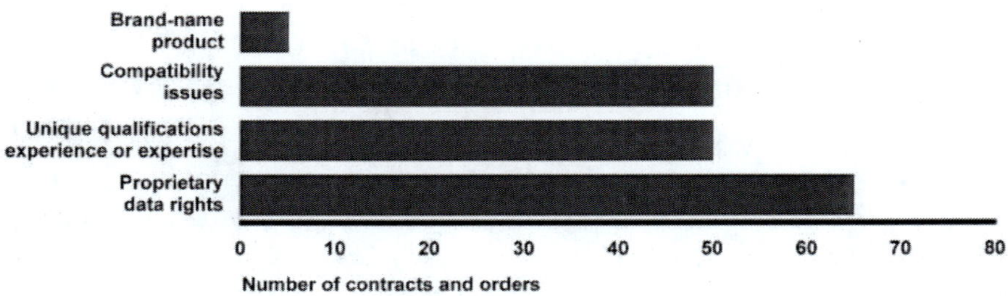


Source: GAO analysis of Federal Procurement Data System – Next Generation data GAO-19-63.

Note: In some cases, contract and order documentation, such as the justification and approval document, cited more than one reason as to why only one contractor could meet the agency's need. Therefore, the number of reasons exceeds the 79 contracts and orders reviewed by GAO.

Figure 5. Reasons Cited by Departments of Defense, Homeland Security, and Health and Human Services as to Why Only One Contractor Could Meet Their Needs.

For 79 of the 142 contracts and orders we reviewed, agencies cited that only one source could meet the need. We found that this exception was the most commonly cited reason for a sole-source IT contract or order at DOD and DHS, but not at HHS. At HHS, the most common reason was that the contract or order was awarded on a sole source basis to an 8(a), which we discuss in more detail later. Agencies justified use of the "only one source" exception on the basis that the contractor owned the proprietary technical or data rights; the contractor had unique qualifications or experience; compatibility issues; or that a brand-name product was needed (see Figure 5). The following examples illustrate the reasons cited by the agencies as to why only one contractor could meet their needs:

- *Proprietary data rights issues and compatibility issues.* The Navy issued a 9-month, approximately $350,000 order under an IDIQ contract for two data terminal sets. The terminal sets, which according to Navy officials, have been used by the Navy since the 1990s to exchange radar tracking and other information among airborne, land-based, and ship-board tactical data systems and with certain allies. The Navy's J&A document noted that the contractor owned the proprietary data rights to the transmitting equipment and software, and the Navy required the equipment to be compatible and interchangeable with systems currently fielded throughout the Navy. Furthermore, the document noted that seeking competition through the development of a new source would result in additional costs that would far exceed any possible cost savings that another source could provide and would cause unacceptable schedule delays. This example illustrates that decisions the program officials make during the acquisition process to acquire or not acquire certain rights to technical data can have far-reaching implications for DOD's ability to sustain and competitively procure parts and services for those systems, as we have previously reported.[39] In our May 2014 report on competition in defense contracting, we found that 7 of 14 justifications we reviewed explained that the awards could not be competed due to a lack of technical data. All 7 of these justifications or supporting documents described situations, ranging from 3 to 30 years in duration, where DOD was unable to conduct a competition

---

[39] GAO, Defense Acquisitions: DOD Should Clarify Requirements for Assessing and Documenting Technical Data Needs GAO-11-469 (Washington, D.C.: May 11, 2011).

because data rights were not purchased with the initial award.[40] We recommended in May 2014 that DOD ensure that existing acquisition planning guidance promotes early vendor engagement and allows both the government and vendors adequate time to prepare for competition. DOD concurred with our recommendation. In April 2015, DOD updated its acquisition guidance to incorporate new guidelines for creating and maintaining a competitive environment. These guidelines emphasize acquisition planning steps including involvement with industry in obtaining feedback on draft solicitations, market research, and requirements development.[41]

- *Unique qualifications and experience.* DHS placed four separate orders under an IDIQ contract for data center support totaling approximately $7 million. The requirement was to maintain mission critical services during a data center support pilot, prototype, and transition period starting in fiscal year 2015. Among other things, DHS's J&A noted that no other contractors had sufficient experience with DHS's infrastructure and requirements necessary to maintain services at the required level during the transition period. HHS awarded an approximately $4 million contract to buy support services for an IT center for a 12-month ordering period, including options. HHS's J&A noted that only the incumbent contractor had the requisite knowledge and experience to operate and maintain the mission and business systems in the IT center during the transition of operations from one location to another. The justification further stated that HHS had no efforts underway to increase competition in the future as this requirement is not anticipated to be a recurring requirement.

[40] GAO, Defense Contracting: Early Attention in the Acquisition Process Needed to Enhance Competition GAO-14-395 (Washington, D.C: May 5, 2014).

[41] See Defense Federal Acquisition Regulation Supplement (DFARS) Procedures, Guidance, and Information (PGI) 206—Competition Requirements (added Apr. 20, 2015).

Program officials stated that they are migrating from legacy IT systems to a new commercial off-the-shelf system.

- *Brand-name products.* DOD awarded a 5-month, approximately $500,000 contract for brand name equipment and installation that supported various video-teleconference systems. The J&A stated that this particular brand name product was the only product that would be compatible with current configurations installed in one of its complexes. To increase competition in the future, the J&A stated that technical personnel will continue to evaluate the marketplace for commercially available supplies and installation that can meet DOD's requirements.

For 42 of the 142 contracts and orders we reviewed, we found that agencies awarded a sole-source contract or order to 8(a) small business participants.[42] HHS awarded 13 of its 23 sole-source contracts and orders we reviewed to 8(a) small business participants, DOD awarded 25 of 95, and DHS 4 of 24. We found that all contracts and orders in our review that were awarded on a sole-source basis to 8(a) small business participants were below the applicable competitive thresholds or otherwise below the FAR thresholds that require a written justification.[43]

As previously discussed, agencies may award contracts on a sole-source basis to eligible 8(a) participants, either in coordination with SBA or when they are below the competitive threshold.[44] While agencies are generally not required to justify these smaller dollar value sole-source 8(a) awards, contracts that exceed a total value of $22 million require a written justification.[45] Since none of the 8(a) sole source contracts and orders in

---

[42] See FAR subpart 19.8.

[43] See FAR § 19.805-1.

[44] GAO has conducted prior work on the 8(a) program, for example: GAO, *DOD Small Business Contracting: Use of Sole Source 8(a) Contracts Over $20 Million Continues to Decline*, GAO-16-557 (Washington, D.C.: June 8, 2016); and GAO, *Federal Contracting: Slow Start to Implementation of Justifications for 8(a) Sole-Source Contracts*, GAO-13-118 (Washington, D.C.: Dec. 12, 2012); FAR § 19.805-1.

[45] FAR § 19.808-1.

our review required written justifications, the contract files generally did not provide the rationale behind the sole-source award.

Policy and contracting officials from all three agencies we reviewed stated they made sole-source awards to 8(a) small business participants to help meet the agency's small business contracting goals and save time. HHS officials further stated that they consider their awards to 8(a) small business participants a success because they are supporting small businesses. Officials stated that once a requirement is awarded through the 8(a) program, the FAR requires that requirement be set aside for an 8(a) contractor unless the requirement has changed or that an 8(a) contractor is not capable or available to complete the work.[46]

For 23 of the 142 contracts and orders we reviewed, we found that agencies cited other reasons for awarding contracts and orders noncompetitively. For example:

- *Urgent and compelling need.* DHS's Coast Guard awarded an approximately 10-month, $6.5 million order (encompassing all options) for critical payroll services in its human resources management system under a GSA federal supply schedule contract. The Coast Guard justified the award based on an urgent and compelling need.[47] A Coast Guard official explained that the efforts to competitively award a follow-on contract had been delayed as the Coast Guard had not developed a defined statement of work in a timely manner, and that the agency had received a larger number of proposals than initially anticipated. Therefore, the evaluation process took longer than expected. In addition, the Coast Guard's competitive follow-on contract, which was awarded in June 2018, was protested. In October 2018, GAO denied the

---

[46] Specifically, the FAR says: "Once a requirement has been accepted by SBA into the 8(a) program, any follow-on requirements shall remain in the 8(a) program unless there is a mandatory source (see 8.002 or .003) or SBA agrees to release the requirement from the 8(a) program in accordance with 13 C.F.R. 124.504(d)." FAR § 19.815(a).

[47] FAR § 8.405-6.

protest and the Coast Guard is currently planning to transition to the newly awarded contract.[48]

- *International agreement.* The Army placed an approximately 8-month, $1 million order under an IDIQ contract for radio systems and cited international agreement as the reason for a noncompetitive award.[49] This order was part of a foreign military sales contract with the Government of Denmark.
- *Authorized or required by statute.* The Defense Logistics Agency (DLA) cited "authorized or required by statute" when it placed an approximately $1.5 million, 12-month order under an IDIQ contract for sustainment support services for an application that is used for planning and initiating contracting requirements in contingency environments.[50] DLA noted that this model was contracted under the Small Business Innovation Research Program, which supports scientific and technological innovation through the investment of federal research funds into various research projects.[51]
- *National security.* The U.S. Special Operations Command (SOCOM) placed an approximately 8-month, $1 million order for

---

48 This contract award was protested to GAO. GAO provides an objective, independent, and impartial forum for the resolution of disputes concerning the awards of federal contracts. GAO's role in resolving a bid protest is an adjudicative process handled by GAO's Office of General Counsel.

49 Contracting officers may award a contract without providing for full and open competition when precluded by the terms of an international agreement or treaty between the United States and a foreign government or international organization or the written directions of a foreign government reimbursing the agency for the cost of the acquisition of the supplies or services for such government. FAR § 6.302-4(a)(2).

50 Contracting officers may award a contract without providing for full and open competition when (i) a statute expressly authorizes or requires that the acquisition be made through another agency or from a specified source; or (ii) the agency's need is for a brand name commercial item for authorized resale. FAR § 6.302-5(a)(2).

51 Small Business Innovation Research Program projects are managed through a three-phase program structure. Phase 1 projects are competitively selected based on scientific and technical merit; Phase 2 expands on efforts for phase 1 projects focusing on technology efforts to prototype; Phase 3 known as commercialization transitions a technology into commercial product or process for sale to government or private-sector customers. For GAO's prior work on the Small Business Innovation Research Program, see GAO, *Small Business Research Programs: Agencies Have Improved Compliance with Spending and Reporting Requirements, but Challenges Remain* GAO-16-492 (Washington, D.C.: May 26, 2016).

radio spare parts and cited national security as the reason for a noncompetitive award.[52]

## An Estimated Eight Percent of Fiscal Year 2016 IT Noncompetitive Contracts and Orders Were Bridges, and Agencies Have Difficulty Managing Them

We estimate that about 8 percent of contracts and orders above $150,000 in fiscal year 2016 at DOD, DHS, and HHS were bridge contracts.[53] Consistent with our October 2015 findings, agencies we reviewed face continued challenges with oversight of bridge contracts, based on 15 contracts and orders we reviewed in-depth.[54] For example, we found that in 9 of the 15 cases, bridge contracts were associated with additional bridges not apparent in the documentation related to the contract and order we reviewed, such as a J&A, and corresponded with longer periods of performance and higher contract values than initially apparent. Agency officials cited a variety of reasons for needing bridge contracts, including acquisition planning challenges, source selection challenges, and bid protests.

### An Estimated Eight Percent of IT Noncompetitive Contracts and Orders in Fiscal Year 2016 Were Bridge Contracts

Based on our generalizable sample, we estimate that about 8 percent of contracts and orders above $150,000 in fiscal year 2016 at DOD, DHS, and

---

[52] Contracting officers may award a contract without providing for full and open competition when the disclosure of the agency's needs would compromise national security. FAR § 6.302-6(a)(2).

[53] The 95 percent confidence interval for this estimate ranges from 3.9 percent to 13.4 percent.

[54] GAO-16-15.

HHS were bridge contracts.[55] We verified, using our definition of bridge contracts as criteria, that 13 of 142 contracts and orders in our generalizable sample were bridge contracts based on reviews of J&As, limited source justifications, or exceptions to fair opportunity, among other documents.[56] In addition, we found two additional bridge contracts related to our generalizable sample while conducting our in-depth review, bringing the total number of bridge contracts we identified during this review to 15.

## Agencies Face Continued Challenges with Oversight of Bridge Contracts

We found that the bridge contracts we reviewed were often longer than initially apparent from our review of related documentation, such as a J&A, and sometimes spanned multiple years. Bridge contracts can be a useful tool in certain circumstances to avoid a gap in providing products and services, but they are typically envisioned to be used for short periods of time. When we conducted an in-depth review of the bridge contracts, such as by reviewing the contract files for the predecessor, bridge, and follow-contracts, we found that in most cases, these involved one or more bridges that spanned longer periods and corresponded with higher contract values than initially apparent. Specifically, we found that 9 of the 15 bridge contracts had additional bridges related to the same requirement that were not initially apparent from documents requiring varying levels of approval by agency officials, such as the J&As. Collectively, agencies awarded bridge contracts associated with these 15 contracts and orders with estimated contract values of about $84 million (see Table 3).

---

[55] The 95 percent confidence interval for this estimate ranges from 3.9 to 13.4 percent.

[56] Three bridge contracts identified did not fully meet our definition of a bridge contract because they were not awarded to the incumbent contractor. In addition, we also identified one bridge contract that was not "short-term." For the purposes of our report, we considered these awards to be bridge contracts, as they were intended to bridge a gap in service due to a delay in the award of a follow-on contract.

## Table 3. Periods of Performance and Associated Contract Values for 15 Bridge Contracts for Information Technology (IT) GAO Reviewed

| Department | Component | Requirement | Total estimated dollar value of bridge contracts (in millions) | Total estimated period of performance of bridge contracts (in months) |
|---|---|---|---|---|
| Department of Defense (DOD) | Air Force | Enterprise-based logistics services and support | 1.9 | 9 |
| DOD | Army | Operations and maintenance of the Army Training Requirements Resource System | 0.4 | 5 |
| DOD | Defense Information Systems Agency (DISA)[a] | IT systems and support services | 2.5 | 12 |
| DOD | DISA/Air Force[b] | Installation and operational support of IT hardware and systems | 0.2 | 12 |
| DOD | Defense Logistics Agency | IT infrastructure support services | 7.8 | 29c |
| DOD | Navy | IT supplies | 0.4 | n/ad |
| DOD | Air Force | High speed data acquisition system and ground support equipment for testing | 6.9 | 5 |
| DOD | U.S. Special Operations Command | Radio supplies and services | 7.0 | 12 |
| Department of Homeland Security (DHS) | Customs and Border Protection | IT engineering and operations services | 23.6 | 25 |
| DHS | Coast Guard | Data monitoring and maintenance support services | 0.9 | 9 |

| Department | Component | Requirement | Total estimated dollar value of bridge contracts (in millions) | Total estimated period of performance of bridge contracts (in months) |
|---|---|---|---|---|
| DHS | Coast Guard | Direct access support services | 19.2 | 32 |
| Department of Health and Human Services (HHS) | Assistant Secretary for Administration | IT support services | 6.9 | 20 |
| HHS | Food and Drug Administration | Database and application server support | 0.3 | 12 |
| HHS | National Institutes of Health | Text mining software subscription and maintenance services | 1.7 | 77 |
| HHS | Indian Health Service | Project management and support services for the resource and patient management system | 4.7 | 18 |

Source: GAO analysis of agency contract documentation. | GAO-19-63. (Continued …)

Note: Although some organizations included in this table, such as DISA and DLA, have a bridge contract policy and definition, other entities, such as DHS and HHS, do not. For consistency, we applied GAO's definition of bridge contracts in GAO-16-15 to our analysis of all the bridge contracts included in our review. In some instances, we included bridge contracts that were not awarded to the incumbent contractor.

[a]The bridge contract consolidates requirements and includes extensions to three separate predecessor contracts.

[b]DISA was the contracting office for this bridge contract, but it supports an Air Force requirement.

[c]DLA contracting officials told us that from their perspective, only 3 of the 29 months were bridge contracts. DLA did not consider 26 of the 29 months to be bridges since they were in the 8(a) program and sole-sourced, and the follow-on task order was sole-sourced within the 8(a) program. We included these contracts in our analyses since our understanding of the intent of those 8(a) contracts was to bridge a gap in services until they could consolidate requirements and award a follow-on indefinite-delivery indefinite-quantity contract to meet their needs. We acknowledge that in the absence of a government-wide definition, agencies may have differing views of what constitutes a bridge contract.

[d]This bridge contained delivery dates rather than a period of performance.

The following examples illustrate contracts we reviewed in which the periods of performance were longer than initially apparent:

- HHS's Indian Health Service (IHS) awarded a 4-month, approximately $1.6 million bridge order for project management and support services for IHS's resource and patient management system. We found, however, that the predecessor contract had already been extended by 6 months before the award of the bridge order due to acquisition planning challenges associated with delays in developing the acquisition package for the follow-on contract. Subsequently, the 4- month bridge order was extended for an additional 6 months, in part because the follow-on award—which had been awarded to a new contractor—was protested by the incumbent contractor due to concerns over proposal evaluation criteria. Ultimately, the protest was dismissed. Following the resolution of the bid protest, officials awarded an additional 2-month bridge order for transition activities. In total, the bridge orders and extensions spanned 18 months and had an estimated value of about $4.7 million. Figure 6 depicts the bridge orders and extensions and indicates the 4-month bridge and 6-month extension we had initially identified.

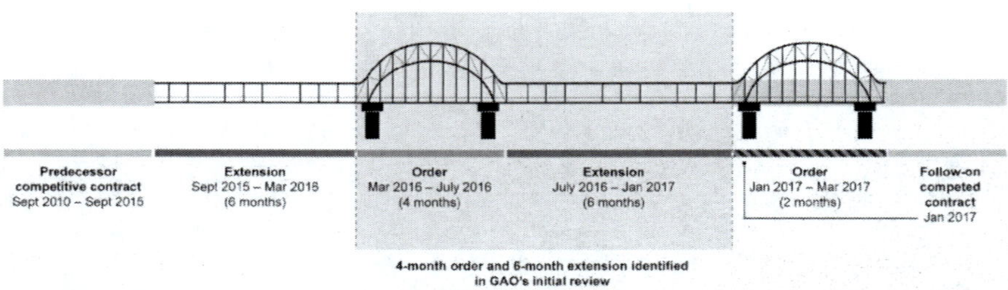


Source: GAO analysis of Federal Procurement Data System – Next Generation data GAO-19-63.

Figure 6. Timeline for the Indian Health Service's Project Management and Support Services Bridge.

- The Air Force awarded a 3-month, approximately $630,000 bridge contract to support a logistics system used to monitor weapon system availability and readiness. We found, however, that the Air

Force had previously awarded a 3-month bridge contract due to delays resulting from a recent reorganization, which, according to Air Force officials, made it unclear which contracting office would assume responsibility for the requirement. The Air Force subsequently awarded an additional 3-month bridge contract due to acquisition planning challenges, such as planning for the award of the follow-on sole-source contract. The total period of performance for the bridges was 9 months with an estimated value of about $1.9 million (see Figure 7).

As of August 2018, 13 of the 15 bridge contracts had follow-ons in place—5 were awarded competitively and 8 were awarded noncompetitively. Two bridge contracts do not currently have follow-on contracts in place for various reasons. For example, in one instance, the Coast Guard's requirement for human resources and payroll support services has continued to operate under a bridge contract because the Coast Guard's planned follow-on contract—a strategic sourcing IDIQ— was awarded in June 2018, and subsequently protested, among other delays.[57]

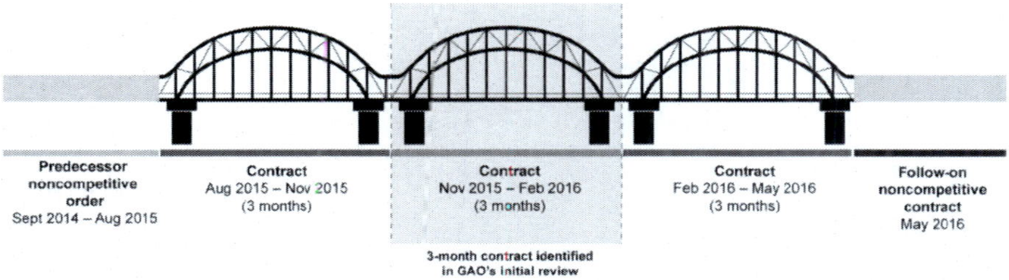


Source: GAO analysis of Federal Procurement Data System – Next Generation data GAO-19-63.

Figure 7. Timeline for Air Force's Enterprise-Based Logistics Services and Support Bridge.

[57] As we noted earlier in the report, in October 2018, GAO denied the protest and the Coast Guard is currently planning to transition to the newly awarded IDIQ contract.

## Officials Frequently Cited Acquisition Planning Challenges as Necessitating the Use of a Bridge Contract

Based on our reviews of contract documentation and information provided by agency officials, we found that acquisition planning challenges were the principal cause for needing to use a bridge contract across the 15 bridge contracts we reviewed. In particular, acquisition packages prepared by program offices to begin developing a solicitation were often not prepared in a timely fashion. Acquisition packages include statements of work and independent government cost estimates, among other documents, and are generally prepared by the program office, with the assistance of the contracting office.[58] In addition to acquisition planning challenges, officials cited delays in source selection and bid protests, among others, as additional reasons justifying the need to use a bridge contract (see Figure 8).

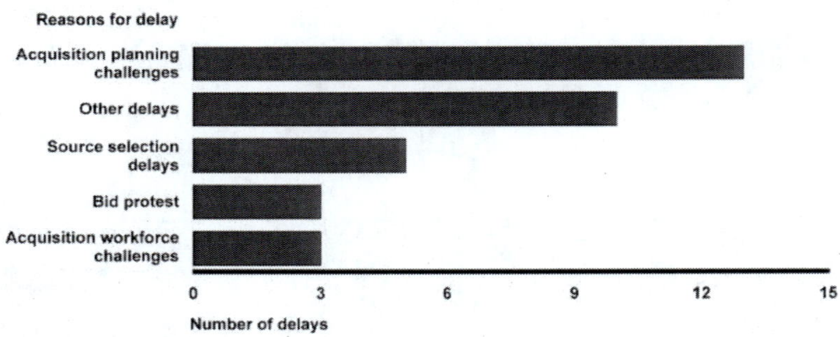


Source: GAO analysis of Federal Procurement Data System – Next Generation data GAO-19-63.

Note: In some cases, more than one reason was cited for using a bridge contract. Therefore, the number of reasons exceeds the 15 bridge contracts included in this analysis. "Other delays" includes requirement consolidation and proprietary issues, among others. We identified each of these reasons in, at most, 2 contracts reviewed.

Figure 8. Reasons for Delays Found in In-Depth Review of 15 Bridge Contracts.

---

58 [58]For our past work on acquisition planning challenges, see GAO, *Acquisition Planning: Opportunities to Build Strong Foundations for Better Service Contracts*, GAO-11-672 (Washington, D.C.: Aug. 9, 2011).

The following examples illustrate reasons officials cited for needing a bridge contract:

- DOD's DISA awarded a bridge contract for IT support services due to acquisition planning challenges, and specifically, the late submission of acquisition packages. According to contracting officials, the bridge contract was originally intended to consolidate 3 of the previous contracts associated with this requirement, but a fourth was added much later in the process. DISA contracting officials said that the program office did not submit acquisition package documentation in a timely manner, and, once submitted, the documentation required numerous revisions. These officials added that they had to award an additional bridge contract to avoid a lapse in service once they received a completed package from the program office because there was not enough time to do a competitive source selection and analysis.
- DOD's SOCOM extended an IDIQ contract for radio supplies and services due to source selection delays and acquisition workforce challenges. For example, contracting officials said they extended the IDIQ for 12 months because the contracting office was working on a source selection for the follow-on contract for modernized radios and simply did not have the manpower to award a new sustainment contract for the existing radios at the same time.
- DHS's Customs and Border Protection (CBP) awarded an approximately 16-month bridge contract in June 2016 for engineering and operations support of CBP's Oracle products and services due to bid protests associated with March 2016 orders for this requirement. We found the protests were filed on the basis that CBP had issued the task order on a sole-source basis, which precluded other contractors from competing for the award. GAO dismissed the protest in May 2016 as a result of CBP's stated intent to terminate the task order and compete the requirement as part of its corrective action plan.

According to CBP contracting officials, they awarded the approximately 16-month bridge contract to the incumbent contractor to continue services until GAO issued a decision and the services could be transitioned to the awardee. In September 2017, CBP officials awarded the competitive follow-on contract to a new vendor, but this award was also protested due to alleged organizational conflicts of interest, improperly evaluated technical proposals, and an unreasonable best-value tradeoff determination. As a result, CBP officials issued a stop-work order effective October 2017. To continue services during the protest, CBP officials extended the existing bridge contract by 3 months and then again by another 6 months. In January 2018, GAO dismissed the protest in its entirety and the stop-work order was lifted. According to a CBP contracting official, CBP did not exercise the final 3 months of options of the 6-month extension. In 2015, we found that the full length of a bridge contract, or multiple bridge contracts, is not always readily apparent from review of an individual J&A, which presents challenges for approving officials, as they may not have insight into the total number of bridges put into place by looking at individual J&As alone.[59] We found a similar situation in our current review. For example, the J&As for the 8 bridge contracts with J&As did not include complete information on the periods of performance or estimated values of all related bridge contracts.[60]

## In the Absence of Government-Wide Guidance, Others Have Taken Steps to Define Bridge Contracts

OFPP has not yet taken action to address the challenges related to the use of bridge contracts that we found in October 2015. At that time, we

---

[59] GAO-16-15.

[60] Of the remaining 7 bridge contracts in our in-depth review, 4 were awarded to 8(a) program participants and written justifications were not required, and 2 did not include written justifications because they were orders placed under existing IDIQ contracts that were extended or had expired. In one instance, the J&A for a bridge contract did include information on periods of performance and estimated value; however, the J&A did not include approval signatures.

recommended that OFPP take appropriate steps to develop a standard definition of bridge contracts and incorporate it as appropriate into relevant FAR sections, and to provide guidance to federal agencies in the interim. We further recommended that the guidance include (1) a definition of bridge contracts, with consideration of contract extensions as well as stand-alone bridge contracts, and (2) suggestions for agencies to track and manage their use of these contracts, such as identifying a contract as a bridge in a J&A when it meets the definition, and listing the history of previous extensions and stand-alone bridge contracts back to the predecessor contract in the J&A. However, as of November 2018, OFPP had not yet done so. As a result, agencies continue to face similar challenges with regard to the use of bridge contracts that we identified in 2015 and there is a lack of government-wide guidance that could help to address them.

In the absence of a federal government-wide definition, others have taken steps to establish a bridge contracts definition. For example, Congress has established a statutory definition of bridge contracts that is applicable to DOD and its components. Specifically, Section 851 of the National Defense Authorization Act for Fiscal Year 2018 defined a bridge contract as (1) an extension to an existing contract beyond the period of performance to avoid a lapse in service caused by a delay in awarding a subsequent contract; or (2) a new short-term contract awarded on a sole-source basis to avoid a lapse in service caused by a delay in awarding a subsequent contract.[61] Section 851 requires that, by October 1, 2018, the Secretary of Defense is to ensure that DOD program officials plan appropriately to avoid the use of a bridge contract for services. In instances where bridge contracts were awarded due to poor acquisition planning, the legislation outlines notification requirements with associated monetary thresholds for bridge contracts.[62]

Acting on this requirement and in response to our prior bridge contracts report, DOD established a bridge contracts policy memorandum in January 2018. The policy defines bridge contracts as modifications to

[61] Pub. L. No. 115-91, § 851(a)(1).

[62] See 10 U.S.C. § 2329(e) (outlining the monetary thresholds for each notification requirement).

existing contracts to extend the period of performance, increase the contract ceiling or value or both, or a new, interim sole-source contract awarded to the same or a new contractor to cover the timeframe between the end of the existing contract and the award of a follow-on contract.[63] The DOD policy excludes extensions awarded using the option to extend services clause as bridge contracts unless the extension exceeds 6 - months.[64] In addition, DOD's bridge contract policy directs the military departments and DOD components to develop a plan to reduce bridge contracts and to report their results annually to the Office of the Under Secretary of Defense for Acquisition and Sustainment. As of August 2018, DHS and HHS did not have component- or department-level policies that define or provide guidance on the use of bridge contracts.

Differing definitions of bridge contracts can lead to varying perspectives as to what constitutes a bridge contract. For example:

- *Differing views on whether a contract within the 8(a) program can be a bridge.* In one instance, we reviewed a 3-month, approximately $1.9 million bridge contract that DLA awarded to the incumbent contractor for a variety of IT contractor support services for DLA's Information Operations (J6). This bridge contract was awarded to continue services until DLA could award a 12-month, roughly $2.9 million sole-source contract (including all options) to an 8(a) small business participant to consolidate

---

[63] Prior to the implementation of DOD's bridge contract policy, the Navy, DISA and DLA established bridge contract policies that include definitions of bridge contracts, but are slightly different and not entirely consistent with DOD's definition. For example, the Navy defines bridge contracts as a noncompetitive contract to bridge the time between the end of one contract action and the beginning of another related contract. DISA defines a bridge contract as a short-term, sole-source contract awarded generally to the incumbent contractor to continue critical services when a follow-on competitive action could not be competed in a timely manner. DISA's guidance states bridge contracts include noncompetitive contract modifications required to bridge performance between an existing contract and the award of a subsequent contract. DLA defines bridge contracts as a noncompetitive contract/order, or contract/order with an existing contractor to bridge the time between the original end of that contractor's contract/order (following exercise of all options or extension provisions meeting the requirements of FAR § 17.207) and the competitive follow-on contract or order.

[64] See FAR § 52.217-8.

tasks from 20 contracts as part of a reorganization effort within J6. After that contract expired, DLA awarded a second 12-month, about $3 million contract (including all options) to the same 8(a) small business participant to continue these task consolidation efforts. DLA subsequently awarded a 2-month $122,000 contract extension to continue services until it could award a follow-on order under DLA's J6 Enterprise Technology Services (JETS) multiple award IDIQ contract, the award of which had also been delayed. Although the 8(a) contracts were not awarded to the incumbent of the initial 3-month bridge, we believe that these contracts could be considered bridge contracts as they were meant to bridge a gap in services until the reorganization efforts were complete and the JETS contract was awarded. DLA contracting officials, however, told us they do not consider the 8(a) contracts to be bridge contracts as these two contracts and the follow-on task order under JETS were awarded sole-source to 8(a) small business participants. DLA officials added that they plan to keep the requirement in the 8(a) program.

- *Differing views as to whether contract extension are bridges.* DOD's policy generally does not include contract extensions using the "option to extend services" clause as bridges, unless the option is extended beyond the 6 months allowed by the clause. Navy policy, however, states that using the option to extend services clause is considered a bridge if the option was not priced at contract award. Similarly, HHS officials stated that the department does not consider contract extensions using the "option to extend services" clause to be bridge contract actions if the total amount of the services covered are evaluated in the initial award, and if the length does not extend beyond the allowable 6 months. The differences among agencies' views and policies may be due to the extent to which the extensions are considered "competitive".[65] For

[65] For example, before an option can be exercised, a contracting officer must determine, among other things, that the exercise of the option meets the competition requirements delineated in FAR Part 6. FAR §17.207(f). An option that was evaluated as part of the initial

the purposes of our definition, if the extension—whether it was competed or not—was used to bridge a gap in service until a follow-on contract could be awarded, then it would be considered a bridge.

Without agreement as to what constitutes a bridge contract, agencies' efforts to improve oversight of and to identify challenges associated with the use of bridge contracts will be hindered. While we are not making any new recommendations in this area, we continue to believe that our October 2015 recommendation to OFPP to establish a government-wide definition and provide guidance to agencies on their use remains valid.

## New Definition Narrows Scope of Legacy IT Noncompetitive Contracts and Orders to About Seven Percent

An estimated 7 percent of IT noncompetitive contracts and orders at selected agencies in fiscal year 2016 were in support of legacy IT systems as newly defined in statute, which is considerably fewer than we found when using the previous definition of legacy IT.[66] At the time our review began, OMB's draft definition for legacy IT systems stated that legacy IT spending was spending dedicated to maintaining the existing IT portfolio, excluding provisioned services such as cloud. Using this definition, and based on our generalizable sample, we estimated that about 80 percent of IT noncompetitive contracts and orders over $150,000 in fiscal year 2016 at DOD, DHS, and HHS were awarded in support of legacy IT systems. In December 2017, however, Congress enacted the Modernizing Government Technology Act (MGT) as part of the National Defense Authorization Act

competition and exercisable at an amount specified in or reasonably determinable from the terms of the basic contract would generally satisfy the requirements of Part 6.

[66] The 95 percent confidence interval for this estimate ranges from 3.3 to 13.0 percent.

for Fiscal Year 2018. This act defined a legacy IT system as an "outdated or obsolete system of information technology."[67]

Using this new statutory definition of a legacy IT system, we requested that each agency reassess how it would characterize the nature of the IT system using the revised definition provided under the MGT Act. For the 142 contracts and orders we reviewed, we found that when using the new definition, agencies significantly reduced the number of contracts and orders identified as supporting legacy IT systems. For example, using the OMB draft definition agencies identified that 118 out of 142 contracts and orders were supporting legacy IT systems. However, when using the more recent MGT Act definition, agencies identified only 10 out of 137 contracts and orders as supporting legacy IT systems (see Figure 9).[68]

Consequently, using the definition provided under the MGT Act, we estimate that about 7 percent of IT noncompetitive contracts and orders over $150,000 in fiscal year 2016 at DOD, DHS, and HHS were awarded in support of outdated or obsolete legacy IT systems.[69]

Agencies' program officials said that they are still supporting outdated or obsolete legacy IT systems (as defined by the MGT Act) because they are needed for the mission, or they are in the process of buying new updated systems or modernizing current ones. For example:

- Army officials awarded a 5-year, roughly $1.2 million contract to install, configure, troubleshoot, and replace Land Mobile Radio equipment at Ft. Sill, Oklahoma. An Army official noted that all equipment is older than 12 years and is nearing its end of life. The radio equipment, however, is required to support first responder and emergency service personnel critical communications. An Army official did not indicate any plans to modernize, but noted that the impact of this system not being supported would

[67] See Pub. L. No. 115-91, §§ 1076-1078.

[68] We received the requested information on how agencies would characterize the nature of the IT system, using the revised definition provided under the MGT Act for 137 of the 142 contracts and orders in our generalizable sample; however, HHS was unable to provide us with the requested information for 5 of its contracts and orders.

[69] The 95 percent confidence interval for this estimate ranges from 3.3 to 13.0 percent.

significantly affect all of Fort Sill's land mobile radio communications.

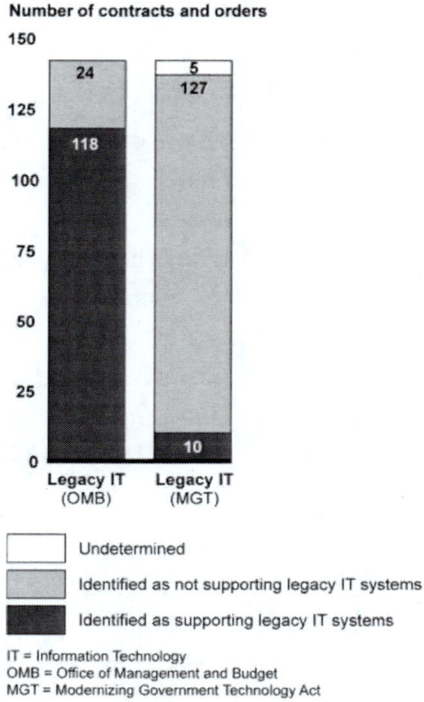


Source: GAO analysis of agency contract documentation and information provided by agency officials | GAO-19-63.

Note: We assessed whether 142 contracts and orders supported legacy IT systems using the OMB definition, i.e., spending dedicated to maintaining the existing IT portfolio but excluding provisioned services such as cloud. We assessed whether 137 of the contracts and orders in our review supported legacy IT systems using the MGT definition, i.e., outdated or obsolete IT systems. For those contracts and orders that were undetermined, the Department of Health and Human Services was unable to provide us with the requested information as to whether 5 contracts and orders were in support of legacy IT using the MGT definition.

Figure 9. Number of Contracts and Orders GAO Reviewed That Supported Legacy Information Technology (IT) Systems Under Two Different Definitions.

- The Air Force awarded a $218,000 order to buy repair services for the C-130H aircraft's radar display unit and electronic flight instrument. An Air Force official noted that legacy hardware that was bought through the order is part of critical systems that are required to safely fly the aircraft. The system, however, is obsolete and the associated hardware is no longer supported by the vendor. The official told us that there is currently a re-engineering effort to modernize the systems that use this hardware.
- HHS issued a 12–month, nearly $2.5 million order to buy operations and maintenance support for a Food and Drug Administration (FDA) system used to review and approve prescription drug applications. According to an FDA program official, efforts are underway to retire the system by gradually transferring current business processes to a commercial-off-the-shelf solution that can better meet government needs. This official, however, told us that the system currently remains in use because FDA's Office of New Drugs is still heavily reliant on the system.

## CONCLUSION

Competition is a cornerstone of the federal acquisition system and a critical tool for achieving the best possible return on investment for taxpayers. In the case of information technology, federal agencies awarded slightly under a third of their contract dollars under some form of noncompetitive contract. Further, our current work was able to quantify that about a tenth of all information technology-related contracts and orders were made under some form of a noncompetitively awarded bridge contract, which provides new context for the issues associated with their use. The challenges themselves, however, remain much the same since we first reported on the issue in 2015. OFPP has yet to issue guidance or promulgate revised regulations to help agencies identify and manage their use of bridge contracts, and our current work finds that the full scope of bridge contracts or the underlying acquisition issues that necessitated their use in the first place may not be readily apparent to agency officials who are approving their use. We continue to believe that our 2015 recommendation would improve the use of bridge contracts, and we encourage OFPP to complete its ongoing efforts in a timely fashion.

The frequency of the errors in reporting and their concentration within a specific type of contract action signals the need for more management attention and corrective action. These errors resulted in the potential misreporting of billions of dollars awarded under orders as being noncompetitively awarded when, in fact, they were competed. One agency included in our review—DHS—has taken steps to address the problems that underlie the errors in coding and provided additional training to its staff. DOD and HHS could benefit from additional insight as to the reasons behind the high rates of miscoding to improve the accuracy of this information.

## RECOMMENDATIONS FOR EXECUTIVE ACTION

We are making a total of two recommendations, one to DOD and one to HHS.

- The Secretary of Defense should direct the Under Secretary of Defense for Acquisition and Sustainment to identify the reasons behind the high rate of miscoding for orders awarded under multiple award contracts and use this information to identify and take action to improve the reliability of the competition data entered into FPDS-NG (Recommendation 1).
- The Secretary of Health and Human Services should direct the Associate Deputy Assistant Secretary for Acquisition to identify the reasons behind the high rate of miscoding for orders awarded under multiple award contracts and use this information to identify and take action to improve the reliability of the competition data entered into FPDS-NG (Recommendation 2).

## AGENCY COMMENTS AND OUR EVALUATION

We provided a draft of this chapter to DOD, DHS, HHS, and OMB for review and comment. DOD and HHS provided written comments and concurred with the recommendation we made to each department.

In its written response, reproduced in appendix II, DOD stated it will analyze FPDS-NG data in an effort to identify why the miscoding of orders on multiple award contracts occurs, and use the information to advise the contracting community of actions to improve the reliability of competition data.

In its written response, reproduced in appendix III, HHS stated that the Division of Acquisition within HHS's Office of Grants and Acquisition Policy and Accountability uses a data quality management platform to ensure data accuracy. HHS is currently in the process of performing the annual data validation and verification of the acquisition community's contract data for fiscal year 2018. Once this process is complete the Division of Acquisition will contact contracting offices that produced records that were flagged as containing errors and provide recommendations that should help improve the fiscal year 2019 accuracy rating. HHS added that it will closely monitor those checks and all others to ensure contract data are accurate. However, in its letter, HHS did not specify how its annual data validation and verification process would specifically address the fact that we found a high rate of miscoding of competition data for certain orders.

OMB staff informed us that they had no comments on this chapter DHS, HHS and the Air Force provided technical comments, which we incorporated as appropriate.

Timothy J. DiNapoli
Director, Contracting and National Security Acquisitions

## List of Requesters

The Honorable Ron Johnson
Chairman

The Honorable Claire McCaskill
Ranking Member
Committee on Homeland Security and Governmental Affairs
United States Senate

The Honorable Trey Gowdy
Chairman

The Honorable Elijah E. Cummings
Ranking Member
Committee on Oversight and Government Reform
House of Representatives

The Honorable Mark Meadows
Chairman

The Honorable Gerald E. Connolly
Ranking Member
Subcommittee on Government Operations
Committee on Oversight and Government Reform
House of Representatives

# Appendix I: Objectives, Scope, and Methodology

Our report examines (1) the extent to which agencies used noncompetitive contracts to procure Information Technology (IT) products and services for fiscal years 2013 through 2017; (2) the reasons for using noncompetitive contracts for selected IT procurements; (3) the extent to which IT procurements at selected agencies were bridge contracts; and (4) the extent to which noncompetitive IT procurements at selected agencies were in support of legacy systems.

To examine the extent to which agencies used noncompetitive contracts and orders to procure IT products and services, we analyzed government-wide Federal Procurement Data System-Next Generation (FPDS-NG) data on IT obligations from fiscal years 2013 through 2017.[70] To define IT, we used the Office of Management and Budget's (OMB) Category Management Leadership Council list of IT products and service codes, which identified a total of 79 IT-related codes for IT services and products. Data were adjusted for inflation to fiscal year 2017 dollars, using the Fiscal Year Gross Domestic Product Price Index. To assess the reliability of the FPDS-NG data, we electronically tested for missing data, outliers, and inconsistent coding. Based on these steps, we determined that FPDS-NG data were sufficiently reliable for describing general trends in government-wide and IT contract obligations data for fiscal years 2013 through 2017.

In addition, as we later describe, we compared data for a generalizable sample of 171 noncompetitive contracts and orders to contract documentation, and we determined that 29 of these had been inaccurately coded in FPDS-NG as noncompetitive. As such, we determined that the data were not reliable for the purposes of reporting the actual amount agencies obligated on noncompetitive contracts and orders for IT products and services. Specifically, we determined, that data for IT noncompetitive obligations awarded under multiple award contracts that cited "follow-on action following competitive initial action" or "other statutory authority" as the legal authority for using an exception to fair opportunity for the Departments of Defense (DOD), Homeland Security (DHS), and Health

---

[70] For the purposes of our report, we are considering noncompetitive contracts and orders to be those that use the exceptions to full and open competition listed in FAR § 6.302, orders awarded in accordance with FAR § 8.405-6 and FAR § 13.106-1, contracts and orders awarded on a sole-source basis in accordance with FAR subpart 19.8 under the 8(a) small business program, and orders awarded under multiple award contracts that use the exceptions to fair opportunity listed in FAR § 16.505.

and Human Services (HHS) in fiscal year 2016 were not reliable.[71] Evidence from our review of this sample suggests there was a high rate of miscoding for these orders; thus, we applied these findings to the remaining agencies and fiscal years because we do not have confidence that the data were more reliable than what we had found.

To determine the reasons for using noncompetitive contracts for selected IT procurements, we selected the three agencies with the highest reported obligations on IT noncompetitive contracts for fiscal years 2012 through 2016 (the most recent year of data available at the time we began our review)—DOD, DHS and HHS. These three agencies collectively accounted for about 70 percent of all noncompetitively awarded contracts for IT during this period. From these agencies, we selected a generalizable stratified random sample of 171 fiscal year 2016 noncompetitive contracts and orders for IT above the simplified acquisition threshold of $150,000.[72] The sample was proportionate to the amount of noncompetitive contracts and orders for IT at each agency.

Based on our review of documentation collected for the generalizable sample, we excluded 29 contracts and orders because they were awarded competitively, but had been miscoded as noncompetitive or as having an exception to fair opportunity. As a result, our sample consisted of 142 contracts and orders. See Table 4 for a breakdown by agency.

---

[71] For the purposes of this report, contracts include definitive contracts, purchase orders, and blanket purchase agreements; single-award contracts include an indefinite-delivery vehicle or blanket purchase agreement to one vendor; multiple-award contracts include those that have been awarded under an indefinite-delivery vehicle or blanket purchase agreement to two or more vendors. Orders refer to task orders as defined in FAR 2.101.

[72] Since all our contracts and orders were awarded in fiscal year 2016, the prior simplified acquisition threshold of $150,000 applies to our generalizable sample. In 2016, the simplified acquisition threshold was generally $150,000. See 80 FR 38293 (Oct. 1, 2015). In December 2017, the simplified acquisition threshold increased to $250,000. See 41 U.S.C. § 134 (2018). Although DOD and DHS issued class deviations implementing this increase, and the Civilian Agency Advisory Council (CAAC) issued guidance permitting civilian agencies to issue class deviations to implement the increased threshold, this change has not yet been implemented in the FAR. FAR Case 2018-004, Increased Micro-Purchase and Simplified Acquisition Thresholds (open as of Nov. 26, 2018).

**Table 4. Number of Noncompetitively Awarded Contracts and Orders GAO Reviewed**

| Agency | Number of contracts | Number of orders on single award contracts | Number of orders on multiple award contracts | Total number of contracts and orders initially reviewed | Excluded due to miscoding in the Federal Procurement Data System | Revised total |
|---|---|---|---|---|---|---|
| Department of Defense | 36 | 54 | 21 | 111 | 16 | 95 |
| Department of Homeland Security | 10 | 10 | 10 | 30 | 6 | 24 |
| Department of Health and Human Services | 10 | 10 | 10 | 30 | 7 | 23 |
| Total | 56 | 74 | 41 | 171 | 29 | 142 |

Source: GAO analysis of Federal Procurement Data System-Next Generation data and agency documentation | GAO-19-63.

Note: Contracts include definitive contracts, purchase orders, and blanket purchase agreements; noncompetitive orders refer to task and delivery orders as defined in FAR § 2.101 and orders off of blanket purchase agreements. Single award describes indefinite-delivery vehicles or blanket purchase agreements awarded to one vendor and those awarded to more than one vendor are referred to as multiple award.

To determine the extent to which IT procurements at selected agencies were bridge contracts or in support of legacy systems, agencies provided information as to whether the contracts and orders met GAO's definition of a bridge contract—which we defined as an extension to an existing contract beyond the period of performance (including base and option years) or a new, short-term contract awarded on a sole-source basis to an incumbent contractor to avoid a lapse in service caused by a delay in awarding a follow-on contract—and whether they met the definitions of legacy IT systems in OMB's draft IT Modernization Initiative and the Modernizing Government Technology Act (MGT).[73] OMB's draft IT

[73] The MGT Act was enacted as part of the Fiscal Year 2018 National Defense Authorization Act on December 12, 2017. National Defense Authorization Act for Fiscal Year 2018, Pub. L. No. 115-91, div. A. title X, subtitle G, 131 Stat. 1283, 1586-94 (Dec. 12, 2017).

Modernization Initiative defined legacy systems as spending dedicated to maintaining the existing IT portfolio but excluding provisioned services, such as cloud, while the MGT Act defines them as outdated or obsolete.[74]

We verified the agencies' determinations of whether a contract or order was a bridge by reviewing documentation, such as justification and approval and exception to fair opportunity documents, for the contracts and orders in our generalizable sample, and conducting follow-up with agency officials as needed. We verified agencies' determination of whether or not a contract or order was in support of a legacy system, as defined in OMB's draft IT Modernization Initiative by reviewing the agencies' determination and comparing these determinations to additional documentation, such as the statement of work, and conducting follow-up with program officials about the nature of the requirement where needed. We verified agencies' determination of whether a contract or order was in support of a legacy system as defined in the MGT Act by reviewing agencies' rationale for these determinations and following up with agency officials where we identified discrepancies between the determination and rationale. To obtain additional insights into bridge contracts and legacy systems, we selected a nonprobability sample of 26 contracts and orders from our generalizable sample of 142 contracts and orders for in-depth review. We selected these contracts based on factors such as obtaining a mix of bridge contracts and other contracts used in support of legacy IT systems and location of the contract files.

For our in-depth review of contracts and orders, we collected and analyzed contract file documentation for the selected contracts and orders and interviewed contracting and program officials to gain insights into the facts and circumstances surrounding the awards of IT noncompetitive contracts and orders. In cases where we selected a potential bridge contract, we also reviewed the predecessor contract, additional bridge

---

[74] OMB's definition of legacy system was in place at the time we began our review. In December 2017, the MGT was enacted and we requested that each agency reassess how it would characterize the nature of the IT systems using the revised definition provided under the MGT Act.

contracts (if any), and, follow-on contract, if awarded at the time of our review. For bridge contracts and orders, we asked about the reasons why bridges were needed and the status of follow-on contracts. We verified, using the definition of bridge contracts that we developed for our October 2015 report as criteria, that 13 of 142 contracts and orders in our generalizable sample were bridge contracts based on reviews of justification and approval documents, limited source justifications, or exceptions to fair opportunity, among other documents.[75] We acknowledge, however, that in the absence of a government-wide definition, agencies may have differing views of what constitutes a bridge contract.

In addition, we found 2 additional bridge contracts not included in our generalizable sample while conducting our in-depth review. For example, we selected three noncompetitive orders from our generalizable sample for in-depth review that were used to buy accessories and maintenance for the U.S. Special Operations Command (SOCOM) PRC-152 and 117G radios. We found that although the three orders were not bridge contracts, the underlying indefinite delivery/indefinite quantity (IDIQ) contract—which outlines the terms and conditions, including pricing for the orders—had been extended 12 months to continue services until the follow-on IDIQ could be awarded. We also selected an Air Force order for equipment for the Joint Strike Fighter instrumentation pallet for in-depth review. Further analysis revealed that the underlying IDIQ was extended for 5 additional months to continue services until officials could award a follow-on contract for this requirement. Including these 2 additional bridge contracts brings the total number of bridge contracts we identified during this review to 15. For legacy contracts and orders we asked about the nature of the requirement and plan to move to newer technologies or systems. The selection process for the generalizable sample is described in detail below.

---

[75] Three bridge contracts identified did not fully meet our definition of a bridge contract because they were not awarded to the incumbent contractor. In addition, we also identified one bridge contract that was not "short-term." For the purposes of our report, we considered these awards to be bridge contracts, as they were intended to bridge a gap in service due to a delay in the award of a follow-on contract.

## Selection Methodology for Generalizable Sample

We selected a generalizable stratified random sample of 171 contracts and orders from a sample frame of 3,671 fiscal year 2016 IT noncompetitive contracts and orders, including orders under multiple award indefinite delivery/indefinite quantity contracts over $150,000 to generate percentage estimates to the population. We excluded contracts and orders with estimated values below the simplified acquisition threshold of $150,000 as these contracts have streamlined acquisition procedures. We stratified the sample frame into nine mutually exclusive strata by agency and type of award, i.e., contract, order, and multiple award order for each of the three agencies.

**Table 5. Fiscal Year 2016 Noncompetitive Contracts and Orders for Information Technology over $150,000 at the Departments of Defense (DOD), Homeland Security (DHS) and Health and Human Services (HHS)**

| Stratum | Agency | Type | Population size | Sample Size |
|---|---|---|---|---|
| 1 | DOD | Contracts | 901 | 36 |
| 2 | DOD | Orders on Single Award Contracts | 1,378 | 54 |
| 2.5 | DOD | Orders on Multiple Award Contracts | 728 | 21 |
| 3 | HHS | Contracts | 79 | 10 |
| 4 | HHS | Orders on Single Award Contracts | 42 | 10 |
| 4.5 | HHS | Orders on Multiple Award Contracts | 134 | 10 |
| 5 | DHS | Contracts | 64 | 10 |
| 6 | DHS | Orders on Single Award Contracts | 155 | 10 |
| 6.5 | DHS | Orders on Multiple Award Contracts | 190 | 10 |
| Total | n/a | n/a | 3,671 | 171 |

Source: GAO analysis of Federal Procurement Data System-Next Generation data and agency documentation | GAO-19-63.

Note: Noncompetitive contracts and orders were awarded in accordance with FAR §§ 6.302, 8.405-6, 13.106-1, 16.505, and those awarded on a sole-source basis in accordance with FAR subpart 19.8. Contracts include definitive contracts, purchase orders, and blanket purchase agreements; noncompetitive orders refer to task and delivery orders as defined in FAR § 2.101.

Single award describes indefinite-delivery vehicles or blanket purchase agreements awarded to one vendor and those awarded to more than one vendor are referred to as multiple award.

We computed the minimum sample size needed for a proportion estimate to achieve an overall precision of at least plus or minus 10 percentage points or fewer at the 95 percent confidence level. We increased the computed sample size to account for about 10 percent of the population to be out of scope, such as competitive or non-IT contracts or orders. We then proportionally allocated the sample size across the defined strata and increased sample sizes where necessary so that each stratum would contain at least 10 sampled contracts or orders. The stratified sample frame and sizes are described in Table 5 above. We selected contracts and orders from the following components:

- DOD: Air Force, Army, Navy, Defense Information Systems Agency, Defense Logistics Agency, Defense Security Service, Defense Threat Reduction Agency, U.S. Special Operations Command, and Washington Headquarter Services;
- HHS: Centers for Disease Control, Centers for Medicare and Medicaid Services, Food and Drug Administration, Indian Health Service, National Institutes of Health, and the Office of the Assistant Secretary for Administration;
- DHS: Federal Emergency Management Agency, Office of Procurement Operations, U.S. Citizenship and Immigration Services, U.S. Coast Guard, U.S. Customs and Border Protection, and the U.S. Secret Service.

We excluded 29 contracts and orders as we determined they had been miscoded as noncompetitive or as not having an exception to fair opportunity. Based on these exclusions, we estimate the number of noncompetitive contracts and orders in this population was about 3,000 (+/- 6.7 percent). All estimates in this chapter have a margin of error, at the 95 percent confidence level, of plus or minus 9 percentage points or fewer.

We conducted this performance audit from April 2017 to December 2018 in accordance with generally accepted government auditing standards. Those standards require that we plan and perform the audit to obtain sufficient, appropriate evidence to provide a reasonable basis for our findings and conclusions based on our audit objectives. We believe the evidence obtained provides a reasonable basis for our findings and conclusions based on our audit objectives.

# APPENDIX II: COMMENTS FROM THE DEPARTMENT OF DEFENSE

OFFICE OF THE UNDER SECRETARY OF DEFENSE
3000 DEFENSE PENTAGON
WASHINGTON, DC 20301-3000

ACQUISITION
AND SUSTAINMENT

NOV 19 2018

Mr. Timothy J. DiNapoli
Director, Contracting and National Security Acquisitions
U.S. Government Accountability Office
441 G Street, N.W.
Washington, DC 20548

Dear Mr. DiNapoli:

This is the Department of Defense (DoD) response to the GAO Draft Report, GAO-19-63, 'Information Technology: Agencies Need Better Information on the Use of Noncompetitive and Bridge Contracts,' dated October 15, 2018 (GAO Code 102032). Enclosed is the Department's response to the report recommendation.

Sincerely,

Kim Herrington
Acting Principal Director,
Defense Pricing and Contracting

**GAO Draft Report Dated October, 15 2018**
**GAO-19-63 (GAO CODE 102032)**

**"INFORMATION TECHNOLOGY: AGENCIES NEED BETTER INFORMATION ON THE USE OF NONCOMPETITIVE AND BRIDGE CONTRACTS"**

**DEPARTMENT OF DEFENSE COMMENT TO THE GAO RECOMMENDATION**

**RECOMMENDATION 1:** The Secretary of Defense should direct the Under Secretary of Defense for Acquisition and Sustainment to identify the reasons behind the high rate of miscoding for orders awarded under multiple award contracts and use this information to identify and take action to improve the reliability of the competition data entered into FPDS-NG.

**DoD RESPONSE:** Concur, we will analyze the FPDS-NG data in an effort to identify why the miscoding of orders on multiple award contracts occurs, and use the information to advise the contracting community of actions to improve the reliability of the competition data.

# APPENDIX III: COMMENTS FROM THE DEPARTMENT OF HEALTH AND HUMAN SERVICES

DEPARTMENT OF HEALTH & HUMAN SERVICES

OFFICE OF THE SECRETARY

Assistant Secretary for Legislation
Washington, DC 20201

NOV 15 2018

Tim DiNapoli
Director, Contracting and National Security
Acquisitions
U.S. Government Accountability Office
441 G Street NW
Washington, DC 20548

Dear Mr. DiNapoli:

Attached are comments on the U.S. Government Accountability Office's (GAO) report entitled, "*Information Technology: Agencies Need Better Information on the Use of Noncompetitive and Bridge Contracts*" (GAO-19-63).

The Department appreciates the opportunity to review this report prior to publication.

Sincerely,

Matthew D. Bassett
Assistant Secretary for Legislation

**GENERAL COMMENTS FROM THE DEPARTMENT OF HEALTH & HUMAN SERVICES ON THE GOVERNMENT ACCOUNTABILITY OFFICE'S DRAFT REPORT ENTITLED – INFORMATION TECHNOLOGY: AGENCIES NEED BETTER INFORMATION ON THE USE OF NONCOMPETITIVE AND BRIDGE CONTRACTS (GAO-19-63)**

The U.S. Department of Health & Human Services (HHS) appreciates the opportunity from the Government Accountability Office (GAO) to review and comment on this draft report.

**Recommendation 2**

The Secretary of Health and Human Services should direct the Associate Deputy Assistant Secretary for Acquisition to identify the reasons behind the high rate of miscoding for orders awarded under multiple award contracts and use this information to identify and take action to improve the reliability of the competition data entered into FPDS-NG.

**HHS Response**

HHS concurs with GAO's recommendation.

The Division of Acquisition (DA) within HHS's Office of Grants and Acquisition Policy and Accountability utilizes FedDataCheck, a data quality management platform, to ensure data accuracy. This platform combs through each record reported to FPDS-NG with over 120 data accuracy checkpoints and provides instant feedback to the acquisition community on how those records are reported and if those records are in compliance with the Federal Acquisition Regulations (FAR). Any record that doesn't pass those checkpoints produces a flag. We are currently in the process of performing the annual validation and verification of the acquisition community's contract data for FY 2018. Once the process is complete, the DA will contact the contracting offices that produced any records with an error flag and provide recommendations that should help improve the FY 2019 accuracy rating. We will be sure to closely monitor those checks and all others to ensure HHS contract data is accurate.

# APPENDIX IV: ACCESSIBLE DATA

## Data Tables

### Accessible Data for Reported Competition on Information Technology Contract Obligations, Fiscal Years 2013-2017 (fiscal year 2017 dollars)

| Fiscal year | Competed | Coded as noncompetitive but undetermined due to unreliable data | Noncompeted |
|---|---|---|---|
| "2013 | 36.8 | 2.75 | 12.81 |
| "2014 | 38.2 | 2.96 | 12.7 |
| "2015 | 38.29 | 3.37 | 12.65 |
| "2016 | 41.59 | 2.98 | 12.68 |
| "2017 | 43.34 | 2.56 | 12.8 |

## Accessible Data for Figure 1: Government-wide Information Technology (IT) Contract Obligations in Comparison with Total Contract Obligations, Fiscal Years 2013-2017 (fiscal year 2017 dollars)

| Fiscal year | Government-wide obligations | IT obligations |
|---|---|---|
| 2013 | 490.1 | 53.5 |
| 2014 | 463.7 | 53.9 |
| 2015 | 450.5 | 54.4 |
| 2016 | 481.3 | 57.3 |
| 2017 | 507.7 | 58.7 |

## Accessible Data for Figure 2: Comparison of Information Technology Contract Obligations by Agency, Fiscal Years 2013 through 2017 (fiscal year 2017 dollars)

| Fiscal year | Other | HHS | DHS | DOD |
|---|---|---|---|---|
| 2013 | 17.97 | 3.59 | 3.48 | 27.46 |
| 2014 | 19.73 | 4.31 | 3.59 | 26.27 |
| 2015 | 20.42 | 4.7 | 3.89 | 25.34 |
| 2016 | 20.98 | 4.86 | 4.05 | 27.39 |
| 2017 | 21.79 | 5.23 | 4.06 | 27.64 |

## Accessible Data for Figure 3: Reported Competition on Information Technology Contract Obligations, Fiscal Years 2013-2017 (fiscal year 2017 dollars)

| Fiscal year | Competed | Coded as noncompetitive but undetermined due to unreliable data | Noncompeted |
|---|---|---|---|
| 2013 | 36.8 | 2.75 | 12.81 |
| 2014 | 38.2 | 2.96 | 12.7 |
| 2015 | 38.29 | 3.37 | 12.65 |
| 2016 | 41.59 | 2.93 | 12.68 |
| 2017 | 43.34 | 2.56 | 12.8 |

## Accessible Data for Figure 4: Fiscal Year 2017 Information Technology Noncompetitive Obligations by Spending Category

| Consulting | Security | Telecommunications | Software | Hardware | Services |
|---|---|---|---|---|---|
| 0.3 | 0.5 | 0.5 | 2.3 | 3.1 | 6.1 |

## Accessible Data for Figure 5: Reasons Cited by Departments of Defense, Homeland Security, and Health and Human Services as to Why Only One Contractor Could Meet Their Needs

| Category | Number of contracts and orders |
|---|---|
| Brand-name product | 5 |
| Compatibility issues | 50 |
| Unique qualifications experience or expertise | 50 |
| Proprietary data rights | 65 |

## Accessible Data for Figure 6: Reasons for Delays Found in In-Depth Review of 15 Bridge Contracts

| Reasons for delay | Number of delays |
|---|---|
| Acquisition planning challenges | 13 |
| Other delays | 10 |
| Source selection delays | 5 |
| Bid protest | 3 |
| Acquisition workforce challenges | 3 |

## Accessible Data for Figure 7: Number of Contracts and Orders GAO Reviewed That Supported Legacy Information Technology (IT) Systems Under Two Different Definitions

| Category | Identified as supporting legacy IT systems | Identified as not supporting legacy IT systems | Undetermined |
|---|---|---|---|
| Legacy IT (Office of Management and Budget definition) | 118 | 24 | 0 |
| Legacy IT (Modernizing Government Technology Act definition) | 10 | 127 | 5 |

# INDEX

## D

## E



## F



## G

## H



## I



## J



## L



## M

## N



## O



## P

## T



## U



## W

## Related Nova Publications

### General National Security: Background, Issues and Legislation

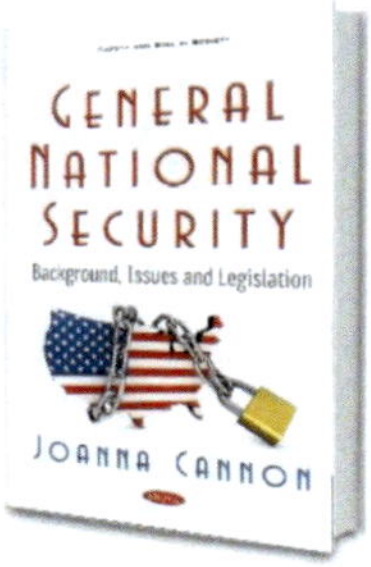


**Editor:** Joanna Cannon

**Series:** Government Procedures and Operations

**Book Description:** This book is comprised of 2018 and 2019 CRS reports on general national security of the United States. The first report provides a background and status on Overseas Contingency Operations Funding.

**Hardcover ISBN:** 978-1-53615-412-2
**Retail Price:** $160

### United States Embassies: Construction, Security and Evacuations

**Editor:** Toma Jović

**Series:** Safety and Risk in Society

**Book Description:** Following terrorist attacks against the U.S. embassy in Beirut, Lebanon, in 1983, the U.S. Department of State began an embassy construction program—known as the Inman program—to protect U.S. personnel.

**Hardcover ISBN:** 978-1-53614-976-0
**Retail Price:** $195

*To see complete list of Nova publications, please visit our website at www.novapublishers.com*